An Introduction to the Science of Metaphysics

By HENRY J. KOREN, C.S.Sp., S.T.D.

WIPF & STOCK · Eugene, Oregon

Wipf and Stock Publishers
199 W 8th Ave, Suite 3
Eugene, OR 97401

An Introduction to the Science of Metaphysics
By Koren, Henry J., CSSp
Copyright © 1955 by Koren, Henry J., CSSp All rights reserved.
Softcover ISBN-13: 979-8-3852-4050-0
Hardcover ISBN-13: 979-8-3852-4051-7
eBook ISBN-13: 979-8-3852-4052-4
Publication date 12/2/2024
Previously published by B. Herder Book Co., 1955

This edition is a scanned facsimile of the original edition published in 1955.

"Let youth not hesitate to philosophize, nor old age get tired of philosophy. For it is suitable for any period of life, and there is no age which is unfit for sanity of mind."

     Epicurus, *Ep. ad Menoeceum*

Preface

✢✢✢ The purpose of this text is to serve as an introduction to the Thomistic theory of being in undergraduate schools where three or four credits can be devoted to this purpose. Because of its introductory nature, the text lays emphasis upon the fundamentals of the Thomistic theory, especially the theory of potency and act and its application to the problems under consideration.

The study of metaphysics is avowedly difficult and exacting. It would be useless to flatter ourselves with the illusion that every student will easily understand all problems and the proposed solutions. There is no such thing as "Metaphysics Without Tears." But it would be disastrous if for the sake of the few who, through lack of interest, application, or capacity, are unable to derive any benefit from the course, we would abstain from offering true metaphysics to the others and consider our duty done when a number of terms have been defined and classified, while all problems are neatly avoided because they are "too abstract and too difficult." It is a matter of experience that a study of metaphysics not only makes the student acquainted with this fundamental science, but also is most powerful in developing his power of independent thinking. The ever-increasing tendency to water down courses and to cater to

PREFACE

the lowest grade of intelligence contains a grave injustice to the more gifted who are thus deprived of the opportunity to advance beyond the lowest level. A student who can derive no benefit whatsoever from a study of metaphysical problems simply does not belong in a college.

A fairly large number of references are given to Aristotle and St. Thomas in the hope that the better students will be induced to become personally acquainted with the works of these masterminds. Excellent translations of most of the works quoted are available nowadays in any self-respecting library; hence ignorance of Greek and Latin no longer offers any difficulty in this respect. However, a word of warning concerning the reading of ancient philosophers may not be amiss: the student is bound to come across numerous passages which reveal utterly antiquated physical theories, especially in the examples with which St. Thomas illustrates his philosophical theories. He should keep in mind that metaphysics is independent from physical science, hence no matter how silly and out of date ancient philosophical writings may be with respect to science, their philosophical views may be just as valid now as on the day they were written. Often the student will be able to separate philosophy from antiquated science by using his own judgment; at other times, however, recourse has to be had to the guidance of an experienced professor.

At the end of each chapter or section a short summary has been added to make it easier to obtain a comprehensive view of the matter. Perhaps it will not be superfluous to warn the student that his studies are not to be limited to these summaries. Two chapters and a number of minor divisions are marked with an asterisk (*). They may be omitted, at the discretion of the teacher, without a serious break in continuity of thought if the time allotted does not permit a complete study of all that is offered. As a matter of fact, one of these chapters, the one on supposit and person, has been inserted rather as a concession to tradition (and possible use by seminarians) than as a matter of intrinsic necessity. The problem of supposit and person is very important for theology and is usually treated in philosophy, because all seminarians study philosophy as a preparation for theology, but I do not see why non-seminarians should be burdened with this profound problem.

Because this text is meant as an introduction for beginners, little time is spent on historical and polemical considerations, except in a few questions where it would not have been justifiable to omit the history of the problem. Nevertheless, at the end of each problem the opinions of other philosophers are briefly recorded, not so much in order to introduce these views to the student, as to give him a clearer idea of the position taken by Thomistic philosophy. These brief notes could be utilized to show what is so beautifully stated by Lactantius: "There is no body of philosophers however wrong, no individual however stupid, who has not had at least a glimpse of the truth. What is more, if there had been anyone with the ability to collect and systematize all the partial truths which are so widely scattered throughout the various schools, then I am sure he would see life as we do. But no one could undertake such a task without a thorough grasp of the truth; and this can come only to a man who is taught by God." (*Inst. Div.*, VII,7; M.L.6,758). St. Thomas was such a man. Of course, we do not mean that St. Thomas possessed the whole truth and nothing but the truth, so that for later generations there would be nothing left to investigate. Philosophy is, in the first place, a work of personal wisdom. Hence, even if nothing could be added to St. Thomas, we would not be exempted from the duty of making a personal investigation of philosophical problems. Secondly, not even the most "fanatical" Thomist would assert that all philosophical problems have been considered and solved by St. Thomas. After all, every age has its own preferences in philosophy; therefore, modern man may be interested in problems for which St. Thomas showed scant interest. All we want to assert is that, in our conviction, St. Thomas gives a coherent, carefully considered answer to the problems he investigated, and the main principles of this solution, for the writer, bear the stamp of truth.

The order to be followed in an introductory study such as this is a difficult problem. I do not think that it is possible to find an order which will be satisfactory from both the logical and the psychological points of view. To plunge headlong into the theory of potency and act at the very beginning of the course, when the student has had no training at all in metaphysical thinking, runs the risk that most of the theory will not be sufficiently assimilated. For this reason I have decided upon a logical approach, which seems also to be better suited psychologically to the student's capacity. After the introduction there follows the explanation of the concept of being and its primary determinations. This will take a few weeks, so that the student will have had an opportunity to do some philosophical thinking [1] before the theory of potency and act is presented to him. Moreover, the application of this theory to the order of activity, *viz.*, the distinction of substance and accidents, is given its logical place in the section on the supreme classes of finite being; hence there is an opportunity

---

[1] I suppose that a course in fundamental metaphysics precedes the study of special metaphysical problems, such as those which are commonly called cosmology, rational psychology, and theodicy.

to review the theory when substance and accidents are considered, which should be in the second half of the semester. However, if one insists that the course should start with act and potency, it will be possible to begin with the Chapters 3, 4, and 5, provided that a sufficient preliminary explanation of the concept of being is given.

To aid the student in preparing for examination, a number of review questions have been added at the end of the book. Besides, as a possible aid for term papers, Suggested Readings in English are given at the end of each chapter or section of a chapter.

A last remark. On several occasions references are made to God. General metaphysics does not presuppose God or take His existence for granted. In a special section of metaphysics, called theodicy, God's existence and nature are discussed. However, there are certain problems of general metaphysics which can be fully answered only if God is taken into consideration. Consequently, it would be necessary either to revert to these problems after studying theodicy so as to supplement whatever was missing, or to give at once the complete answer upon the assumption that there is a God. For obvious practical reasons, the second method of procedure has been chosen.

My sincere thanks are due to the Rev. J. A. J. Peters, C.SS.R., professor of philosophy at the Charlemagne University of Nijmegen, Holland, who has read the manuscript and volunteered many pertinent remarks and valuable suggestions, although he disagreed with me in many points; also to the Very Reverend John L. Callahan, O.P., S.T.M., for his aid in preparing the manuscript for publication, and to the Oxford University Press for permission to quote from their publication, *The Works of Aristotle*.

Henry J. Koren, C.S.Sp.

Duquesne University

Table of Contents

	PAGE
PREFACE	vii

INTRODUCTION

The Names Given to Metaphysics – Scientific Knowledge and Metaphysics – The Object of Metaphysics – The Division of Metaphysics – The Importance of Metaphysics – The Origin and History of Metaphysics – Epistemological Presuppositions – Summary . 1

Suggested Readings 16

PART ONE

The Philosophy of Being in General

CHAPTER

1. THE NATURE OF BEING

    I. The Concept of Being. Senses of the Term "Being" – Being Is the Most Common and Most Simple of All Concepts – No Strict Definition of Being Is Possible – Being Is Ontologically the First of All Concepts – * Historical Notes – Summary   19

    II. The Unity of the Concept of Being. The Abstraction of Universal Concepts – The Abstraction of Being – The Contraction of Being – Being Is Not a Genus – * Historical Notes – Summary .   24

TABLE OF CONTENTS

CHAPTER   PAGE

    III. The Analogy of Being. Univocal, Equivocal, and Analogous Terms – Modes of Analogy – Being Is Neither Univocal nor Equivocal but Analogous – * Historical Notes – Summary   31

    IV. Logical Being. The Nature of Logical Being – Kinds of Logical Beings – Summary 44

    Suggested Readings 47

2. THE TRANSCENDENTAL PROPERTIES OF BEING

    I. Transcendental Properties in General. Explanation of Terms – Derivation of Transcendental Concepts – Transcendental Properties – * Historical Notes – Summary   48

    II. Otherness (The Principle of Contradiction). Preliminary Notions – The Principle of Contradiction – * Historical Notes – Summary   54

    III. Transcendental Unity. The Concept of Transcendental Unity – Every Being Is "One" – * Historical Notes – Summary   63

    Appendix: Identity and Distinction. Nature and Kinds of Identity – Nature and Kinds of Distinction – * Historical Notes – Summary   67

    IV. Transcendental Truth. Nature and Kinds of Truth – Every Being Is True – * How Truth Is in Beings – * The "True" Adds to Being as Such a Purely Logical Relation – Truth of Speech – * Phenomenal Truth – * Eternal and Unchangeable Truth – Falsity – * Historical Notes – Summary   74

    V. Transcendental Goodness. The Concept of Goodness – * What Does the "Good" Add to Being? – Every Being Is Good – * How Goodness Is Found in Finite and Infinite Beings – Kinds of Goodness – Evil:

TABLE OF CONTENTS

CHAPTER		PAGE
	Its Notion, Division, and Cause – * Historical Notes – Summary	86
	* Appendix: Beauty. Notion of Beauty – Is Every Being Beautiful? – Historical Notes – Summary	96
	Suggested Readings	102
3.	ACT AND POTENCY	
	I The Problem of Becoming. Statement of the Problem – The Answer of Parmenides – The Answer of Heraclitus – The Answer of Aristotle – The Objectivity of Change	104
	II. The Problem of Limitation. Statement of the Problem – The Answer of Plato – The Answer of St. Thomas	108
	III. Synthesis of Aristotle's Theory of Potency and Act with the Theory of Limitation by Participation. Act Is Limited Only by Potency – Potency Is Limited of Itself – Corollaries of the Limitation of Act by Potency – Potency and Act Are Really Distinct – Potency and Act Enter Into a Real Composition – Potency and Act Adequately Divide Real Being – Definition of Act and Potency – Divisions of Act and Potency – * Historical Notes – Summary . . .	112
	Suggested Readings	126

PART TWO

The Philosophy of Finite Being

SECTION I

THE NATURE OF FINITE BEING

4. MULTIPLICATION OF "TO BE"

Essence and "To Be" – The Multiplication of "To Be" Can Be Explained Only by the Reception of "To Be"

TABLE OF CONTENTS

CHAPTER	PAGE

in a Limiting Essence – "To Be" and Its Limiting Essence Are Really Distinct – Distinctions Admitted by All – What Is Not Implied by the Real Distinction – Proof of the Real Distinction – A Finite Essence and Its "To Be" Enter Into a Real Composition – Importance of the Real Distinction – * Historical Notes – Summary 130

Suggested Readings 140

5. MULTIPLICATION OF ESSENCE

I. How Can an Essence be Multiplied? The Multiplication of a Specific Essence Can Be Explained Only by the Reception of the Specific Perfection in a Limiting Potency – Matter and Form – Matter and Form Are Really Distinct and Enter Into a Real Composition – There Is No Limitation of Form Without Matter 142

II. The Principle of Individuation. The Concept of Individual – The Concept of "Principle of Individuation" – Matter Is the Principle of Individuation – How Matter Is the Principle of Individuation – Matter Made Distinct by Quantity – * Individuation of Unreceived Forms and Pure "To Be" – * Historical Notes – Summary . . . 147

Suggested Readings 160

6. POSSIBLE BEING

The Concepts of Possible Being and Possibility – The Ultimate Foundation of Extrinsic Possibility Can Be Found Only in a Being Whose Essence Is Its "To Be" – The Ultimate Foundation of Intrinsic Possibility Can Be Found Only in a Being Whose Essence Is Its "To Be" – What Kind of a "To Be" do the Possibles Have? – Historical Notes – Summary . . . 161

Suggested Readings 170

xvi

TABLE OF CONTENTS

CHAPTER PAGE

SECTION II
THE SUPREME CLASSES OF FINITE BEING

7. THE CATEGORIES IN GENERAL

    The Meaning of the Term "Category" – The Number of Categories – No Category Is a Purely Extrinsic Denomination – Categories Have No Common Genus – * Historical Notes – Summary 172

    Suggested Reading 178

8. SUBSTANCE

    I. The Necessity of Distinguishing Between Substance and Accidents. A Being Which Is Subject to Change While Remaining the Same Individual Is Composed of Potency and Act in the Order of Activity – Union of Substance and Accidents . . 179

    II. The Concept of Substance. How the Concept Is Acquired – The Existence of Substance – Definition of Substance – * Is God a Substance? – Meaning of the Term "To Be in Itself" – A Misconception – * Division of Substance – * Historical Notes – Summary 182

    Suggested Readings 198

9. * SUPPOSIT AND PERSON

    Meaning of the Terms "Supposit" and "Person" – Individual Substance or Nature and Supposit Are Really Distinct – The Nature of Subsistence or Personality – Consciousness and Personality – Historical Notes – Summary 199

    Suggested Readings 209

10. ACCIDENTS IN GENERAL

    Definition and Division of Accidents – The Reality of Accidents – Accidents Have Their Own "To Be" – In-

xvii

TABLE OF CONTENTS

CHAPTER		PAGE
	dividuation of Accidents – * Historical Notes – Summary	210
	Suggested Readings	215
11.	RELATIONS	
	The Nature of Relation – Transcendental and Predicamental Relations – Conditions Required for a Predicamental Relation – Existence of Predicamental Relations – Distinction of Predicamental Relations from Their Subject, Term, and Foundation – * Multiplication of Relation – A Misconception – * Historical Notes – Summary	216
	Suggested Readings	226

SECTION III
THE CAUSES OF FINITE BEING

12.	CAUSES IN GENERAL	
	I. The Concept of Cause. Cause and Principle – Cause and Condition – Cause and Occasion – Cause and Sufficient Reason of Being	228
	II. The Existence of Causes	232
	III. Genera of Causes – * Historical Notes – Summary	234
	Suggested Readings	239
13.	EFFICIENT CAUSALITY	
	I. The Principle of Causality. Formulas of the Principle of Causality – Certainty of the Principle of Causality – Some Axioms of Efficient Causality – * Historical Notes – Summary	240
	II. The Causality of Finite Beings. Division of Efficient Causes – Primary and Secondary Causes – Instrumental Causes – * Historical Notes – Summary	247
	Suggested Readings	256

xviii

TABLE OF CONTENTS

CHAPTER PAGE

14. FINAL CAUSALITY
    The Final Cause Is a True Cause – The Principle of Finality – The Nature of Final Causality – Chance – * Historical Notes – Summary 257
    Appendix: The Exemplary Cause 265
    Suggested Readings 266

15. THE MUTUAL RELATIONS OF CAUSES
    Reciprocal Causality – * Two or More Causes of the Same Effect 268
    Review Questions 271
    Some Translations of St. Thomas' Writings . . . 282
    Index of Names 285
    Index of Subject Matter 288

Introduction

The Names Given to Metaphysics

✢✢✢ 1. In the course of time, several names have been given to the department of philosophy which we are about to study. Aristotle himself called it either "First Philosophy," [1] because "other sciences, which take their principle from it, come after it," [2] or "Theology," [3] because it leads to the consideration of the First and Supreme Principle, which is God.[4] When Aristotle's manuscripts, damaged by mildew and bookworms, reached Rome in the first century before Christ, Andronicus of Rhodes, according to a report related by Strabo, Plutarch and Porphyry, published a new edition of Aristotle's works in which he placed the books of the first philosophy after those concerned with physics, under the general title μετὰ τὰ φυσικά, i.e., *After the Physics*. Hence the name "metaphysics," which since then has been the commonly accepted name for this science. The term "ontology" was rendered popular by the German philosopher Christan Wolff (1679–1754), who divided metaphysics into general metaphysics, or ontology,

---
[1] *Metaphysics*, bk. VI, ch. 1; 1026a, 24.
[2] St. Thomas, *In Boethium de trinitate*, q. V, a. 1.
[3] *Metaphysics*, bk. XI, ch. 7; 1064b, 2.
[4] *Ibid.*; 1064a 37.

and special metaphysics, in which he placed theodicy, cosmology, and psychology. The term "Philosophy of Being" is a translation of the term "ontology."

Scientific Knowledge and Metaphysics

2. Even in its most abstract form, "human knowledge takes its starting point from sense experience,"[5] but the level on which this knowledge terminates may be different. For "sometimes it is in the *senses,* sometimes in the *imagination,* and sometimes in the *intellect* alone."[6] Hence we must distinguish three levels of scientific knowledge according as the terminus of knowledge is in the senses, the imagination, or the intellect.[7] These three levels of scientific knowledge correspond to three degrees of abstraction from matter which can be made by the human intellect in its consideration of reality.

3. On the *first level,* scientific knowledge "terminates in the senses," for "the properties and accidents of the thing which are shown by the senses sufficiently express the nature of the thing. In this case, the judgment of the intellect concerning the truth of the thing must be conformed to that which the senses reveal about the thing."[8] The science which is concerned with this level of knowledge is called *physical* or "*natural science,* i.e., we judge of nat-

[5] St. Thomas, *op. cit.*, q. VI, a. 2.
[6] *Ibid.*
[7] This does not mean that on the first and the second levels the intellect does not play any role. It is needed on all three levels, just as the imagination is needed on both the first and the second levels. Note the word "alone" in the text of St. Thomas.
[8] St Thomas, *ibid* Attention is drawn to the fact that according to St. Thomas scientific knowledge on this level reaches the *nature* of the sensible object.

ural things according as they are revealed by sense experience . . . and whoever disregards sense experience with respect to the realm of nature falls into error." [9] Hence the conclusions of physical sciences must always be open to verification by sense experience. From this it follows that physical sciences must retain something which is subject to sense experience; for otherwise no verification by means of the senses would be possible.

It is clear, therefore, that scientific knowledge on this level may make abstraction only from so-called *"individual matter,"* i.e., from the differences which distinguish this man from that man, this sample of sodium from that sample of sodium, etc.[10] But it must retain the common *"sensible matter"* which enters into the definition of the things it considers. By sensible matter is meant matter "insofar as it is subject to sensible qualities, such as being hot or cold, hard or soft, and such like." [11] *Common* sensible matter refers to those sensible qualities which are found in individuals insofar as they belong to a certain group or class. That common sensible matter is retained in physical science should be clear. For questions referring to such matter are meaningful in physical science. For instance, it makes sense to ask questions about the temperature, hardness, density, etc. of a physical object.

Knowledge on this level is said to be on the *first degree of abstraction*. The intellect considers such things as water in general, man in general, plants in general, or a certain type of water, man or plant, etc., without being particu-

[9] *Ibid.*
[10] All scientific knowledge must make some kind of abstraction, because all scientific knowledge is intellectual knowledge, and all intellectual knowledge is obtained by means of abstraction.
[11] St. Thomas, *Summa theol*, Ia, q. 85, a. 1, ad 2.

INTRODUCTION

larly interested in the individual as such. The object is always something which can *neither exist nor be understood without sensible matter.*[12] Experimental sciences, such as physics, chemistry, biology, experimental psychology, etc., belong to this level of scientific knowledge.[13]

4. On the *second level*, scientific knowledge "terminates in the imagination," for "when abstraction is made from the sensible conditions of a thing, there still remains something imaginable; so that with respect to such objects judgment must be made according to what the imagination shows."[14] This "something imaginable" is quantity, i.e., extension and number, which are abstracted from all sensible qualities. A simple consideration will make this clear. If a man inquires about the temperature of a triangle or the softness of number ten, the listener will conclude, no doubt, that the fellow must have escaped from an asylum, because such questions do not make sense. The reason why they are meaningless is precisely that quantity abstracts from all sensible matter. The study of mathematics belongs to this level of scientific knowledge. "In mathematics the judgment of knowledge must be terminated in the imagination and not in sense experience because a mathematical judgment exceeds the apprehen-

[12] St. Thomas, *In Boethium de trinitate*, q. V, a. 1.
[13] St. Thomas has an interesting remark about the use of mathematics in physical science. "The natural body adds sensible matter to mathematical magnitude. Hence it is not incongruous if the physicist uses mathematical principles in his demonstrations; for [his science] is not an entirely different genus but somehow contained under the other science [i.e., mathematics]." *In I de coelo et mundo, lect.* (3 no. 24 in the Spiazzi edition).
[14] St. Thomas, *In Boethium de trinitate*, q. VI, a. 2.

sion of the senses." [15] The lines, figures, numbers, etc. considered in mathematics are not objects of sense experience but exist only in our imagination, although it is true that sense-perceptible representations of them on paper or a blackboard may be used to aid our imagination. Hence verification by sense experience is not possible with respect to mathematical objects.

Scientific knowledge on this level is said to be on the *second degree of abstraction* from matter. It abstracts not only from individual matter, but also from common sensible matter, and retains only quantity, which "can be understood in a substance before there is understanding of the sensible qualities by which matter is called sensible; hence according to the nature of its substance quantity does not depend upon sensible matter, but only upon intelligible matter." [16] By *"intelligible matter"* is meant "substance insofar as it is subject to quantity." [17] Intelligible matter has to be retained because numbers, dimensions and figures "cannot be considered unless the substance which is their subject is considered." [18] The object of scientific knowledge on this level *"depends upon* [sensible] *matter for its existence, but can be understood without it* because sensible matter does not enter into its definition." [19] All mathematical sciences belong to this level of scientific knowledge.[20]

[15] *Ibid.*

[16] *Cp cit.*, q. V, a. 3.

[17] *Summa theol*, Ia, q. 85, a. 1, ad 2.

[18] *Ibid.* The intelligible matter retained on this level is not individual but common, i.e., not this or that material subject, but a material subject, as St. Thomas explains, *ibid.*

[19] *In Boethium de trinitate*, q. V, a. 1.

[20] Regarding the position of modern mathematics, cf. Andrew G.

INTRODUCTION

5. On the *third level*, scientific knowledge "terminates in the intellect," for "there are things which transcend both that which falls under the senses and that which falls under the imagination"; [21] not that we obtain knowledge of these things independently from sense experience and imagination, but rather that "the judgment of knowledge must not be terminated in either imagination or sensation." [22]

On this level, knowledge abstracts not only from all individual matter, as in experimental sciences, and from common sensible matter, as in mathematics, but from *all* matter. Thus we reach the highest or *third degree of abstraction* from matter. Scientific knowledge on this level considers "either things which never exist in matter, such as God and angels, or things which in some cases exist in matter but not in others, such as substance, quality, potency and act, the one and the many, and things of this sort," [23] or in general "separate [i.e., immaterial] substances, and whatever is common to all beings" [24] and therefore most universal. In other words, the object of scientific knowledge here is *"wholly independent from matter, both as to its existence and as to its understanding."* [25] Science on this level is called metaphysics.

---

van Melsen, *The Philosophy of Nature* (Pittsburgh: Duquesne University, 1954), p. 97.

[21] St. Thomas, *op. cit.*, q. VI, a. 2.

[22] *Ibid.*

[23] *Op. cit.*, q. V, a. 1. Nowadays angelology is no longer treated in metaphysics.

[24] *Op. cit.*, q. VI, a. 1, q. 2, ad 2.

[25] *Op. cit.*, q. VI, a. 2. The objects considered in metaphysics can be either positively immaterial, as God, or abstractively immaterial, as finite being In the second case, no attention is paid to the material aspect of the being in question.

The Object of Metaphysics

6. In every science we must distinguish the material and the formal object. By the *material* object of a science is meant the things which are considered in that science, and by the *formal* object is meant that aspect under which the material object is considered.[26] For instance, the human body is the material object of medical science, and health is its formal object.

One and the same material object may be considered from several points of view or by several sciences. For example, water is considered by the chemist, the physicist, the physician, the philosopher, the brewer, and the sailor, but each of them considers it from a different point of view. Hence sciences will be distinguished according to their point of view or formal object.[27]

All sciences are concerned with beings, but they do not consider all beings, but only a particular type of being, such as plants, minerals, or quantified being. Metaphysics differs from all other human sciences because of the *extension of its material object*. It embraces everything that is or can be, whether it be material or immaterial, limited or unlimited.

With respect to the *formal object*, no other science considers beings precisely insofar as beings, as metaphysics does. Hence metaphysics differs from all other sciences because of its formal object, which is being itself.

By taking the material and the formal object together,

---

[26] Strictly speaking, we should distinguish the so-called formal objects "quod" and "quo." The formal object "quod" is the material object taken under a certain aspect; the formal object "quo" is precisely that aspect under which the material object is considered.

[27] *In I analytica posteriora,* lect. 39.

we obtain the definition of metaphysics as *the science of being as being.*[28]

The Division of Metaphysics

7. It cannot be denied that metaphysics is one science,[29] for wherever there is unity of formal object there is only one science. Nevertheless, for convenience it is permissible to divide metaphysics into several sections, provided we do not lose sight of its fundamental unity. It is in this sense that we may speak of *general* metaphysics when our study of being is concerned with the concept of being, the general properties of being, its primary divisions, etc. *Special* metaphysics will be concerned with finite and infinite being, and with the applications of general metaphysical principles to the various types of finite beings. Sometimes special names are given to these sections of metaphysics. Thus it is a common practice to speak of the metaphysics of infinite Being as science of *theodicy;* of the metaphysics of inanimate nature as *cosmology;* of the metaphysics of animate nature as (rational) *psychology,* and of the metaphysics of man in particular as *philosophical anthropology.* Moreover, the metaphysics of being in general and the metaphysics of finite being in general are often joined together under the name of *ontology.* In addition, there is a preliminary metaphysical investigation which considers being as it is related to the human mind, i.e., whether or not our mind is capable of attaining knowledge of being as it is in itself. This investigation is called *epistemology.* Logically, it should precede the other sections of metaphysics, for the conclusions reached in epistemology decide about the value of metaphysics as a whole.

[28] Cf. Aristotle, *Metaphysics,* bk. IV, ch. 1, 1003a 21.
[29] Cf. St. Thomas, *In metaphysic.,* prooemium.

8. In ancient times and even in the Middle Ages, the whole of experiential data was rather small and did not allow the immediate development of an autonomous system of knowledge on the first level. Consequently, the available data were drawn into the sphere of philosophy and formed together with the metaphysics of nature the so-called philosophy of nature. But St. Thomas clearly indicates that certain questions of natural philosophy belong to the metaphysical level. A special science, he says, "may be called a part of this science [i.e., of metaphysics] insofar as it is concerned with potency and act, with unity, and with anything of the sort. For these things have the same manner of consideration as being which is dealt with in metaphysics." [30] Nowadays, the subject matter formerly considered in the philosophy of nature has been divided into a number of autonomous sciences which limit themselves to the level of sense experience, and philosophy proper, i.e., the application of general metaphysical principles to material nature.

The Importance of Metaphysics

9. *Metaphysics Is a Speculative Science.* From the foregoing it should be clear that metaphysics is a speculative science and does not serve a utilitarian purpose. It is not studied because it teaches us *how to do* certain things, but because man seeks to know *for the sake of knowing*. To quote Aristotle: "It is owing to their wonder that men both now begin and at first began to philosophize; . . . therefore since they philosophized in order to escape from ignorance, evidently they were pursuing science in order to know, and not for a utilitarian end. And this is con-

---

[30] *In Boethium de trinitate,* q. V, a. 1, ad 6.

firmed by the facts; for it was when almost all the necessities of life and the things that make for comfort and recreation had been secured, that such knowledge began to be sought. Evidently then we do not seek it for the sake of any other advantage; but . . . we pursue this as the only free science, for it alone exists for its own sake." [31] Although we may disagree with Aristotle on the necessities and comforts of life, it is clear that metaphysics does not serve any utilitarian purpose.

10. *Metaphysics Has Absolute Value.* As a pure science, the value of metaphysics can hardly be overrated. For metaphysics is concerned with being in general; hence its conclusions will apply to everything which falls under the extension of the concept of being. Consequently, whatever conclusions metaphysics reaches will have *absolute value;* they apply to the objects considered in any branch of human knowledge and not only in philosophy. For the objects of other sciences are things which fall under the extension of the concept of being.

11. *Metaphysics Renders Secure the Ultimate Foundation of All Science.* Without metaphysics the ultimate foundations of all other sciences are left insecure. In other sciences we presuppose and take for granted such things as the principles of contradiction and of causality, the multiplication of individuals in the same species, the pos-

[31] *Metaphysics,* bk. I, ch. 2; 982b 11 ff. It is to be noted that the term "philosophy" had a wider meaning in the time of Aristotle than it has now. Therefore, philosophy in the modern sense of the term is not the only "free science." This and the other translations of Aristotle are taken from *The Works of Aristotle,* translated into English under the editorship of W. D. Ross. All quotations are made with the kind permission of the publishers, Oxford University Press.

INTRODUCTION

sibility of change, etc. If we accept all these things without examining their value, the whole structure built upon them stands on insecure grounds and thus leaves everything open to doubt. On the other hand, if we do not accept them, scientific knowledge of any kind will be impossible. Hence in order to make true science possible, these principles and presuppositions must be examined, and their validity established. This, however, does not mean that it would be impossible to study any other science without a previous study of metaphysics; for man quite spontaneously accepts the validity of certain metaphysical principles without any critical examination. But it is quite obvious that such an examination must be made if we do not wish to leave everything open to doubt. The task of evaluating these principles does not belong to any special science but to metaphysics. St. Thomas clearly shows us the reason why: these principles, he says, "should not be dealt with in any particular science; for they are needed for the [complete] knowledge of any genus of being; hence any particular science would be equally entitled to deal with them. Consequently, it follows that such principles must be dealt with in one general science [i.e., metaphysics], which . . . is the norm of all others." [32]

12. *It Is the Task of Metaphysics to Examine All Absolute Principles.* Man is naturally inclined to philosophize, even if he has not received any training in philosophy. Hence it may easily happen that in the course of other sciences one will tacitly assume, or explicitly formulate, metaphysical principles which sound reason cannot accept. It is the task of metaphysics to analyze and evaluate any absolute principles which are assumed or put forward

[32] St. Thomas, *In metaphysic.*, prooemium.

INTRODUCTION

in the study of other sciences. It is to be noted however, that we say "any *absolute* principles," i.e., principles which by their very nature are applicable to all things. For it is obvious that metaphysics is neither entitled to nor equipped for the examination of the relative principles and laws particular to any special science, i.e., a principle or law which applies only within the limits of a special science or group of cognate sciences. For instance, metaphysics should not attempt to examine purely physical principles, e.g., the law of gravitation or the law of conservation of energy.[33] Hence this claim of metaphysics does not jeopardize the hard-won autonomy of the other sciences.

13. *The Norms of Life Ultimately Depend Upon Metaphysical Principles.* Man is guided in his life by certain practical philosophic principles, whether these principles be embodied in an established religious system or remain purely ethical and personal. Now, ultimately, even practical philosophic principles are based upon metaphysical principles. Therefore, whether we are aware of it or not, the principles which govern the way we want to live and act ultimately depend upon our metaphysical principles. Of course, we may continue to live and act according to principles whose ultimate basis we have never subjected to a rational analysis; for we can accept them on authority

---

[33] However, one should not forget that often so-called physical laws are expressed in such a way that a certain philosophical background, which may be either true or false, is discernible. In such a case, it is the task of a well-trained, philosopher-scientist to disentangle the physical law from its quasi-philosophical formulation. Cf. Andrew G. Van Melsen, *From Atomos to Atom* (Pittsburgh: Duquesne University, 1952), pp. 160 ff., 187 ff. and passim.

or even as quite natural, without scientific examination, just as in experimental science we may continue our research without examining the metaphysical foundation of these sciences. However, it should be clear that in doing so we remain exposed to the danger of being more easily led astray by false principles.

The Origin and History of Metaphysics

14. As far as historical records go, *Parmenides* of Elea (born about 540 B.C.) seems to have been the first philosopher to consider all things under the common aspect of being and thus well deserves to be called the first metaphysician. *Aristotle* (384–322 B.C.), however, was the first to systematize a comprehensive theory of being. His works became the object of countless commentaries, first in the Greek world, and later among Arabian philosophers, such as *Avicenna* and *Averroes*. As a result of the conquest of Toledo in 1085, his writings became better known to the medieval West, although only in translations from corrupt Arabian and Hebrew versions, which themselves were but translations of Syrian translations of the original Greek. But after the fall of Constantinople in 1204 the West was able to obtain direct translations from the Greek. In the course of the thirteenth century the Schoolmen, especially *St. Thomas*, widened the scope of Aristotelian metaphysics by adding to it many other elements, especially from Neoplatonic philosophy. From the fourteenth century on, it became generally accepted in the European universities, though not without an intense struggle. But after a period of splendor the study of metaphysics declined, due to the Renaissance and other causes which guided man's quest of knowledge into different directions. This decline became still more pronounced through the efforts of the

nascent physical sciences to obtain their autonomy. Lack of insight into the true nature of both philosophy and the sciences of nature must be held responsible for the subsequent confusion of philosophic and physical theories, which was and still is a hindrance for the study and development of scientific knowledge on both levels.

In modern times, outside scholastic schools of philosophy agnosticism is fairly prevalent. Phenomenalists, such as *Hume,* and positivists, such as *Comte,* refuse to recognize metaphysics as a science because in their view only that exists which can be perceived by the senses; hence according to them metaphysics does not have an object. On the other hand, idealists, such as *Kant,* claim that metaphysics is impossible, either because objective reality does not exist or because it cannot be known even if its existence is admitted. However, this is not the place to discuss these theories. They have been, or will be, discussed in epistemology.

Epistemological Presuppositions

15. The complexity of modern epistemology makes it impossible for us to include a study of epistemological problems in a general course of metaphysics. Hence we suppose here as valid and proven the epistemological system of *mitigated realism,* which hold the following propositions:
1. There is a real world outside the mind, i.e., a world which does not depend upon our mind for its existence.
2. Our senses are trustworthy with respect to their proper objects.
3. Our intellectual knowledge is derived from sense experience without being altered by any *a priori* elements

which would make it impossible for us to know the world as it is in reality; hence our universal concepts have objective value.

SUMMARY

16. All scientific knowledge begins with sense experience. Scientific knowledge which abstracts only from individual matter is open to verification by sense experience. To this level of knowledge belong all of the experimental sciences.

Scientific knowledge which abstracts from all sensible matter is not open to verification by the senses. Its terminus is in the imagination, and its object is quantity. All the mathematical sciences belong to this level of scientific knowledge.

Scientific knowledge which abstracts from all matter can be examined and verified only by the reflection of the intellect. Its object is being as being. Scientific knowledge on this level is called metaphysics.

The material object of metaphysics embraces all things; its formal object is the aspect of being. Hence metaphysics may be defined as the science of being *qua* being.

The division of metaphysics into general metaphysics and special metaphysics, such as theodicy, cosmology, etc. is justifiable only if one does not lose sight of the fundamental unity of metaphysics.

Metaphysics is a speculative science. Its importance lies in this that its conclusions have absolute value for all sciences, that it examines the ultimate foundations of all sciences, that it analyzes and evaluates all absolute principles proposed in the course of other sciences (without, however, claiming control over the relative principles

INTRODUCTION

proper to other sciences), and that it examines and renders secure the ultimate foundations of the normative moral principles which direct man in his actions.

SUGGESTED READINGS

17. R. J. Henle, *Method in Metaphysics* (*Aquinas Lecture, 1950*) Marquette University Press, 1951.
G. Buckley, *The Nature and Unity of Metaphysics*, Catholic University of America Press, 1946.
V. J. Bourke, "Experience of Extramental Reality as the Starting Point of St. Thomas' Metaphysics," in *Proceedings of the American Catholic Philosophical Association*, 1934, pp. 134–148.
A. G. Van Melsen, *The Philosophy of Nature* (*Duquesne Studies, Philosophical Series*, vol. 2), Duquesne University Press, 1954, Ch. 3 (on degrees of abstraction).
Thomas Aquinas, *The Division and Method of the Sciences* (English translation of *in Boethium de Trinitate q. V and VI*, by A. A. Maurer), Pontifical Institute of Mediaeval Studies, Toronto, 1953.
J. T. Casey, *The Primacy of Metaphysics*, Catholic University of America Press, 1935.
E. Gilson, *The Unity of Philosophical Experience*, Scribners, 1950, Ch. 12.
L. de Raeymaeker, *Introduction to Philosophy*, Wagner, 1948, pp. 70–162 (survey of history of metaphysics). *The Philosophy of Being*, Herder, 1954, Ch. I (man's natural tendency to metaphysics).

PART ONE

The Philosophy of Being in General

THIS PART is divided into three chapters. First, we shall study the nature of the concept of being, its unity and analogy. In the second chapter we shall consider the properties consequent upon being. The last chapter of this section shall consist of a study of the theory of act and potency.

CHAPTER 1

The Nature of Being

I. THE CONCEPT OF BEING

Senses of the Term "Being"

✲✲✲ 18. The verb "to be" and its derivative "being" can be used in different senses.[1] *In the logical order* "to be" is used as a verbal copula which connects two ideas in our mind; for example, when we say that man is a species. Taken in this sense, "to be" does not express that a thing exists in reality, but may refer to anything which is conceived as if it were existing, even if in itself it does not exist. Hence in this sense "to be" and "being" may be used with respect to anything about which a proposition can be formed, although the thing in question is a mere negation or privation. Thus we say that blindness *is* in the eye, or even that a square circle *is* a contradiction. In doing so, we do not intend to attribute real "to be" to the square circle, but we merely connect in our mind the ideas "square circle" and "contradiction."

In the real order "to be" implies extramental existence. It is obvious, for instance, that in the proposition, "Peter

---

[1] Cf. St. Thomas, *Quodlibet* 9, a.3; *De ente et essentia*, c.1; *In V metaphysic.*, lect. 9 (nos. 889–896 in the Cathala and Spiazzi editions).

is fat," the value of the term *"is"* is absolutely different from that in the proposition "a square circle is square and round at the same time." The first *"is"* refers to something extramental, or real, whereas the second "is" merely is a verbal copula. Hence the term "being," insofar as it refers to the real order, cannot be used for things which cannot have an extramental existence.

19. However, even when "being" is used to refer to the order of reality, we must distinguish its use as a participle and as a noun.

As a participle "being" implies the actual exercise by a subject of the action indicated by the verb "to be," just as the participle "walking" implies the actual exercise by a subject of the action indicated by the verb "to walk." Hence when the term "being" is used as a participle in the real order, it can be attributed only to things which actually exist, or are considered to exist here and now in the order of reality.

As a noun "being" does not indicate actual "to be," or existence, but merely indicates a subject which has a reference to "to be," i.e., something which exists, has existed, will exist, or at least can become existent. This use of the term "being" is similar to that of other verbal nouns.[2] For example, expressions such as "the writings of Julius Caesar" and "the musings of a sage" do not indicate that Julius Caesar is actually writing here and now, or that the sage is here and now deeply engrossed in thought, but only that the things indicated by these expressions are subjects having a reference to an act of writing on the part of Caesar, or an act of musing on the part of the sage.

[2] Cf. St. Thomas, *In Boethium de hebdomadibus*, lect. 2.

When we speak of real being in metaphysics, it is in this sense that the term is used, unless there is positive indication to the contrary.[3] Hence "being" applies not only to actually existing things, but to anything which possesses a reference to existence, whether it be considered as actual or not.

Being Is the Most Common and Most Simple of All Concepts

20. It is obvious that being is the *most common* of all concepts. For a concept is more common if it extends to a larger number of things; now being applies to absolutely everything which has a reference to "to be"; in other words, nothing is excluded from the extension of being because what has no reference to "to be" simply is not. Hence being is the most common of all concepts.

From this it follows that being is also the *most simple* of all concepts. For in order to be most common, a concept must have no determinations which limit its extension; now a concept which is most indeterminate is most simple. *However, notwithstanding its simplicity, *the concept of being is not entirely without composition.* For it expresses a subject whose act is "to be," i.e., a composite of essence and "to be." Hence the objection could be raised that the concepts of essence and "to be" are more simple than the concept of being. To this we may answer that it is impossible to conceive an essence without a relation to "to be"; hence the concept of essence is not more simple than the concept of being. And with regard to "to be," it is con-

[3] For instance, it should be clear that we mean "being" as a participle when we say that being is predicated essentially of God and accidentally of creatures. Cf. St. Thomas, *Quodlibet.* 2, a.3.

ceived as if it were a determination of the essence; hence its concept includes essence and is not as simple as the concept of essence itself.

*Thus it is clear that the human mind is not capable of forming an *absolutely simple* concept. The reason is that the human intellect which is united to a body derives all its concepts from material things, in which there is always a composition of a subject with a form.[4] In passing, we may note that this is the reason why, even if there exists a being which is without any composition, our concept of this being cannot be simple but will have to remain composite, although we know that the object of our concept has no composition in itself.

No Strict Definition of Being Is Possible

21. Since being is most common, a strict definition of it is impossible. For a strict definition consists of the genus of a thing and a specific difference which is not actually contained in the genus; for instance, the strict definition of man is "rational (specific difference) animal (genus)." Being, however, is not contained in any *genus;* for whatever would be named as a genus would fall under "being" and therefore could not be its genus.

Moreover, it is impossible to find any *specific difference.* For whatever would be named as a specific difference would be something having a reference to "to be," and therefore would fall under the concept of being; hence it could not be something which determines a genus to the species "being."

All we can do, therefore, is give descriptions of being— being is *that which is; or that whose act is "to be"; or that*

---

[4] Cf. I *Contra gentes,* c. 30.

to which is due a "to be";[5] or *that which has a reference to "to be."*[6] It is to be noted that these descriptions imply two elements in the subject which is called a being, viz., a reference to "to be" and this "to be" itself. The reference to "to be" may be called the *essence,* and "to be" itself is often spoken of as *existence.*

Being Is Ontologically the First of All Concepts

22. The concept of being is first ontologically inasmuch as it is the foundation of all other concepts. Other concepts, such as man, weight, God, blue, etc., are obtained by adding something to being.[7] The only concept which does not express any being at all is "nothing," but nothing is the negation of being, and thus it, too, presupposes the concept of being.

*Historical Notes

23. *Monistic philosophers* claim that being in general exists as such outside the mind, and that all things are but modifications of this one being. The *nominalists* and *conceptualists* consider the concept of being as a pure figment of our intellect and therefore without any objective value. This position makes true metaphysics impossible.

SUMMARY

24. In the logical order "to be" is a verbal copula and does not express that a thing exists in reality. In the real

[5] Cf. St. Thomas, *In Boethium de hebdomadibus,* lect. 2; *Quodlibet.* 2, a 3; *De natura generis* (the authenticity of this work is not certain, although it is generally considered to be Thomistic in spirit).

[6] This reference should be conceived as a transcendental relation. Cf. no. 218.

[7] Cf. *De veritate,* q.I, a.1. Concerning the sense of the term "adding," see below, no. 30.

order "to be" implies extramental existence. As a participle, "being" implies actual existence; as a noun, it means something which has a reference to "to be."

Being is the most common of all concepts because it applies to everything that has a reference to existence. It is most simple because it is most indeterminate. Nevertheless, it implies a composition of a subject with its "to be."

A strict definition of being is impossible because being has neither a genus nor a specific difference.

Being is ontologically first inasmuch as it is the foundation of all other concepts of reality.

II. THE UNITY OF THE CONCEPT OF BEING

25. Having determined the meaning of the concept of being, we must now see whether this concept possesses any internal unity or not. The answer to this question is important; for if being does not have any unified meaning but is altogether different whenever applied to reality, it will be nothing but an empty word, void of any meaning. Three answers are possible to our question: either being possesses internal unity or its unity is merely external; and if its unity is internal, it can be either perfect or imperfect. In the following pages we shall see that the unity of the concept of being is internal but imperfect. This unity is obtained by a process of abstraction, but not by the same type of abstraction as that by which we obtain universal concepts which have always the same definite meaning, such as man, animal, or plant.

The Abstraction of Universal Concepts

26. Briefly, the process by which universal concepts are obtained is the following.[8] When our intellect is presented

[8] Cf. St. Thomas, *In II de anima*, lect. 12 (nos. 377–380 in the Pirotta edition).

with a sense image of a concrete material thing, an intellectual power dematerializes this image, and this dematerialized image actuates the intellectual power by which we understand by impressing itself upon this power. The resulting act of understanding terminates in the production of a concept of an immaterial and therefore universal nature. It makes no difference whether the sense image of Peter or John is presented to the intellect, for the concept resulting from the activity of the intellect leaves out of consideration everything by which Peter and John are different, such as their weight, size, degree of intelligence, etc. It focuses its attention upon those characteristics which are common. Thus it apprehends a definite nature which can exist in many precisely because it prescinds from all individual differences. This cognitive process is called "*abstraction.*"

It is to be noted that in abstracting the universal concept of man we leave behind, out of consideration, all differences by which Peter, John, and others are distinct. Hence it is clear that our universal concept does not *actually* contain the differences of its inferiors,[9] but is *perfectly abstracted* from them and therefore *perfectly unified*. It is true, of course, that the universal nature expressed in our concept remains capable of being further determined by these differences. For this reason we may say that these differences are *potentially* included in the concept. But it should be clear that such a determination cannot come from within, from anything actually contained in the concept of man, but has to come from without, through the addition of a new element. For instance, the nature expressed by the concept "animal" can be further determined by the addition of the differentiating

[9] By the inferiors of a concept are meant all things to which the concept can be applied.

element "rational"; but this element is not actually included in the concept of animal because otherwise all animals would have to be rational.

The Abstraction of Being

27. We must now see whether this process of abstraction can be used to form the concept of being.[10] It should already be clear that such an abstraction is impossible. When we abstract "being" from its inferiors, we cannot leave behind any determinations or characteristics; for each and everyone of these characteristics is something which has a reference to "to be"; each of them, in a sense, is a being. Hence it is impossible to form the concept of being in the same way as we form the concept of man; for our concept of being will have *to retain actually* all the differences between its inferiors.

28. *How "Being" Retains the Differences of Its Inferiors.* There would seem to be two ways in which "being" could actually retain the differences of its inferiors: they could be retained either explicitly or implicitly. If they are retained *explicitly,* being will contain them precisely insofar as they are differences, without any internal unification. Thus the differences would be in "being" in the manner in which a book contains a number of pages or a jar a number of cookies. Consequently, being would be merely a collective name covering a plurality of entirely different modes of being. Let us illustrate our intention with an example. Take the propositions: God is a being, and Peter is a being. If being is without any internal unification, its meaning as predicated of God will be entirely different from the meaning it has when predicated of

[10] Cf. Cajetan, *Enarratio de ente et essentia,* I, 2.

Peter. As applied to various beings, the predicate "being" would have nothing in common but the name. As a result, we should be committed to an undisguised form of nominalism, which is untenable, as we have seen in epistemology.

29. This leaves us with the other alternative, viz., that the concept of being actually contains the differences of its inferiors, not explicitly, but *implicitly*. Obviously, this alternative is possible only if these differences can be unified to some extent. *Absolute* or *perfect* unification is impossible for the following reason. Our concept of being is a concept of reality, and things as they exist in reality are different. Now we can obtain an absolutely unified concept only by leaving behind the differences between things as they exist in reality. The concept of being, however, may not leave behind any differences. Hence the only kind of unity we will be able to retain will be a *relative* or *imperfect* unity. Examples of relative unity may be found in proportional expressions, such as double weight, double windows, double power, double work, etc. These terms are absolutely different save insofar as they express an equal proportion.[11] Likewise, half the weight, half the size, half the power, etc. It will be possible to find a type of relative unity in the concept of being if the differences between its inferiors can be retained, not insofar as they are differences, but insofar as each of them expresses a similar proportion. Now it is clear that each of

[11] From "double windows," "double weight," etc. it is possible to abstract a univocal concept of quantity, namely, "double," because the proportion implied by these terms is not merely similar but equal. In analogous concepts, however, the proportion is similar but not equal.

these differences is something having a reference to "to be"; for otherwise we should not call them beings. Of course, the nature of this reference to "to be" varies according to the type of being considered; for example, in "man" we do not find the same relationship to "to be" as in "yellow" or "heavy," because man does not exist in the same way as yellow or heavy. Nevertheless, in everything to which the term "being" can be applied we shall always find that the thing has a definite nature, and that this nature is proportioned to its "to be." Hence as long as we conceive things by a concept which does *not determine the nature of this relationship* but leaves it indeterminate, our concept can be applied to everything which has a relation to "to be." Now, our concept of being does not determine this relationship, for we described being merely as that which has a reference to "to be."

In a certain sense, therefore, it is true that our concept of being abstracts from the differences of its inferiors, but not in the same manner as concepts such as man, which make perfect abstraction from these differences. Being abstracts from the differences of its inferiors only insofar as it abstains from determining the exact nature of the relation between these inferiors and their "to be." This abstraction may be called *imperfect abstraction,* abstraction of indetermination or abstraction of con-fusion.[12] It terminates in a concept endowed with true internal, though imperfect, unity.

The Contraction of Being

30. Since being actually contains the differences of its inferiors, it is impossible to contract or limit the concept

[12] Cf. Cajetan, *De nominum analogia,* c.5.

of being by the addition of something from without; for outside being nothing is. Hence the only way in which we can contract being to a particular type of being is by adding something to being from within, i.e. by making *explicit* what is contained implicitly in being.[13] For instance, we can contract the concept of being to the type of being called "substance" by explicitly mentioning a mode of being implicitly contained in being, viz., "to be in itself." Or we can limit the concept of being to "man" by making explicit the attributes rational, sentient, living, corporeal, and substance. However, it is evident that these attributes express things which fall under the extension of the concept of being.

Being Is Not a Genus

31. From the foregoing it should be clear that being is not a genus. For, as is evident from logic, a genus is contracted to a species by the addition of differences which are not actually contained in the genus.[14] Since being actually contains all differences of its inferiors it follows that it is not a genus.

*Historical Notes

32. *Parmenides* maintained the perfect unity of being, even in the order of reality, notwithstanding the testimony of the senses to the contrary. He reasoned as follows: in order to be many, beings have to be different; now outside being nothing is; therefore being cannot be differentiated and is perfectly unified. We shall come back upon the position of Parmenides in chapter 3.

Duns Scotus (1274–1308) maintained that the concept

[13] Cf. St. Thomas, *De veritate*, q. I, a. 1.
[14] Cf. St. Thomas, *In III metaphysic.*, lect. 8, no. 433.

of being is perfectly unified because it prescinds perfectly from the differences of its inferiors. It does not contain these differences actually, but only potentially. Hence being is contracted to its inferiors by the addition from without of differentiating modes. Nevertheless it is not a genus, because these modes do not add anything to being: formally speaking they are not being, though really they are. It is only fair to add that according to many modern Scotists Scotus' concept of being is de-essentialized and thus means nothing but the act of existence taken by itself.

Francis Suarez (1548–1617) tried to take a middle course between St. Thomas and Scotus by asserting on the one hand that the concept of being does not contain the differences of its inferiors because it prescinds perfectly from them; and on the other that the differences of the inferiors are formally being.

The *nominalists* deny that being possesses any internal unity and admit only a unification of the name or term "being" inasmuch as the same term is used to indicate the whole collection of beings.

SUMMARY

33. Universal ideas, such as man, are obtained by a process of perfect abstraction from the differences existing between the inferiors. Hence such a concept is perfectly unified and includes these differences only potentially inasmuch as they can be added to being from without.

The concept of "being" cannot be abstracted in the same way because being must actually retain the differences of its inferiors. But it cannot retain them explicitly; for otherwise it would be nothing but a name without any real meaning. Hence it may retain them only implicitly, by a kind of unification. Absolute unification, however, is not possible because an absolutely unified concept perfectly abstracts from the differences of its inferiors. But relative unification is possible because each of the differences is something which has a relation to "to be." Although this relation varies from being to being, yet my concept of being will remain the same, applicable to all beings insofar as it does not determine the nature of this relation. Hence the abstraction by which the concept of being is obtained is not as perfect as that which leads to universal concepts such as man. It is called abstraction of indetermination or con-fusion, and terminates in a concept with a true internal, though imperfect unity.

Being is not contracted to a particular type of being by the addition of something from without, but by making explicit something which is implicitly contained in it.

Being is not a genus, for a genus does not actually contain the differences of its inferiors.

III. THE ANALOGY OF BEING

The unity of the concept of being is intimately connected with the question whether the concept of being is analogous or not, and if so by what kind of analogy. Before, however, we can attempt to answer this question, we must first study the nature of analogy.

Univocal, Equivocal, and Analogous Terms

34. As will be recalled from logic, with respect to predication terms are divided into three types: univocal, equivocal, and analogous terms. A term is *univocal* "when it is predicated of diverse things according to exactly the same concept. For instance, the term "animal" as applied

to a horse and an ox signifies an animated, sensitive, substance." [15] In univocal predication not only the spoken or the written term remains the same, but the very *concept* of which this term is a symbol remains exactly the same. The reason is that such a concept abstracts perfectly from the differences of its inferiors; consequently, it is defined in an absolute way, i.e., independently from any relation to its inferiors.

35. A term is *equivocal* when it "is predicated of diverse things according to an entirely different concept." [16] A clear example is the term "coach" as applied to an instructor of athletics and to a certain type of vehicle. In equivocal predication the term itself remains the same, but the *concept* of which the term is a symbol is entirely different. It is purely accidental that two or more entirely different concepts are indicated by one and the same spoken or written symbol. For this reason such terms are said to be *equivocal by chance* or *by accident*.

It is to be noted that there can be no question of equivocal *concepts*. For by its very nature a concept has only one thought-content; hence an equivocal concept would be a contradiction in terms. Equivocity occurs only in the external term because the same symbol may be chosen to express entirely different concepts.[17]

[15] St. Thomas, *In XI metaphysic.*, lect. 3, nos. 2195 ff. Cf. also *In IV metaphysic.*, lect. 1, nos. 535 ff.; *De principiis naturae* (c. VI in the edition prepared by John J. Pauson and published by Nauwelaerts, Louvain, 1950).

[16] *Ibid.*

[17] Because being is the foundation of all concepts, no concepts are entirely different in themselves. But we may call them entirely different, inasmuch as in the choice of their external symbol no attention is paid to any common characteristics.

When we want to determine whether a term is univocal or equivocal (or analogous), we must take into consideration the *subjects of which the term is predicated*. If, for instance, the term "pen" is taken only insofar as it is predicable of a certain instrument for writing, it is univocal; but if it is taken as predicable of such an instrument and of an enclosure for animals, it is equivocal.

36. A term is *analogous* if "one and the same name is predicated of many according to concepts which are not entirely different, but agree in some common point." [18] In analogous predication the external term remains the same, but the concept of which the term is a symbol neither remains exactly the same, as is the case in univocal predication, nor becomes entirely different, as happens in equivocal predication, but *varies*, i.e., while changing it retains something. The reason why it does not remain exactly the same is that such a concept does not completely abstract from the differences of its inferiors. As a result, these differences have to be taken into consideration when the concept is predicated of different subjects. Thus the unity of such a concept is not absolute but only relative. For example, when my eyes perceive a sense object, I can say: "I see"; and when my intellect understands a problem, I can say: "I see." The act of sense perception is absolutely different from that of intellectual perception; nevertheless there is a certain relative unity because as the eye is related to sense perception, so the intellect is related to intellectual perception. Consequently, one and the same term may be used to express both actions. But when I predicate this term of the eye and of the intellect, the concept signified by the term "to see" has to be adjusted according

[18] St. Thomas, *In I ethic.*, lect. 7 (no. 95 in the Spiazzi edition).

as required by the subject (the eye or the intellect). In this way, one concept can be predicated of things which are absolutely different insofar as they are relatively the same.

Analogous terms are said to be *equivocal by design* or *intentionally* because man chooses the same term for the avowed purpose of expressing the relative unity which he discovers in absolutely different things.

Modes of Analogy

37. Not all analogous terms are analogous in the same manner.[19] We may distinguish analogy of attribution, metaphorical analogy, and analogy of proportionality. Before explaining these modes of analogy, let us first state that by the term *"analogate"* we mean that of which an analogous term is predicated. The *primary* analogate means the analogate to which such a term belongs principally, and *secondary* analogates are analogates of which such a term is predicated in dependence upon the primary analogate. For example, if I predicate "healthy" of man, fresh air, and medicine, man is the primary analogate, and fresh air and medicine are the secondary analogates.

38. *Analogy of Attribution.* In analogy of attribution the nature signified by the concept is *intrinsically* realized in the primary analogate, but attributed to the others only insofar as they have a *relationship* to the primary analogate. The traditional example is the concept of health. We say: Peter is healthy; fresh air is healthy; his complexion is healthy. In its proper and accepted meaning health means that the various parts of a living body function properly in relation to the whole. Hence the perfection of

[19] Cf. Cajetan, *De nominum analogia,* cc. 2 and 3.

health is intrinsically realized in the primary analogate, Peter. When health is predicated of fresh air and complexion, it is attributed to them merely because in fresh air and in a rosy complexion there is something by which they are related to the health of a living body, either as a contributing cause or as an effect which reveals this health.[20] Hence in calling them healthy I merely want to affirm this relationship. For this reason fresh air, complexion, etc. are said to be healthy by relation, attribution, or extrinsic denomination. Whence also analogy of attribution may be called analogy of relation or proportion.

It is clear that it would be impossible to define health as predicated of the secondary analogates without the primary analogate being taken into consideration. The reason is that the secondary analogates are not "healthy" in an absolute sense, but only relatively to the primary analogate.

It should be noted also that in analogy of attribution, strictly speaking, it is not the concept which varies in meaning. For even when we predicate healthy of the secondary analogates, we are still thinking about the same health as when we predicate it of a living body. It is rather the external term expressing this concept which is widened so as to make possible its application to things which have a relationship to the primary analogate. Hence we may conclude that a concept which is analogous by analogy of attribution is *analogous only in a wider sense* of the term, for when the perfection expressed by the term is realized, it is realized in a strictly univocal sense. Nevertheless, there is no pure equivocation in the use of such terms with respect to secondary analogates; for the widen-

---

[20] Cf. *Summa theol.*, Ia, q. 16, a. 6.

ing of the application of the terms is not done arbitrarily, but because there is a basis for it in the secondary analogates. As we have seen above, this basis is in the causal relation existing between the primary and the secondary analogates.

39. *Metaphorical Analogy.* In this analogy, which is also called analogy of improper proportionality, the nature signified by the term is realized *formally and intrinsically* in one of the analogates, and in the other or others *intrinsically and virtually*, i.e., only with respect to a secondary characteristic, such as the activity, proper to this nature. Take for example, the term "lion." The nature signified by this term is realized formally and intrinsically only in the animal which we call a lion. We cannot call a man a lion in the formal sense, for a lion is essentially irrational, whereas man is essentially rational. However, it is proper to the nature of a lion to act courageously in the face of danger, or at least we consider this to be so. Hence we may fix our attention upon this secondary aspect of the nature of a lion and predicate the term "lion" of a man who is courageous. In doing so we merely want to convey the idea that in the face of danger this man acts in the same way as a lion is supposed to act. Hence we say that he is a lion because of his resemblance to a lion in the order of activity. As far as the predication of the term "lion" is concerned, it is clear that only a certain type of brute animal formally and intrinsically realizes the nature expressed by this term. Hence in predicating "lion" of a man we have to keep in mind the subject of our predication and to make an adjustment in the predicate. Again, however, this adjustment is rather in the term than in the

concept; for the nature signified by the term is realized formally and intrinsically only in the animal. Nevertheless, pure equivocation is avoided because we see a basis for predicating the same term of both animal and man. This basis lies in a similiarity of both subjects in a secondary aspect of the nature "lion," namely, in the order of activity.

It should be clear that it is impossible to define "lion" as predicated of a man without the primary analogate (the brute animal) being taken into consideration. For the reason of the predication is precisely some aspect flowing from the nature of the primary analogate.

40. *Analogy of Proportionality.* In analogy of (proper) proportionality the nature signified by the concept is *formally and intrinsically* realized in *each* of the analogates according to a proportional similarity. Let us explain this definition.

In the first place, the nature signified by the concept is *intrinsically* realized in each of the analogates. This characteristic distinguishes analogy of proportionality from analogy of attribution, for in the latter only the primary analogate realizes this nature intrinsically. An example to the point would be the concept of life as predicated of plants, animals, man, and pure spirits. Obviously, the life of plants, animals, man, and pure spirits is very different; yet the perfection signified by the concept of life is found in each of them.

In the second place, the nature signified by the concept is *formally* realized in each of the analogates. This feature distinguishes analogy of proportionality from metaphorical analogy, in which only one of the analogates realizes this

THE NATURE OF BEING

nature formally. Life, for instance, is found in plants, animals, and man in a formal sense, and not merely as a figure of speech.

In the third place, the nature must be realized in the analogates according to a *proportional similarity*. This characteristic distinguishes analogy of proportionality from univocity. A nature can be realized formally and intrinsically either in exactly the same manner or according to a proportional similarity. If it is realized in exactly the same manner, the concept cannot be analogous, but is univocal because it does not vary. But a perfection can be realized also according to a proportional similarity. By this term we mean that in each of the analogates there exists a proportion or relation between two perfections or notes, and that these proportions or relations are similar. stance, we predicate the term "living" of plants, animals, Hence it is no longer a question of one analogate being related to another, as is the case in analogy of attribution, but of a relation in one analogate being similar to a relation or proportion in another analogate. When, for in- and men, we do not consider the relations which these forms of life have to one another, but the fact that man's nature is proportioned to the human mode of life as an animal's nature is proportioned to a sentient mode of life, and the nature of a plant is proportioned to a vegetative mode of life. Thus in each of the analogates the concept of life is realized formally and intrinsically, but the content of this concept varies according to the subject under consideration. Hence we have here analogy in the strictest sense of the term, for it is the concept itself which has to be adjusted in the predication.

It should be clear that such an analogy is possible only in concepts which express a nature *indeterminately*, in such a way that the concept can be determined from within.[21] This determination takes place when the concept is predicated of one of the analogates. The concept "living," for example, implies a nature which is proportioned to self-movement, but it does not determine the kind of self-movement. But as soon as we predicate this concept of particular living things, we are referring to a definite type of self-movement, so that our concept undergoes a determination which makes it unsuitable for predication of another type of self-movement without being readjusted.

After this rather lengthy study of analogy, we must now see whether the concept of being is univocal, equivocal, or analogous.

Being Is Neither Univocal nor Equivocal but Analogous

41. At first sight it is clear that *being is not a univocal concept*.[22] For a univocal concept abstracts from the differences of its inferiors, whereas being actually includes these differences. A substance, for instance, is a being in the sense of something whose "to be" is a "to be in itself"; an accident is a being in the sense of something whose "to be" is a "to be in another"; again, God's "to be" is different from that of any creature because unlike any creature He is His own "to be." Hence "it is clear that the diversity of relationship to "to be" prevents the univocal predication of being." [23]

---

[21] If the concept can be determined from without, it will be purely univocal.

[22] Cf. St. Thomas, *In III metaphysic.*, lect. 8, no. 433; *De potentia*, q. 7, a. 7.

[23] *De potentia*, q. 7, a. 7.

THE NATURE OF BEING

42. *The Term "Being" Is Not Equivocal.*[24] For equivocity occurs when there is no foundation in reality why diverse things should be called by the same name. But we predicate the name "being" of diverse things because each of them is something which has a reference to "to be"; hence there is a foundation of reality for the predication of the term, so that "being" is not equivocal.

43. Consequently, it follows by exclusion that the concept of *being is analogous*. Since above we have distinguished three modes of analogy, we must now investigate which mode of analogy applies to the concept of being. For obvious reasons we can immediately exclude that beings would be analogous by a mere *metaphorical analogy*. For otherwise many beings would be beings only according to a secondary aspect; consequently, with regard to their primary aspect these beings would be non-beings, which is impossible.

Being is analogous by *analogy of proportionality*. For according to our definition a term is analogous by analogy of proportionality if the perfection signified by the term is realized intrinsically and formally in each of the analogates according to a proportional similarity. Now the perfection of being is realized in each of the analogates thus:

a) *intrinsically;* for each of them has in itself a reference to "to be";

b) *formally;* for each being is called a being not merely as a figure of speech (with regard to a secondary aspect), but in a strict and proper sense;

c) *according to a proportional similarity;* for the reference to "to be" does not remain exactly the same, but varies in accordance with the nature of the subject of which

[24] *Ibid.*

being is predicated; hence in each analogate we find a mode of being which is proportioned to the nature of the subject.

44. Is being analogous also by *analogy of attribution?* As we have seen above, a term is analogous by analogy of attribution if the perfection signified by it is found intrinsically in the primary analogate, and is attributed to the others only because of a consideration of their causal relationship to the primary analogate. Now the perfection of being is realized intrinsically in each of the analogates; hence it is clear that, formally speaking, being cannot be said to be analogous by analogy of attribution. On the other hand, it is true that created beings have a relationship of causal dependence to God. Hence it follows that we can attribute the perfection of being to them precisely insofar as we consider this relationship of causal dependence. In other words, when we analyze the reason why created beings have the perfection of "to be," we find that they have it by participation, i.e., their "to be" is caused by God, who has "to be" by His very essence.[25] Accordingly, although, *formally speaking,* we do not predicate being of creatures because of their causal dependence on God, yet, *as a matter of fact,* their analogous manner of being implies such a dependence and thus offers a basis for attributing to them the perfection of being.

* *Historical Notes*

45. The *nominalists,* who do not admit any universal concepts, hold, at least implicitly, that being is equivocal.

Duns Scotus and his followers, who claim that the con-

[25] Cf. *Summa theol.,* Ia, q. 44, a. 1, ad 1.

cept of being is perfectly unified, logically admit that this concept is univocal.

Suarez admitted the analogy of the concept of being. But being unable to accept the Thomistic analogy of proportionality, he invented the so-called analogy of intrinsic attribution.[26] According to his theory, all analogy of proportionality has something metaphorical, but analogy of attribution may be either intrinsic or extrinsic (health). In analogy of intrinsic attribution the analogous perfection exists intrinsically in each of the analogates, in one absolutely, and in the others by reason of an intrinsic relation to the first. While we do not deny that creatures have a relation of dependence on God, we cannot admit that this relation constitutes their very being, for "the relation to its cause does not enter into the definition of the caused thing." [27]

St. Thomas held that being is analogous by analogy of proportionality and of attribution.[28] Unfortunately, St. Thomas never wrote a treatise of analogy, but he speaks about it quite frequently when needed by the particular problem under consideration.[29] Since analogy of proportionality often coincides *materially* with analogy of attribution, it is not surprising that his statements about analogy have become a source of confusing interpretations. It was *Cajetan* (1469–1534) who systematized and de-

[26] *Disputationes metaphysicae*, disp. XXVIII, sect. 3.

[27] *Summa theol*, Ia, q. 44, a. 1, ad 1.

[28] Cf. *In I sentent.*, prolog., ad 2, *In I sentent.*, d. 19, q. 5, a. 2, ad 1, *De principiis naturae*, c. VI, *De veritate*, q. 2, a. 11; *De potentia*, q. 7, a. 7, *Summa theol*, Ia, q. 13, aa. 5 and 6.

[29] In addition to the texts quoted in the preceding footnote, cf. I *Contra gentes*, cc. 32–34; *In IV metaphysic.*, lect. 1, nos. 535–39; *In XI metaphysic.*, lect. 3, nos. 2195–96; *In I ethic.*, lect. 7, no. 95; *Compend. theol.*, c. 26.

veloped the Thomistic theory of analogy in his work *de Nominum Analogia*.

SUMMARY

46. A univocal term is predicated of diverse things according to exactly the same concept because it abstracts completely from the differences of its inferiors. An equivocal term is predicated of diverse things according to entirely different concepts. No concept can be equivocal, but equivocity may occur in the written or spoken term. An analogous term is predicated of its inferiors according to concepts which are absolutely different and relatively the same. An analogous concept does not abstract from the differences of its inferiors; hence its meaning varies according to the subject.

In analogy of attribution the nature signified by the concept is realized intrinsically in the primary analogate only, but is attributed to the others insofar as they have a relation to the first. In metaphorical analogy the nature signified by the concept is realized intrinsically and formally in the primary analogate, and in the others intrinsically and virtually, i.e., according to a secondary aspect, usually that of activity. In analogy of proportionality the nature signified by the concept is realized intrinsically and formally in each of the analogates according to proportional similarity.

Being is not a univocal concept because it actually includes the differences of its inferiors. Neither is being equivocal because each being is something which has a reference to "to be." Hence it is analogous. This analogy is not metaphorical because otherwise the secondary analogates would be beings only in a secondary aspect, so that with regard to their primary aspect they would be non-beings, which is impossible. Being is analogous by analogy of proportionality because each of its inferiors has a reference to "to be," and this reference varies according to the nature of the subject. Moreover, since created beings depend upon God for their existence, the analogous perfection of being contains an analogy of attribution insofar as God exist by His very essence and a creature exists merely by participation in dependence upon God as the cause of its being.

IV. LOGICAL BEING

The Nature of Logical Being

47. At the end of our study of the concept of being, a few words may be added about the distinction of real and logical being, which was touched upon briefly when we distinguished the uses of the term "to be" in the logical and in the real order.[30] The term *"real"* always has the same meaning, viz., it always refers to something which belongs to the extramental order of things, the order of things which do not depend upon the consideration of the mind for their "to be." Hence a *real being* is something which has a reference to "to be" in the extramental order; it is or can exist independently of the consideration of the mind. It is real being with which we are primarily concerned in metaphysics.

By *logical being* or *being of reason* we mean something which has a reference to "to be" only as an object of the intellect; in other words, its whole "to be" consists in being considered by the intellect. It is to be noted that logical

[30] Cf. above, nos. 16 f., and St. Thomas, *In IV metaphysic.*, lect. 4, no. 574.

being is *not the same as nothing.* For nothing, as such, does not have any "to be" at all, not even in the intellect; whereas a logical being has a "to be" in the intellect by which it is conceived. Of course, such a being exists only as long as the mind considers it and is not capable of existence in the extramental world. For instance, a dentist will tell his patient that there is a cavity in one of his molars. He speaks about the cavity as if it were something real, although in reality a cavity is nothing but a lack of tooth. Obviously, the defective tooth is something real, but this defect conceived as if it were a positive reality is a logical being, for it exists only as an object of the mind.

It should be noted that our intellect does not arbitrarily form such logical beings. There must be a foundation in reality, such as the defective tooth, which allows us to form a logical being. Other similar examples are sickness, paralysis, death, vacuum, evil, tunnel.

Kinds of Logical Beings

48. St. Thomas divided logical being into negative and relative logical being.[31] If something which is unable to exist extramentally is *negative,* it will be the absence of a perfection conceived as if it were something positive, as is clear from the examples given above. Such a negative logical being can be either *purely negative* or *privative* according as the perfection which is absent does not belong to the nature of its subject or somehow belongs to it. Examples of purely negative logical beings are the sightlessness of a stone or the speechlessness of a fly, conceived as if they were something real. And when we say that John Doe has contracted pneumonia or takes part in a cam-

[31] Cf. *De veritate,* q. 21, a. 1.

paign to stamp out infantile paralysis, we speak about these privations as if they were positive realities.

If a thing which is unable to exist extramentally is positive, it must be a *relation*. For only a relation can be conceived as something positive without being real.[32] The reason is that anything positive which is absolute (non-relative) includes in its very nature at least a capacity for extramental existence and therefore is not a logical but a real being; whereas the essence of a relation consists merely in a respect to another. Such a respect does not of necessity have to exist outside the intellect, for the intellect itself can establish such a respect by comparing one thing with another.[33] To use the example of St. Thomas,[34] "left" and "right" in a column are purely logical relations for which the column itself does not offer any foundation. More important are the logical relations which exist in our mind between concepts of realities. For example, we express the relations existing between the concepts "animal" and "man" by saying that animal is the *genus* of man or that man is a *species* of animal. These and other similar relations constitute the object of logic.

[32] The objection could be raised that the mind is capable of conceiving something positive which is incapable of extramental existence although it is not a relation, e g., a centaur, a gremlin, or a ghost. The answer is that such *imaginary* things may be called logical beings in a wider sense. Strictly speaking, they are not logical beings because they have no foundation in reality, but are merely erroneous concepts if their existence outside the imagination is implied. However, insofar as they exist in the imagination, they may be called real beings, for phantasms are real.

[33] Cf. St. Thomas, *Summa theol.*, Ia, q. 28, a. 1. Concerning relations, cf. Chapter XI.

[34] *Summa theol.*, Ia, q. 13, a. 7.

THE NATURE OF BEING

SUMMARY

49. A real being is something which has a reference to "to be" in the extramental order. A logical being has a reference to "to be" only as an object of the intellect. It is not the same as nothing because nothing, as such, has no reference to "to be." Logical beings are either negations or relations. Negative logical beings are either purely negative or privatively negative.

SUGGESTED READINGS

50. J. Maritain, *A Preface to Metaphysics,* Sheed and Ward, 1939, pp. 1–89.
J. F. Anderson, "On Being; its Meaning and its Role in Philosophy," in *The Thomist,* 1941, pp. 579–587.
J. F. Anderson, *The Bond of Being,* Herder, 1949 (analogy).
V. E. Smith, "On the Being of Metaphysics," in *The New Scholasticism,* 1946, pp. 72–84.
J. J. Toohey, "The Term Being," in *The New Scholasticism,* 1942, pp. 107–129.
G. B. Phelan, *St. Thomas and Analogy* (*Aquinas Lecture, 1943*), Marquette University Press, 1943.
Cajetan, *The Analogy of Names and The Concept of Being,* tr. by Edward A. Bushinski in collaboration with Henry J. Koren (*Duquesne Studies, Philosophical Series,* vol. 4), Duquesne University Press, 1953.
Louis de Raeymaeker, *The Philosophy of Being,* Herder, 1954, Ch. III (the analogy and identity of being).

CHAPTER 2

The Transcendental Properties of Being

I. TRANSCENDENTAL PROPERTIES IN GENERAL

Explanation of Terms

✢✢✢ 51. In scholastic [1] philosophy we may call *transcendental*:

1) that which is above the categories, i.e., above the supreme classes of finite being; e.g., God.

2) that which is found in all or at least in several categories; for such a thing transcends the categories; e.g., change or plurality.[2]

3) that which can be predicated of being as such and therefore of every being. It is in this sense that the term is taken here.

A *property* in general is a predicate which does not

---

[1] In Kant's philosophy the term "transcendental" usually is taken as the opposite of "empirical."

[2] This is also the sense of "transcendental" in the expression, "transcendental relation," for such a relation expresses *any* absolute reality which by itself is related to another reality.

belong to the essence of its subject but flows from the essence of necessity. Thus, for instance, the power of laughter is a property of man, for it flows necessarily from the nature of man as a rational animal. Notice, however, that, strictly speaking, the term "property" applies only to predicates which are consequent on a genus or a species. Since being is neither a genus nor a species, it should be clear that the term is used here in a wider sense to indicate a predicate which is not identical in concept with being but flows from it of necessity. Moreover, the term *"transcendental property"* is reserved for those properties of being which flow from the concept of being not only of necessity but also *immediately*.[3]

52. *Predicamental and Transcendental Concepts.* When we speak of the transcendental properties of being it is clear that we do not mean predicates which are not contained in the concept of being. Being, as we have seen above, is the first concept, and all other concepts of the intellect are obtained by the addition of something to being. "Nothing, however, can be added to being as extrinsic to it;"[4] for being actually contains everything. "Hence things add something to being insofar as they express a mode of being which the term "being" itself does not express. Now this may happen in two ways. In one way, insofar as the expressed mode is a *special mode of being*."

---

[3] An example of a property of being which is not transcendental in the sense in which the term is used here is "otherness," taken as expressing the opposition of one being to another; for in this sense it does not flow immediately from the concept of being, but from that of unity.

[4] This and the subsequent quotations are taken from *De veritate,* q. 1, a. 1.

TRANSCENDENTAL PROPERTIES OF BEING

For instance, if we add to being the mode "in itself," we limit the extension of our concept to those things which are indicated by the term "substance." Evidently, such a concept is not transcendental, for it does not apply to being as such. Most concepts which limit the extension of being express a special mode of being which is predicated univocally of a class of beings. Such concepts are called *predicamental* or *categorical* concepts.[5] At present, we are not concerned with them, but later in Chapter VII we shall study these predicamental modes of being.

"In another way, [something can be added to being] insofar as the expressed mode is a *mode which flows from every being in general.*" It expresses something which can be attributed to each and every being; hence it is truly *transcendental,* for its extension is the same as that of being itself. However, not every transcendental *concept* is a *property* of being, as a little reflection will show. A concept which has the same extension as being itself is either entirely synonymous with being or not. If it is entirely synonymous with being, it cannot be said to be a property of being; for the attribute expressed by it cannot be said to *flow from* being, but *is* being itself, just as "rational animal" cannot be said to flow from "man," but is "man." Consequently, a property of being must be an attribute which is not entirely synonymous with being. The reality expressed by it is the same as the reality expressed by being, but it expresses this reality in its own way. The reality of being contains aspects which the concept of being itself does not express. Our intellect can turn its attention to each of these aspects and express the real-

---

[5] If a mode of being is not univocal but analogous without, however, applying to being as such, it will be transcendental in the second sense; e.g., "finite."

ity implied by being in a new concept which has such an aspect as its focal point. Hence this new concept merely expresses in a special way being in general, and the attribute which it represents is distinct from being by a logical (virtual) distinction. Obviously, such a concept will be analogous in the same way as being itself, i.e., by analogy of proportionality.

Derivation of Transcendental Concepts

53. Apart from being itself, philosophers enumerate five transcendental concepts. They are: *thing, one, otherness, true,* and *good*. St. Thomas shows how they are arrived at in the first question (art. 1) of *de Veritate:*[6] A mode of being which flows from every being "may be understood in two ways: In one way, according as it flows from every being considered in itself [*absolutely*]; in another way, according as it flows from every being with respect to something else [*relatively*]. If it is taken in the first way, [the mode of being] expresses something in being either *affirmatively* or *negatively*. Now it is impossible to find any *affirmative* and absolute predicate in every being save the essence, according to which a thing is said to be. This gives us the term *"thing,"* which . . . differs from *"being"* in this that "being" is taken from the act of existing, whereas "thing" expresses the quiddity or essence of the being. The *negation* which follows every being absolutely is indivision; it is expressed in the term *"one,"* for "the one" is nothing else than being undivided. If the mode of being is taken in the second way, i.e., according to the *relation* of one being to another, it may be understood in two ways: first according to the *division* of one thing from

[6] Cf. also *De natura generis* (c. II in the Parma edition). The authenticity of this work is not certain.

another, which is expressed by the term *"otherness"* (*aliquid*); for otherness is spoken of as some other thing (*aliud quid*). Hence just as being is said to be "one" insofar as it is undivided in itself, so also is it called "other" insofar as it is divided from other things. Secondly, according to the *agreement* of one being with another. Such an agreement is possible only if we consider something which is naturally capable of agreeing with every being. Such a thing is the [rational] soul, which·in some way is everything. . . . Now the soul has a cognitive and an appetitive power. Accordingly, the agreement of being with the appetite is expressed by the term *"good,"* and the agreement with the intellect is expressed by the term *"true."*

However, it is to be noted that *"otherness"* can be understood either as opposed to other beings (*some other thing*) or as opposed to nothing (*not-nothing*), for "taken in a certain sense being is predicated of non-being inasmuch as non-being is apprehended by the intellect."[7]

Putting the whole argument into a schematic form, we get the following: The reality of *being* can be considered:

{
  absolutely { affirmatively: *thing*
             { negatively: *one*
  relatively { as disagreeing with { nothing: *otherness* (*not-nothing*)
             { (divided from)   { other beings: *otherness* (*some other thing*)
             { as agreeing with { the intellect: *true*
                                { the will: *good*
}

Hence, inclusive of being itself, there are *six* transcendental concepts, but one of these (otherness) can be understood in two ways. We must now see which of these

[7] *De veritate*, q 1, a. 1, ad 7.

transcendental concepts are transcendental properties of being.

Transcendental Properties

54. As we have seen above, a transcendental property may not be entirely synonymous with being and must flow immediately from the concept of being. Now *"thing"* is generally considered to be synonymous with being; it merely puts the stress on the essence of being rather than on the act of being. *"Being"* itself cannot be a property; for nothing is a property of itself. *"One"* is a property; for it adds to being the negation of division, which being itself does not express. *"Otherness,"* if it is taken in the sense of *"not-nothing"* adds to being a comparison with the concept of non-being and thus may be considered to be a transcendental property. If, however, "otherness" is taken in the sense of *"some other thing,"* it is not a transcendental property; for it does not flow immediately from the concept of being but rather from the concept of "one," which means undivided in itself and divided from everything else. *"True"* and *"good"* add to being something which the concept of being itself does not express, and flow immediately from the comparison of being with the intellect and the will; hence they are transcendental properties. Thus we see that there are four transcendental properties, viz., not-nothing, one, true, and good. We shall study them separately in the subsequent parts of this chapter.

*Historical Notes

55. The one, the true, and the good are generally admitted as transcendental properties. Some philosophers, such as the *Pseudo-Dionysius,* add the beautiful, but most

others consider the beautiful merely as a special kind of goodness and refuse to admit it as a distinct transcendental property. Concerning otherness, there is no agreement: some simply reject it as a transcendental property, whereas others, such as *Gredt,* distinguish between "not-nothing" and "some other thing." *Van Steenberghen* adds likeness to the four properties of being enumerated above, because every being as such gives rise to a relationship of ontological likeness to every other being.

SUMMARY

56. A transcendental concept is a concept which can be predicated of every being. A transcendental property of being is a transcendental concept which is not entirely synonymous with being and flows immediately from the concept of being. Apart from being itself, there are five transcendental concepts; they are: thing, one, otherness, true, and good. Thing, however, is generally not considered as a property because it is practically synonymous with being. Otherness, in the sense of "not-nothing," may be considered as a transcendental property, but in the sense of "some other thing" it is not a property because it does not flow immediately from the concept of being itself. One, true, and good add to being something which is not expressed by being itself and flow immediately from the concept of being; hence they are transcendental properties of being.

II. OTHERNESS (THE PRINCIPLE OF CONTRADICTION)

57. Above we have seen in what sense otherness may be considered to be a transcendental property of being; namely, insofar as it adds to being the formal considera-

TRANSCENDENTAL PROPERTIES OF BEING

tion of its distinction from its opposite, non-being, which distinction being itself does not formally express. Once this distinction is perceived it gives rise to the judgment: *Being is not non-being.* This judgment is called the principle of contradiction, or sometimes and more correctly, the principle of non-contradiction. This principle may be considered to be the first or most fundamental principle which must guide the mind in its quest for truth. Because of its importance, we shall devote a few pages to it.

Preliminary Notions

58. *Principle.* By a principle in general we mean "that from which something proceeds in any way whatsoever."[8] This definition is rather vague, but a more explicit determination cannot be made because of the vast range of things to which the term "principle" can be applied. For instance, we must distinguish principles in the order of reality, such as causes, and principles in the order of cognition. At present, however, we are concerned only with a principle which flows immediately from the comparison of the concept of being with its opposite, non-being.

59. *Logical, Ontological or Epistemological Principle?* A principle in the order of cognition may be called a *logical principle,* provided that we do not misunderstand the term. If by a logical principle we mean merely a law which the mind must follow in its operation, a law of thought, but not a law which applies to reality, a law of being, we should have to call the principle of contradiction an ontological principle; for it is a principle which applies to reality as it is outside the mind.

On the other hand, the term *"ontological principle"*

---
[8] St. Thomas, *Summa theol.,* Ia, q.33, a.1.

makes one think of a reality from which another reality proceeds, such as a cause from which an effect comes forth. Hence both terms are open to a certain amount of confusion. However, in view of the fact that we have accepted the epistemological presupposition that our intellect is capable of knowing reality as it is outside the mind, it should be clear that by the principle of contradiction we mean a principle which applies to things known and not merely to the working of our intellect. Therefore, in order to avoid confusion, it will perhaps be better to call this principle an *epistemological principle;* for this term shows that the principle in question is concerned with our knowledge of reality as it is.

60. *First Principle.* It should be noted that the term "the first principle in the order of cognition" may have two meanings. It could mean a most perfect principle which *actually contains all truth* in such a way that in it all truths would be known to the intellect, or at least could be derived from it by a deductive process. However, the term can also be taken to mean a most fundamental principle which *is contained in all truths,* in the sense that all other true judgments of the intellect are based upon it. Hence the denial of such a fundamental principle would make knowledge of any truth impossible because it would take away the very foundation of every judgment and thus destroy itself. It is in the second sense, as a principle contained in all truths, that we speak here of the principle of contradiction as the first principle.

Complex and Incomplex Principles. In a certain sense the concept of being itself may be called the first principle in the order of cognition; for, as we have seen above, all our concepts are based upon the concept of being. We say "in a certain sense"—namely, if we limit our consideration to the first act of the human mind, apprehension. At present, however, we are concerned with the second act of the mind; for we are investigating the judgment which arises from the comparison of being with non-being. As will be recalled from logic, a judgment consists of a subject, a predicate, and a verbal copula, whereas an act of simple apprehension terminates in a single concept. If we want to stress the difference betwen the concept of being and the judgment "being is not non-being" with respect to the term "principle," we may say that being is the first *incomplex* principle, and that the judgment "being is not non-being" is the first *complex* principle.

The Principle of Contradiction

61. *Formulas of the Principle.* There are several formulas in which this principle is expressed:
"The same attribute cannot at the same time belong and not belong to the same subject and in the same respect." [9]
"The same thing cannot be affirmed and denied at the same time." [10]
"It is impossible for a thing to be and not to be at the same time." [11]
Being is not non-being, or, being is not nothing.
To be and not to be is not the same.
In the second and the third formula, the words "at the same time" should not be understood merely with respect to time, but in the sense of "in the same respect." For in

---

[9] Aristotle, *Metaphysics,* bk. IV, ch. 3; 1005b 18.
[10] St. Thomas, *Summa theol.,* Ia IIae, q.94, a.2.
[11] St. Thomas, *In IV metaphysic.,* lect. 6, no. 606.

TRANSCENDENTAL PROPERTIES OF BEING

different respects one and the same thing can be and not be at the same time; for example, the sun can be shining and not shining at the same time with respect to different places.

62. *The Principle of Contradiction Is the First Principle.* To prove this assertion we must show that the principle of contradiction flows *immediately* from the concept of being and that it is the *foundation* of all other principles. With regard to the first point, it is clear that the first principle will have to express a relationship of the concept of being to another concept. For by its very nature a complex principle must be concerned with the relationship of two concepts. Now from the concept of being the intellect derives immediately the concept of non-being as its contradictory. Upon apprehending these concepts the intellect sees at once that one is not the other, that being is not non-being. Hence the principle of contradiction flows immediately from the concept of being.

The second point, that the principle of contradiction is the *foundation* of all other principles, follows from the first. For if the principle of contradiction flow immediately from the first concept, it is clear that no other principle is prior to it. Moreover, any other principle either presupposes the principle of contradiction or is merely a different formula of the same (cf. Nos. 64 f.).

63. *The Principle of Contradiction Is an Analytic Principle.*[12] The question may be asked as to how we know

[12] The expressions "analytic principle" and "analytic proposition" should not be misunderstood. In Kantian philosophy a proposition is analytic if the predicate is contained in the essence of the subject, hence an analytic proposition is purely explicative. In Thomistic philosophy, a proposition is analytic if there is a necessary relation

that the principle of contradiction is true.[13] At first sight it is clear that it will be *impossible to offer any direct demonstration* of this principle. For in a direct demonstration we derive the truth of a conclusion from certain premises, i.e., from truths known to us prior to the truth of the conclusion; now no truth can be prior to the first principle; hence a direct demonstration of the principle of contradiction is not possible.

It is likewise *impossible to demonstrate the principle indirectly*. For in an indirect demonstration we show that the denial of a proposition implies a contradiction, i.e., is against the principle of contradiction. Hence any indirect demonstration presupposes that the principle of contradiction has already been admitted.

However, demonstration is not the only way in which we can be certain of the truth of a judgment. Sometimes a judgment may reveal itself to the mind as true by a mere *analysis* of its terms. To be certain of the truth of such a judgment, we only have to understand its subject and predicate, and our intellect is no longer able to doubt or reject it. Take, for example, the judgment "the whole is greater than any of its parts." Once we understand the meaning of the terms used in this proposition we cannot escape the judgment that the whole is greater than any of its parts. Hence an analytic principle is self-evident.

That the principle of contradiction is such *a self-evident principle* should be clear. Once we understand the meaning of the terms "being" and "non-being," our intellect

---

between the subject and the predicate. Thus the proposition "man is capable of speech" will not be analytic according to Kant, whereas in Thomistic terminology it may be called analytic.

[13] Cf. Aristotle, *Metaphysics*, bk. IV, ch. 3; St. Thomas, *In IV metaphysic.*, lect. 6, nos. 607 ff.

sees at once the truth of the statement that one is not the other. Moreover, it would be impossible to doubt or deny the principle of contradiction. For if I say "I deny or doubt the principle of contradiction," I admit that to deny or to doubt is not the same as not-to-deny or not-to-doubt, and thus my very denial or doubt shows that I admit what I deny or doubt. For this reason this principle has been appropriately nicknamed "the boomerang principle." [14]

64. *The Principle of Identity.* Some recent philosophers claim that the first principle is not the principle of contradiction but the principle of identity, which may be formulated as follows:

Being is being, or, What is, is, and what is not, is not.

They [15] claim that this principle is prior to the principle of contradiction because the latter implies a negation, and negation presupposees affirmation.[16] It would seem, however, that the statement "being is being" can be taken either tautologically or not. If it is taken in a tautological sense, it is true that it is prior to the principle of contradiction. But in this sense it is not a principle for the simple reason that nothing can be deduced from it. Used as a premise in a syllogism, it will have to leave the conclusion identical with the other premise; hence nothing can be derived from it. On the other hand, if it is not used tautologically, it would seem to be merely a different formula

[14] R. P. Phillips, *Modern Thomistic Philosophy*, vol. II, p. 35.

[15] Cf. L. de Raeymaeker, *The Philosophy of Being*, p. 60.

[16] Sometimes a distinction is made. For example, D. Mercier says that the principle of contradiction is first in the order of certitude, and the principle of identity first in the psychological order (genetically). Cf. *Manual of Modern Scholastic Philosophy*, 3rd ed., vol. I, p. 474.

TRANSCENDENTAL PROPERTIES OF BEING

of the principle of contradiction; for it would seem to mean that being is necessarily being, i.e., that being cannot be non-being.

65. *The Principle of Excluded Middle.* This principle is formulated as follows:

A thing is or is not, or: Between being and non-being there is no middle ground.

This principle supplements the principle of contradiction inasmuch as it eliminates the possibility that a thing would neither be nor not be.[17]

*Historical Notes

66. *G. Hegel* (1770–1831) admitted a first logical principle which actually contains all truths.

Idealists in general admit the principle of contradiction as a law of thought, but deny it as a law of being.

Aristotle calls the principle of contradiction "the most certain of all principles," and "the starting-point even for all other axioms."[18]

St. Thomas states that it is "naturally the first principle in the second operation of the intellect," and that "all other principles are based upon it."[19]

---

[17] In recent times the claim has been made that the principle of excluded middle has no absolute value, but applies only in certain logical systems. Upon closer inspection, however, it becomes clear that in systems in which the principle is claimed not to be valid there is no contradictory opposition, but only opposition between "proved to be true" and "proved not to be true." Obviously, there is a middle ground between these two, but this does not prove anything against the principle of excluded middle.

[18] *Metaphysics*, bk. IV, ch. 3; 1005b 22 and 34.

[19] *In IV metaphysic.*, lect. 6, no. 605; *Summa theol.*, Ia IIae, q. 94, a. 2.

G. *Leibnitz* (1646–1716) held that the principle of identity was the first principle.

Modern Scholastics argue whether the principle of identity or that of contradiction is first.

SUMMARY

67. Otherness, in the sense of not-nothing, adds to being a formal consideration of its distinction from non-being, which being itself does not formally express. Thus it gives rise to the judgment: being is not non-being, which is called the principle of contradiction.

A principle is that from which something proceeds in any way whatsoever. By an epistemological principle we mean here a principle in the order of cognition which applies to reality as it is outside the mind. The first complex principle in this order is the principle of contradiction; for this principle flows immediately from the comparison of the concept of being with its contradictory, non-being, and is presupposed by all other judgments of the intellect.

The principle of contradiction cannot be demonstrated either directly or indirectly, but is clear from an analysis of its terms. Denial or doubt is impossible; for the more it is denied or doubted, the more vehemently the principle is asserted.

Some claim that the principle of identity (being is being) is prior to the principle of contradiction. But if the proposition "being is being" is not taken as a tautology but as a true principle, its meaning would seem to be "being is necessarily being"; hence it would seem to be merely a different formula of the principle of contradiction. The principle of excluded middle (a thing either is is or is not) eliminates the possibility that a thing would neither be nor not be.

III. TRANSCENDENTAL UNITY

The Concept of Transcendental Unity

68. Unity or oneness expresses abstractly what "one" expresses concretely, just as humanity is the abstract term for "man." It is important to realize that "one" does not always mean the same. "One is spoken of in two ways, viz., the one which is the principle of number, and the one which is convertible with being." [20] In ordinary speech "one" is used as the principle of number, i.e., as the *mathematical unit of measurement* or *predicamental unity*. As such, it can be applied only to things "in which there is quantitative measurability." [21] Hence in this sense it is limited to quantified things and cannot be the "one" which is considered with respect to being in general. As St. Thomas warns us, "the unity and number which the mathematician considers is not the unity and the multitude which is found in all beings, but merely [unity and number] according as they are found in material beings." [22]

Hence this unit of measurement should be carefully distinguished from *transcendental unity* or the unity of being *qua* being. All unity is negation of division. But apart from division which flows from quantity, "there is a division which transcends the genus of quantity—namely, division by formal opposition, which is not concerned with any quantity. Hence . . . the "one" which deprives of this division must be more general and of a wider application than the genus of quantity." [23] This unity is called transcendental unity or oneness.

[20] St. Thomas, *In I sentent.*, d.24, q.1, a.3, ad 4.
[21] *Ibid.*, in the body of the article.
[22] *Op. cit.*, d.24, q.1, a.1, ad 2.
[23] *De potentia*, q.9, a.7.

TRANSCENDENTAL PROPERTIES OF BEING

It is to be noted that the *plurality* opposed to predicamental or categorical unity is not the same as that opposed to transcendental unity. Plurality opposed to predicamental unity is *number* (two, three, four, etc.), whereas the plurality opposed to transcendental unity is *multitude*. For, as St. Thomas remarks, "every plurality is consequent upon a division. Now division is twofold. One is *material* and according to division of the continuous; and this division results in *number*, which is a species of quantity. Hence number in this sense is found only in material beings, which have quantity. The other division is *formal* and according to opposite or diverse forms; and this division results in *multitude*, which does not belong to a genus but is transcendental in the sense in which being is divided into one and many. Only this kind of multitude is found in immaterial beings." [24]

*69. *The "One" Does Not Add Any Positive Reality to Being.* If the "one" added any positive reality to being, just as "white" adds a positive reality to man, it would follow that "any thing is "one" by something else; since this thing again would be "one" we should have to go on to infinity if this, in turn, would be "one" by something else. Accordingly, we must say that the "one" which is convertible with being does not add anything real to being." [25]

*70. *The "One" Is Not a Purely Negative Concept.* A purely negative concept is a concept which does not posit anything but merely denies something; for example, "non-animal" merely denies "animal" and does not say whether the non-animal is to be identified with nothing or with a being without sentient life. The "one," however, always

[24] *Summa theol*, Ia, q.33, a.3.
[25] *Op. cit.*, Ia, q.11, a.1, ad 1.

implies a subject which is one. Hence although the "one" means being undivided, "it does not signify merely this indivision, but it signifies the substance of being together with indivision. . . . Hence the "one" which is convertible with being posits being itself and adds to it merely a negation of division." [26] Accordingly, the "one" is not purely negative; for it implies being as its subject.

Every Being Is "One"

71. The second property of being gives rise to the important principle that every being is "one" or intrinsically undivided. The *proof* of this assertion is as follows: "Every being is either simple or composite. If it is simple, it is undivided both actually and potentially. If it is composite, it does not have a 'to be' as long as its parts are divided; but [it has a 'to be'] as soon as they make up and compose the composite. Hence it is clear that the 'to be' of any thing consists in indivision. For this reason everything retains its unity just as it retains its 'to be.' " [27]

Hence the "one" and being are *convertible* terms. It should be noted, however, that although the "one" and being are convertible, they "are *not synonymous*. For synonymous are those terms which signify one and the same thing under the same respect; [28] now being and the one are convertible as things which really are the same, but they differ in concept only, inasmuch as the one adds a negation [privation [29]] to being." [30]

[26] *De potentia*, q.9, a.7.
[27] *Summa theol.*, Ia, q.11, a.1.
[28] *De potentia*, q.9, a.7.
[29] A privation, because the "one" conncted being as its subject.
[30] *In I sentent*, d.2, q.1, a.3 Note that "the one is indifferent with respect to essence and "to be"; hence the essence of a thing

TRANSCENDENTAL PROPERTIES OF BEING

72. *Importance of This Principle.* The importance of the principle that every being is "one" lies in the irreconcilable opposition which it shows to exist between being and multiplicity. "To be" as "to be" cannot be multiple. Hence multiplicity and composition are bound to raise problems in metaphysics, as we shall see in subsequent chapters. We may now establish the conclusion that *it is impossible for two actual beings to become perfectly unified,* to become one being. For either actual being is actually one; hence together they are not actually one but two beings. Consequently, a perfect union of two actual beings is impossible; although an imperfect union may take place, such as by unity of place (juxtaposition) or of purpose (as in a machine). This conclusion is frequently stated by St. Thomas. For example:

"Two which are in act are never actually one." [31]

"Several cannot become absolutely one unless there is something in them which is act and something else which is in potency." [32]

"If to a thing which is in act another act is added, the whole will not be absolutely one (*unum per se*) but only accidentally one thing." [33]

The importance of this principle will become clear in the applications of the theory of potency and act.

*Historical Notes

73. *Pythagoras, Plato,* and *Avicenna* did not distinguish the "one" which is the unit of quantitative measurement

---

is one of itself and not by a kind of participation as is the case with being and the good." *De veritate,* q 21, a. 5, ad 8.

[31] *In VII metaphysic.,* lect. 13, no. 1588.
[32] I *Contra gentes,* c. 18.
[33] *De substantiis separatis* (c. 5 in Mandonnet edition).

from the "one" which is convertible with being. Hence *Pythagoras* and *Plato* concluded that the substance of all things is numbers; *Avicenna*, on the contrary, concluded that the "one" which is convertible with being adds a reality to being.

Alexander of Hales and *Bonaventure* thought that the "one" is a purely positive concept.

Duns Scotus denied that two actual beings cannot be perfectly unified to form one being.

SUMMARY

74. Predicamental unity or the mathematical unit of measurement should be distinguished from the transcendental unity or oneness of being *qua* being.

*The "one" in the transcendental sense does not add any positive reality to being, but being is "one" in virtue of itself. The "one" is not purely negative, but posits being itself, to which it adds a negation of division.

Every being is one either because it does not have any parts or because it does not exist as long as its parts are divided. Hence being and "one" are convertible; yet they are not entirely synonymous because the "one" adds a negation of division to being. Since being and "one" are convertible, it follows that it is impossible for two actual beings to become actually "one" except by means of an imperfect, accidental, union.

The opposite of predicamental unity is number, and that of transcendental unity is multitude.

APPENDIX: IDENTITY AND DISTINCTION

With the unity of being we may connect a consideration of the fundamental concepts of identity and distinction, which are connected with unity and multitude.

Nature and Kinds of Identity

75. Identity is not easy to define. Perhaps it may be best described as the sameness of a thing with itself *or* of one thing with another insofar as they have something in common.[34] This description shows that we must distinguish two kinds of identity, viz., real and logical identity.

Real identity is concerned with the order of extramental things. One and the same reality is considered by the intellect as if it were two or more things. For example, this man, Peter, is only one reality, but can be considered either insofar as he is rational or insofar as he is an animal; hence when we speak of his rationality and his animality we are referring to one and the same reality. His rationality and animality are really identical, although it is obvious that they are distinct in concept. Real identity may be metaphysical, physical, and moral. *Metaphysical* is the sameness with itself of a thing which is not subject to any change whatsoever. As we shall see later, such identity exists only in the Pure Act, or God. *Physical identity* is the sameness with itself of a thing whose nature remains the same, although it undergoes changes in secondary respects. A case in point would be the identity with himself of Peter who remains a human being, although in the course of his life he undergoes quite a few changes in size, weight, knowledge, etc. *Moral identity* is spoken of with respect to a moral body, which is considered to remain the same as long as the same bond unites its members, even though the original members have been gradually replaced by others. For example, of the original members of the Catholic Church none survive; yet the Church is

[34] Cf. St. Thomas, *In V metaphysic.*, lect. 11, no. 912.

considered to be the same because all its present members are united by the same bond as the original members whom they replaced gradually.

76. The other kind of identity is concerned with the order of things in the intellect; hence it is called *logical identity*. It refers to things which are many in the order of reality, but are considered to be the same insofar as they agree in something they have in common. For instance, Peter and John are two really distinct human beings; yet they agree in the concept of man which applies to both; hence Peter and John are logically identical. Such identity occurs when really distinct things fall under the extension of one and the same concept. Consequently, there will be as many kinds of logical identity as there are ways in which one and the same concept can apply to different things. The most important of these are essential and accidental identity.

We speak of *essential identity* if things agree in a concept expressing their essence. Thus Peter and Mary are essentially identical because they agree in the concept of man, which expresses their nature. Essential identity may be *generic* or *specific* inasmuch as the concept expressing an essence may express either the whole essence (the species) or that part which is common to several species (the genus). An example of generic identity would be a man and a donkey insofar as they agree in the common concept of animal; of specific identity Peter and Mary insofar as they agree in the common concept of man.

Accidental identity is had when things agree in a concept expressing an attribute which is not part of their essence. For instance, snow and sugar are accidentally identical in the concept "white"; 100 lbs. of lead and 100 lbs. of feathers are accidentally identical insofar as they agree in a common concept of weight.

By putting these types of identity into a schematic form [35] we get the following:

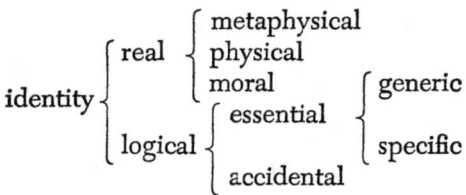

Nature and Kinds of Distinction

77. Distinction is the opposite of identity and may be described as the negation of identity. It is obvious that distinction will always imply at least two terms and thus is based upon plurality. It is divided into real and logical distinction.

A distinction is *real* if it exists independently of the mind. For instance, the distinction between Peter and Paul is real. It is to be noted that in Thomistic philosophy real distinction does not coincide with separation or even separability. Separation occurs only in things that exist apart, and separability will be possible only if really distinct constituent parts of a thing are capable of existing all by themselves. Hence a real distinction is possible even if the constituent parts of a thing cannot be separated. If we wish to indicate this difference, we could call the real distinction which admits separability or separation a real *physical* distinction, and the real distinction which does not admit the separability of the constituent parts of a

[35] This division is not meant as a complete division of identity.

TRANSCENDENTAL PROPERTIES OF BEING

thing a real *metaphysical* distinction.[36] A real distinction between two positive realities, such as Peter and John, is called a *positive* real distinction, whereas the real distinction between a real being (e.g., sight) and its negation (blindness) is called a *negative* real distinction.[37]

78. A *logical* distinction exists only in the consideration of the intellect which apprehends one and the same reality by two or more concepts. If reality itself offers a basis for being conceived by different concepts, the distinction will be called a logical distinction with a foundation in reality or a *virtual* distinction.[38] For example, a man is really one being, but the perfection of his nature is so great that it can be expressed in several concepts, such as rationality, sentiency, life, corporeity, etc. Each of these concepts expresses a different aspect of one and the same reality; hence we say that in one and the same man the perfections expressed by these concepts are virtually distinct. If the concepts expressing different aspects of the same reality do not include one another, the perfections expressed by them are said to be distinct by a *major virtual* distinction because reality offers a perfect foundation for making such a logical distinction. For instance, the perfections of rationality and animality in the same man are distinct by a major virtual distinction, as is clear from the fact that

[36] Cf. L. de Raeymaeker, *The Philosophy of Being*, p. 66.

[37] The distinction between two negative beings, such as blindness and deafness, is sometimes called a real negative distinction.

[38] Gredt, in his *Elementa philosophiae* (Freiburg i. Br.: Herder, 1937), vol. II, no. 801, subdivides the virtual distinction into *intrinsic* and *extrinsic* according as the basis for the distinction is found in the reality under consideration or in some other reality. As an example of a virtual extrinsic distinction he points to the distinction between essence and "to be" in the Pure Act.

animality can be realized separately from rationality in brute animals. If, however, the concepts expressing different perfections of the same reality are such that one includes the other, reality offers no perfect foundation for making a distinction, and in such a case the distinction is called a *minor virtual* distinction. For example, the concepts of being and substance express perfections of this man Peter; but being implicitly contains substance, and a substance which is not a being would be unthinkable; hence the perfections of being and substance in Peter are distinct by a minor virtual distinction.

Even when no foundation can be found in reality, the intellect is capable of making a distinction. This will happen when the same aspect of the same reality is expressed twice. Such a distinction is called a *purely logical* or *verbal* distinction. A case in point is the distinction between the concept of a thing and its definition; e.g., between man and rational animal.

Putting these distinctions into a schematic form we get the following:

$$\text{distinction} \begin{cases} \text{real} \begin{cases} \text{positive} \begin{cases} \text{physical} \\ \text{metaphysical} \end{cases} \\ \text{negative} \end{cases} \\ \text{logical} \begin{cases} \text{virtual} \begin{cases} \text{major} \\ \text{minor} \end{cases} \\ \text{purely logical} \end{cases} \end{cases}$$

*Historical Notes

79. The above distinctions are generally admitted by scholastic philosophers, but *Scotus* and *Suarez* limit the real distinction to things which admit separability.

Moreover, *Scotus*, the "Subtle Doctor," admits, in addition to logical and real distinction his famous formal distinction which is actual on the part of the thing. This distinction is supposed to be prior to the consideration of the intellect; hence it is not logical; yet it is not real because it is not between one thing and another thing, but between different formalities which actually exist in a thing. However, it is impossible to conceive a distinction which is prior to the consideration of the intellect but not real; for whatever is independent of the consideration of the intellect is real. Some modern Scotists interpret Scotus' distinction as equivalent to a virtual distinction.

Descartes admits real, logical and modal distinctions; but what we have called above the real metaphysical distinction is rejected by both *Cartesians* and *empiricists*, who do not admit any metaphysical composition.

SUMMARY

80. Identity is the sameness of a thing with itself or of two things with one another insofar as they have something in common. It is either real or logical. Real identity is metaphysical, physical, or moral. Logical identity occurs when two or more things fall under one concept. If this concept is the concept of the essence of these things, the identity will be essential; otherwise it will be accidental. Essential identity may be either generic or specific.

Distinction is the negation of sameness and is based upon plurality. If plurality exists independently of the consideration of the mind, it is real; otherwise it is logical. Real distinction is not the same as separability; for it may happen that really distinct constituent parts cannot exist separately. Hence real distinction is either physical or metaphysical according as the constituent parts are separable or not. A logical distinction occurs if one and the same reality is apprehended by the mind in two or more concepts. It will be virtual if reality itself offers a basis for making the distinction; otherwise it will be purely logical. A virtual distinction may be either major or minor according as reality offers a perfect foundation for making the distinction or not. A perfect foundation exists if the concepts expressing the reality do not include one another.

IV. TRANSCENDENTAL TRUTH

Nature and Kinds of Truth

81. Truth always implies a relationship of conformity between two extremes, one of which is the intellect. The other is the being which is the object of the intellect. If there is *conformity between this being and the intellect*, there is truth; otherwise there is falsity. The conformity between being and the intellect may be viewed either from the intellect or from being. In the first case, we speak of *ontological truth*, which may be defined as the conformity of a being with the intellect; in the second case, we have to do with *logical truth*, which is defined as the conformity of the intellect with being.[39] That we are justified in speaking of ontological truth is clear from the usage of speech. For example, we speak of a true friend, by which we mean that he possesses the qualities which in our opinion a true friend ought to have; hence a true friend will be one who is in conformity with our idea of a friend.

82. *Logical Truth*. At present, we are primarily concerned with the truth of being or ontological truth; hence

[39] Cf. *Summa theol*, Ia, q.16, a.1. In mathematics, the definition of truth is verified in an analogous sense inasmuch as there is conformity between the mathematical object and the axioms governing mathematics.

a few words about logical truth will have to be sufficient. According to common usage of speech, truth is spoken of in the first place with respect to the intellect which is in conformity with its object, and in the second place with respect to the object which is in conformity with the intellect.[40] For our intellect to know truth means to know its conformity with being or its object. This conformity is not known before the intellect makes a judgment; hence it is "only when the intellect judges that a thing corresponds to the form which it apprehends concerning this thing that it knows and expresses truth."[41] In the senses and in the simple apprehension of the intellect truth may exist as something which is true, but not as known truth. Hence it is clear that "properly speaking, truth is found in the composing and dividing [i.e., the judging] intellect, and not in the senses nor in the intellect which knows what a thing is [i.e., in the apprehending intellect]."[42]

83. *Ontological Truth.* We have seen above that ontological or transcendental truth is the conformity of a being with the intellect. We must now determine what we mean by the term "the intellect." Obviously, "the intellect" cannot refer to the human intellect; for there is no such thing as *the* human intellect. Only individual human intellects exist. Now it is clear that it is impossible for a thing to be

[40] This usage is based upon the fact that the terminus of knowledge is in the knower because a thing is known insofar as it is in the knower. The opposite applies to goodness, which is found primarily in the object of the appetite and secondarily in the appetite itself; for a thing is called "good" inasmuch as it causes an inclination to itself in the appetite. Therefore, the terminus of the appetite is in the object.
[41] *Summa theol.,* Ia, q. 16, a. 2.
[42] *Ibid.*

in agreement with all human intellects, for the obvious reason that all human intellects do not agree about anything. Accordingly, either nothing would be true or contradictory things would be true simultaneously, which is impossible.[43] Hence "the intellect" cannot refer to all human intellects. Secondly, things are capable of causing truth in our intellect, inasmuch as they can cause our intellect to form a judgment which is in agreement with being. Now if things are capable of causing truth in our intellect, they must have truth in themselves prior to causing it in us. Hence the term "the intellect" does not indicate human intellects which reality causes to conform to it.

As St. Thomas says, we must distinguish two intellects to which a thing may be related, viz., the one to which it is related *essentially* (*per se*), and the one to which it is related *accidentally*. A thing is "related essentially to the intellect upon which it depends for its "to be," but accidentally to the intellect by which it can be known." [44] For instance, we may say that a house is related essentially to the intellect of the architect who designed it, and accidentally to the intellect of the "sidewalk-superintendent." Hence the truth of a thing should be taken from its order to the intellect upon which it depends for its "to be," because the order to all other intellects is purely accidental. Thus it follows that a thing is true insofar as it is *in conformity with the intellect of its maker*.[45]

---

[43] *De veritate,* q.1, a.2.
[44] *Summa theol*, Ia, q.16, a.1.
[45] This paragraph applies only to the ontological truth of finite beings. God's essence is true because it is in conformity with His divine intellect by identity, hence God's essence is the "Supreme and First Truth." Cf. St. Thomas, *Summa theol.,* Ia, q.16, a.5, ad 2.

In things which are made by man, such as buildings and machines, we may consider as the maker the one who designed them. Things which are not produced by man are true by being in conformity with the intellect of their cause, i.e., God. *Ultimately,* even the truth of things made by man depends upon the divine intellect. For man's intellect is a true intellect only inasmuch as it is in conformity with God's idea of an intellect. Moreover, man, in making things, can only change pre-existing things into something else. Now the truth of these pre-existing things depends upon God. Hence "even if there were no human intellect, things would still be called true with respect to the divine intellect. But if we were to conceive both intellects as removed, which is impossible, the aspect of truth would nowise remain." [46]

Every Being Is True

84. Everything is a being insofar as it has a "to be." Now "everything is knowable insofar as it partakes in 'to be.'" [47] Whatever is knowable has a relation of conformity with the intellect; hence it is true. As a result "being" and "true" are convertible terms.

Strictly speaking, in order to be true, a thing does not have to be actually known, but it is sufficient that it be potentially known or knowable: "Truth is found . . . in a thing insofar as it has a "to be" which *can be* in conformity with an intellect." [48]

85. *Importance of This Principle.* The thesis that every being is true is called the *principle of intelligibility*, which

---

[46] *De veritate,* q. 1, a. 2.
[47] *Summa theol*, Ia, q. 16, a. 3.
[48] *Op. cit.,* Ia, q. 16, a. 5. Cf. also *De veritate,* q. 22, a. 1.

is usually formulated: Being is intelligible. Hence what is unintelligible, unthinkable, simply is not and cannot be. By "unintelligible" we mean here positively beyond understanding, and not negatively so in the sense that we cannot see how it can be. On the other hand, whatever is, is capable of being understood, although its actual understanding may be beyond the limited capacities of a human intellect.

*How Truth Is in Beings

86. A thing is true insofar as it has a "to be." Now the essence of the infinite Being, God, is identical with its "to be"; hence the infinite Being is true *by its very essence*.[49] But a finite being is not by its very nature but only *by participation,* i.e., shares in "to be" in dependence upon God who is "to be"; hence it cannot be knowable or true by its very essence but only "insofar as it participates in a certain way in the likeness of the divine essence." [50] Insofar as it is a limited imitation of God's essence it has a reference to "to be" and is known to God, who knows His essence "not only as it is in itself but also as it can be participated in by creatures according to a certain manner of likeness." [51]

* The "True" Adds to Being as Such a Purely Logical Relation

87. From the foregoing it follows that "the true adds (to being) a relation to the intellect." [52] Concerning the

---

[49] *Op. cit.,* Ia, q.3, a.4.

[50] *Op. cit ,* Ia, q.15, a.2.

[51] *Ibid.* Cf. Ia IIae q.3, a.8: "Whatever things are beings by participation are true by participation."

[52] *Op. cit.,* Ia, q.16, a.3.

nature of this relation there is no agreement. However, it should be clear that it *cannot be a mere predicamental relation*. For a predicamental relation is a special kind of being; hence if we were to say that being is true by means of a predicamental relation, we would imply that truth is not found in any other predicament save relation.[53] Moreover, if the question were raised why this relation, which is a being, is true, the answer would have to be: By means of another relation, and so on to infinity.

Could it be that the "true" adds to being a *transcendental relation?* It would seem that a distinction has to be made. If we consider being *qua* being, i.e., without determining whether we mean finite or infinite being, the "true" will add to being a purely logical relation to the intellect to which being is referred. The reason is as follows. The intellect in question is either a created or the uncreated intellect. If it is created, it is related to being *qua* being as the perfectible to that which perfects. But such a relation is real only in the perfectible and logical in that which perfects.[54] Hence being as such has only a logical relation to the created intellect. With regard to the uncreated intellect, being as such is neither finite nor infinite; hence it is related to the divine intellect neither as something which depends upon it (as a finite being) nor as something which does not depend upon it (the divine essence), but as something which is undetermined with respect to dependence. Therefore, being as such cannot have a real relation to the divine intellect. Consequently, this relation is *purely logical*. This was also the opinion of St. Thomas, for he wrote: "The true and the good cannot

[53] Cf. *De veritate,* q.21, a.1, ad 3.
[54] *De veritate,* q.21, a.1 (*illa autem relatio*).

add [to being as such] any relation save a logical relation." [55]

If, however, we do not speak of ontological truth as a property of being as such, but with respect to *determined beings,* it must be admitted that *finite* beings have a real relation of dependence to the intellect upon which they depend. This relation is a kind of *transcendental* relation because by its whole entity a finite being is referred to the intellect of its maker, which is its exemplary cause.[56] Moreover, if we consider any *particular* finite being, a *predicamental* relation of dependence to its maker is added to this transcendental relation. The *infinite* Being, however, is related to the divine intellect by a relation of identity; hence its relation to this intellect is purely *logical.*

Truth of Speech

88. Above we distinguished only two kinds of truth, viz., logical and ontological truth. But frequently there is also question of *moral truth,* by which is meant the truth of speech. Is the truth of speech another genus of truth or is it possible to reduce it to logical or ontological truth? In order to answer this question we must distinguish two manners in which speech can be considered. If speech is taken *as a reality,* truth of speech will mean that speech is in conformity with the intellect of the speaker. In this sense it will be considered to be *ontologically true,* just as

[55] *Ibid.*

[56] A transcendental relation would seem to imply merely that the very essence of one absolute reality contains an order to another absolute reality, so that the existence of such a relation in one extreme does not depend upon the existence of the corresponding real relation in the other extreme.

a bridge is ontologically true if it is in conformity with the intellect of its builder. It is to be noted that from the viewpoint of moral truth it does not matter whether or not the intellect of the speaker is in conformity with reality—as long as the speech is in conformity with the mind of the speaker, it is ontologically and morally true. For the same reason, speech will be morally false if it is not in conformity with the mind of the speaker, even if it is in conformity with reality; as happens when the speaker erroneously thinks that what he is saying is not true.

On the other hand, speech may be considered *as a sign* of what is going on in the mind. Taken in this way the truth of speech may be reduced to *logical truth*, inasmuch as speech is a sign that the intellect is in conformity with reality.

*Phenomenal Truth

89 Frequently philosophers speak about phenomenal truth. There would be no serious objection against the use of this term if it were taken to mean that things can be truthfully described according to their external appearances so long as no judgment is implied about their nature. In this sense it is true that the sun rises in the East and sets in the West, or that the sun revolves around the earth, etc. But many post-Kantian philosophers use the term unrestrictedly as if all truth were limited to phenomena and the nature of things would be entirely unknown to us. Taken in this sense, phenomenal truth is a contradiction in terms; for one cannot affirm that truth is entirely phenomenal without making a judgment concerning the nature of phenomena. Besides, even these phenomena "are" and therefore have the nature of being.

*Eternal and Unchangeable Truth

90. Sometimes truth is said to be eternal and unchangeable; hence the question may be asked whether or not these expressions are correct. We must answer with some distinctions.

With regard to *eternal truth, uncreated* truth is both logically and ontologicaly eternal, for God's essence and intellect are identical and eternal. *Created logical* truth is not eternal because created intellects are not eternal. The *ontological* truth of things that are created in time is not eternal because such things did not have any "to be" in themselves before being "created." However, in the sense that from eternity all things are objects of divine knowledge and thus conform to His intellect, we may say that all things are ontologically true from eternity. But it should be clear that this is a purely *extrinsic* mode of being called true from eternity.[57]

With regard to the *immutability of truth,* the *logical* truth of the *divine* intellect is immutable because the divine intellect is always in conformity with its object. The truth, however, of the *human* intellect is subject to change inasmuch as a true judgment of our intellect may become false either because it does not change when reality changes or because it changes when reality does not change. Concerning *ontological* truth, reality is always in conformity with the divine intellect; hence *absolutely* true, although it may change from one form of truth to another. *Relatively,* however, to the human intellect a true thing may become false.[58]

[57] Cf. *De veritate,* q. 1, a. 5.
[58] Cf. *Summa theol.,* Ia, q. 16, a. 8; *De veritate,* q. 1, a. 6.

Falsity

91. Falsity is the contrary [59] of truth and may be defined as the lack of conformity between the intellect and reality. Hence *logical* falsity will be the lack of conformity of the intellect with reality, *ontological* falsity the lack of conformity of reality with the intellect, and *moral* falsity the lack of conformity of speech with the intellect. A logical falsity is called an error or a mistake; a moral falsity is a lie. Concerning the occurrence of logical and moral falsity, there cannot be any doubt. With regard to ontological falsity, "*absolutely* speaking, everything is true, and nothing is false," [60] because every being is in conformity with the divine intellect. "*Relatively*, however, to our intellect, certain things are said to be false" [61]—namely, inasmuch as they are apt to lead us into forming a wrong judgment. For example, we call somebody a false friend when his conduct is such that it can mislead us into thinking that he is a true friend. Moreover, in things made by man we may speak of falsity insofar as things do not agree with the plan in the intellect of their maker.

*Historical Notes

92. According to Aristotle,[62] *Empedocles, Democritus* and other ancient philosophers held that true is what appears to be true.

The classical definition of truth is usually attributed to the Jewish philosopher *Isaac Israeli* (845–940).

---

[59] Not the contradictory. Cf. *Summa theol.*, Ia, q. 17, a. 4.

[60] *De veritate*, q. 1, a. 10.

[61] *Summa theol.*, Ia, q. 17, a. 1. Cf. Aristotle, *Metaphysics*, bk. V, ch. 29, 1024b 19 ff.

[62] *Ibid.*, bk. IV, chaps. 5, 6.

Aristotle wrote extensively about logical truth, but said very little about ontological truth.

Vasquez (1551–1604) thought that ontological truth is a purely extrinsic denomination.

D. Mercier (1851–1926) defines ontological truth as a relation of conformity with an ideal type previously abstracted from sensible reality.[63]

Among *Thomistic* philosophers there is no agreement as to whether ontological truth adds to being a logical or a real relation.

SUMMARY

93. Truth consists in the conformity between intellect and being. It is called logical when it is viewed as the conformity of the intellect with being, and ontological when it is considered as the conformity of being with the intellect. Properly speaking, logical truth is found only in the intellect. Ontological truth is based upon the conformity of beings with the intellect of their maker; hence ultimately all ontological truth depends upon the divine intellect.

Every being is true. For everything is a being insofar as it has a "to be" and is knowable insofar as it has a "to be"; now whatever is knowable has a relationship of conformity with the intellect; hence every being is true. The statement that every being is true is called the principle of intelligibility. As such, it is usually formulated: Being is intelligible. Its importance lies in this that whatever is not intelligible simply is not.

*The infinite Being, whose essence is "to be," is true by its very essence; finite beings, whose essence is not their

---

[63] *A Manual of Modern Scholastic Philosophy, Ontology*, no. 61.

"to be," are true only by participation, precisely because they *are* only by participation.

*The "true" adds to being a relation to the intellect. This relation cannot be a predicamental relation; for such a relation is a being and thus could be true only by means of another predicamental relation, and so on to infinity. To being *qua* being the "true" adds a purely logical relation to the created intellect which is perfected by it, and also to the divine intellect because being as such is neither finite nor infinite; hence it is indeterminate as regards dependence or independence with respect to the divine intellect. To finite being the "true" adds a real relation of dependence upon the intellect of its maker. This relation would seem to be transcendental if we consider finite being as such; but a predicamental relation is added if we consider any particular finite being. To the infinite Being the "true" adds a logical relation of identity to the divine intellect.

The truth of speech can be reduced to ontological truth if we consider speech insofar as it is a reality. If, however, speech is considered as a symbol of what is going on in the intellect, it may be reduced to logical truth.

*There is no objection against the use of the term "phenomenal truth" if it is taken to mean that things can be truthfully described according to their appearances. If, however, the expression is used to express that the nature of things is unknowable, it is a contradiction in terms.

*Uncreated truth is eternal. Created logical and ontological truth is not eternal because created reality and created intellects are not eternal. However, created things are extrinsically eternal insofar as from eternity they are known to God's intellect.

*The logical truth of the divine intellect is immutable; that of the human intellect is not. Reality is ontologically always absolutely true, but relatively to the human intellect a true thing may become false.

Falsity consists in the lack of conformity between a reality and the intellect. Nothing can be ontologically absolutely false, but a thing may be false relatively to man's intellect.

V. TRANSCENDENTAL GOODNESS

The Concept of Goodness

94. The "good" is one of our primary concepts and therefore cannot be properly defined. Its description as *"that which all desire"* was approved by Aristotle.[64] This description indicates the effect produced by the "good": it moves the appetite, which tends towards it as long as the good is not yet possessed and comes to rest in it as soon as it is possessed.

Concerning this definition of the "good," the following points should be noted:

1) "When we say: good is what all desire, we do not mean that every good is desired by all beings, but that *whatever is desired has the nature of the good*." [65]

2) "What all desire should not be understood only with respect to beings endowed with knowledge, which apprehend the good, but also with respect to things deprived of knowledge, which tend to the good by a *natural appetite,* not as if they know the good, but because they are moved to the good by one who knows [the good]." [66]

3) No being tends towards *evil as such.* Those who desire evil "do not desire it save inasmuch as it has an aspect

---
[64] *Nic. Ethics,* bk. I, ch. 1; 1094a 3.
[65] *Summa theol.,* Ia, q. 6, a. 2, ad 2.
[66] *In I ethic.,* lect. 1, no. 11.

of goodness—namely, inasmuch as they consider such a thing good; hence their intention is directly concerned with the good and accidentally with evil." [67]

*What Does the "Good" Add to Being?

95. *The "Good" Does Not Add Anything Real to Being.* "For if anything real were added to being, being would be contracted to a special genus by the nature of the good." [68]

The "Good" Is Not Entirely Synonymous with Being. For "the essence of a thing, taken absolutely, is sufficient to allow a thing to be called a being, but not to allow it to be called good." [69] Hence the "good" adds something logical to being.

The "Good" Adds to Being a Relation of Suitability to the Appetite. Since good is what all desire, it should be clear that the "good" adds something to being, i.e., expresses that a being is suitable for the appetite. Thus "it is clear that the "good" and being are really one and the same, but the "good" expresses the aspect of suitability, which being itself does not express." [70]

Every Being Is Good

96. Every being contains at least some perfection, for "to be" itself is a perfection. Now perfection makes a thing desirable and therefore good. Hence every being is good.[71]

The importance of this thesis lies in the fact that it shows the way towards a correct understanding of the problem of evil.

[67] *Ibid.*, no. 10.
[68] *De veritate*, q. 21, a. 1.
[69] *Ibid.*, ad 1.
[70] *Summa theol.*, Ia, q. 5, a. 1.
[71] *Ibid.*, a. 3.

*How Goodness Is Found in Finite and Infinite Beings

97. The question may be raised whether finite and infinite beings are good in the same way. With St. Thomas, we may answer as follows: "Since good is what all desire, the good has the aspect of an end," [72] i.e., of a final cause or that for the sake of which the agent acts. As far as the *infinite Being*, God, is concerned, "His *essence* is sufficient to allow Him to be called good," [73] for the essence of God is the ultimate end of all things, and the ultimate end is a final cause by its very nature. A *finite being*, however, derives its nature of a final cause from its relationship to God. Hence a finite being "is not good by its very essence but *by participation* . . . inasmuch as its essence is considered to be distinct according to concept from its relationship to God from which it has its nature as a final cause and to Whom it is ordered as to an end." [74] Thus it is "from the First Being, which by its very essence is being and good, that everything can be called good and being inasmuch as it participates in the First Being by way of a certain assimilation, although only in a remote and deficient way." [75]

It should be noted, however, that a finite being is *not good by a purely extrinsic denomination* which does not imply any intrinsic goodness in the thing that is called good. For the First and Supreme Good is also the efficient cause of all good; hence "it impresses its likeness upon its

[72] *Ibid.*, a.4.
[73] *De veritate*, q.21, a.1, ad 1.
[74] *Ibid*
[75] *Summa theol.*, Ia, q.6, a.4.

effects; and thus everything is called good as by an *inherent* form through the likeness to the Supreme Good which is *implanted in it*." [76]

Kinds of Goodness

98. By an analogous division [77] the good is divided, according to the manner in which it is the object of the appetite, into the *disinterested* or *virtuous,* the *pleasant* and the *useful.* For "the thing desired which terminates the movement of the appetite to a certain extent, as a means of tending towards something else, is called the *useful;* that which is desired as the last thing which terminates the movement of the appetite entirely, as a thing towards which the appetite tends for its own sake, is called the *virtuous,* for we call virtuous what is desired for its own sake; and that which terminates the movement of the appetite as a rest in the thing desired is called the *pleasant*." [78]

Concerning this division, it should be noted that it is not a division of things but of *aspects of goodness.* Hence a thing which is a virtuous good may be at the same time also pleasant. "Properly speaking, however, pleasant are those things which have no other aspect under which they are desirable save the pleasant . . . ; whereas useful are called those things which are undesirable in themselves but are desired solely because they are an aid to something else, as for instance the taking of bitter medicine; while

[76] *De veritate,* q.21, a.4.
[77] The good "is predicated primarily of the virtuous good, secondarily of the pleasant, and in the third place of the useful." *Summa theol.,* Ia, q.5, a.6. Cf. *De veritate,* q.21, a.1.
[78] *Summa theol.,* Ia, q.5, a.6.

virtuous are such things as are desired for their own sake." [79]

The *virtuous* good (*honestum*) should not be taken here in the strict sense as the moral good, i.e., as the good which is in conformity with man's objective ultimate end. It is used here in a wider sense as the good which is wanted for its own sake because it confers a perfection; for example, knowledge of metaphysics. For this reason, we called the virtuous good the *disinterested* good, i.e., a good which is not desired because of its usefulness or pleasure, but because of the perfection it confers.

Other divisions of goodness are: a) the *moral* and the *physical* good, according as a thing is good with due regard for the ultimate end or without consideration of the order to the ultimate end;

b) the *absolute* and the *relative* good, according as a thing has all the perfections due to its nature or only some of them.[80]

Evil: Its Notion, Division, and Cause

99. *Evil Is the Privation of Good.* Evil is the opposite of good, just as darkness is the opposite of light and error of truth. Hence the notion of evil must be derived from the notion of the good. As we have seen above, every being is good; hence "it is impossible that evil signify any "to be," any form, or nature. Thus it follows that the term "evil" signifies some *absence of good.* This is what we mean when we say that evil is neither a being nor a good. For, since being *qua* being is good, the absence of the one [goodness] implies the absence of the other [being]." [81]

[79] *Ibid.*, ad 2. Cf. Ia IIae, q.145, a.3.
[80] Cf. *De veritate*, q.21, a.5.
[81] *Summa theol.*, Ia, q.48, a.1.

However, "not every absence of good is evil. For the absence of a good can be understood in a privative and in a negative sense. Taken in a *negative* sense, the absence of good is not evil; for otherwise it would follow that everything would be evil because it does not have the good found in something else. For example, a man would be evil because he does not have the swiftness of the roe or the strength of a lion. But the absence of a good taken in the *privative* sense is called evil; for example, the privation of sight is called blindness." [82] Hence we may define evil as the *privation of good,* i.e., as the absence of a good which is due to a subject.

Evil Can Exist Only in a Good. Evil is something privative; hence it is clear that "evil cannot exist all by itself because it does not have an essence . . . Accordingly, evil has to exist in a subject; now every subject . . . is a good; therefore every evil is in a good." [83]

From this it follows that evil cannot totally corrupt its subject so that no good would be left in it; for otherwise evil would be left without a subject and therefore exist all by itself.[84]

100. *Division of Evil.* Evil is divided into absolute and relative evil. This division can be understood in two senses. In one way, *absolute* evil is "what is deprived of a particular good which belongs to its perfection; for instance, sickness is an evil of an animal. But we call *relative* evil what is not evil with respect to itself but with respect to something else, i.e., it is not deprived of a good which belongs to its own perfection, but to the perfection due

[82] *Ibid*, a. 3.
[83] III *Contra gentes,* c. 11.
[84] Cf. *Ibid.,* c. 12.

to something else." [85] For example, water is evil with respect to fire because it causes fire to be extinguished, and a carnivorous animal is evil with respect to its victims because it deprives them of life. In another way, *absolute* evil is evil which implies merely a privation, such as blindness, whereas *relative* evil is a positive entity which is out of proportion to its subject; for example, fever, which is a degree of body heat which is disproportioned to its subject.

By another division evil is divided into physical and moral evil. *Physical* evil deprives a being of a natural perfection due to it; for instance, sickness. *Moral* evil is the privation of the proper order to the ultimate end in a being endowed with free will. In Christian ethics moral evil is called sin.

101. *Cause of Evil.* It cannot be denied that every *evil in some way or other has a cause.* For evil deprives a being of a good due to it, and a thing can fall short of its nature only because something causes it to fall short. This cause can only be something good; for every cause is a being, and every being is good.

Nevertheless, *evil does not have a direct efficient cause,*[86] i.e., a producing cause which intends evil as such, for "whatever is the object of an appetite is a good." [87] Hence it follows that evil can have only an *indirect* efficient cause, that it is caused by accident.

Evil may result from the action of an agent which in-

[85] *De malo,* q. 1, a. 1, ad 1.

[86] The material cause of evil is the good which is its subject. Evil has no formal cause, for it is the privation of a form, nor a final cause, because it is not intended as such. Cf. *Summa theol.,* Ia, q. 49, a. 1.

[87] *De malo,* q. 1, a. 1, ad 1.

tends to produce a good, because of a certain deficiency. This deficiency may be *a defect in the agent*,[88] which falls short of its intention in the exercise of its causality; for instance, not even Caruso would be able to sing perfectly with a heavy cold, nor can a sick stomach properly digest food. But the deficiency may also be *a defect in the recipient,* insofar as the recipient is not properly disposed to receive all the perfection which would naturally flow from the action of the agent. For instance, not even a first class craftsman can produce a perfect piece of furniture if he has to work with inferior materials.[39]

*102. *Can God Be the Cause of Evil?* Since God is all-perfect, the action of God is without any defect; hence evil which results from a defect in the agent cannot be reduced to God as its cause. However, God can be the direct cause of a good which corrupts another good or is harmful to it; and in this way we may say that God can be, as it were, the *accidental cause of physical evil.*[90] For instance, if God creates birds which feed on insects, the birds are good in themselves but evil for the insects. On

---

[88] If the agent uses an instrument, the deficiency may be found in the principal agent, in the instrument, or in both. For instance, the imperfection of a photograph may result from a defect in the photographer (a lack of skill), a defect in the camera (an inferior lens), or both. Cf. III *Contra gentes,* c.10.

[89] Cf. St. Augustine, *De civitate Dei,* bk. XII, c.7; St. Thomas, *Summa theol.,* Ia, q.49, a.1. Evil may result also from the fact that a good intended by the agent is incompatible with another good existing in the recipient and thus causes it to be corrupted. However, this is not an evil with respect to the effect intended by the agent, but only with respect to something else. Cf. III *Contra gentes,* c.10.

[90] Cf. *Summa theol.,* Ia, q.49, a.2; I *Contra gentes,* c.41.

the other hand, *not even by accident can God be the cause of moral evil.* For moral evil consists in the privation of the proper order to the ultimate end (God); hence it is directly opposed to the fulfillment of the divine will, so that God in willing moral evil would be willing what He does not will.[91] How the occurrence of moral evil can be reconciled with God's will is a very complex problem which will be considered in Theodicy.

*Historical Notes

103. With few exceptions, such as *Cicero,* all philosophers after *Aristotle* have defined the "good" with reference to the appetite.

The convertibility of "good" and being was denied by the Persian philosopher *Zoroaster* (7th or 6th c. B.C.) and by *Manes* (3rd c. A.D.), whose followers are called Manicheans. Zoroaster admitted two supreme principles, the Principle of Good (Ormuzd) and the Principle of Evil (Ahriman), which are forever engaged in a battle for supremacy. All good is caused by the supreme Principle of Good, and all evil comes from the supreme Principle of Evil. This theory is known as *dualism.* In his youth, *St. Augustine,* whose doctrine of evil is now embodied in Christian philosophy, was a follower of Manes. The error of dualism lies in this that it conceives evil as something positive, which therefore requires a positive efficient cause. A supreme Principle of Evil would be a contradiction in terms because every being is good. Moreover, the positive influence of an efficient cause must result in a positive effect; hence it would be impossible to conceive a cause which would produce evil as such.

[91] Cf. *Summa theol.,* Ia, q. 48, a 6, *De malo,* q. 1, a.5.

TRANSCENDENTAL PROPERTIES OF BEING

The existence of evil is denied by *Christian Scientists*. After *Leibnitz* (1646–1716), some philosophers admitted metaphysical evil, by which they meant the absence of a perfection which is not due to a subject. However, a mere negation of a perfection is not an evil.

SUMMARY

104. Good is that which all desire; hence whatever is the object of an appetite is good.

*The "good" does not add anything real to being, nor is it entirely synonymous with being, but it adds to being a relation of suitability to the appetite.

Every being is good, because "to be" itself is a perfection and therefore desirable.

*The infinite Being is good by its very essence; for its essence is the ultimate end of all things and therefore the object of appetite. Finite beings, on the other hand, are good only by participation; for they are an end only through their relationship to God, whom they imitate in a limited way.

By an analogous division the "good" is divided into the disinterested or virtuous good, which is desired for its own sake, the pleasant good, which is desired for the sake of the pleasure it gives, and the useful good, which is desired as a means towards something else. Other divisions of goodness are the moral and the physical good, according as a thing is good with due regard to the ultimate end or without the order to the ultimate end being taken into consideration; the absolute and the relative good, according as a thing has all the perfections due to its nature or only some of them.

Evil is not the mere absence of a good, but the absence of a good which is due to a subject, i.e., the privation of a good. Hence it can exist only in a subject which is good, and is not capable of corrupting its subject entirely so as to make it entirely evil.

Evil is divided into absolute and relative evil, according as it deprives its subject of a good due to its nature or deprives another being of such a good. In another sense, absolute evil is evil which implies merely a privation, whereas relative evil is evil which expresses something positive which is not proportioned to its subject. Physical evil deprives a being of a natural perfection, whereas moral evil deprives its subject of the proper order to the ultimate end.

In some way, every evil has a cause; yet evil does not have a direct efficient cause; hence it can have only an indirect cause. Evil will result from the action of an agent if there is a deficiency in the causality exercised by the agent or in the subject upon which the agent acts.

*God can be the cause of physical evil, as by accident, inasmuch as He can create a good which causes the corruption of another good. But not even by accident can God be the cause of moral evil; for otherwise He would be willing what He does not will.

*APPENDIX: BEAUTY

Notion of Beauty

105. Closely allied to the concepts of truth and goodness is that of beauty. The beautiful is defined by St. Thomas as *"that which pleases when seen,"* [92] or *"that whose apprehension pleases."* [93] It is, indeed, a matter of experience that beauty *pleases*. On the other hand, not everything which pleases is considered to be beautiful;

---

[92] *Summa theol.*, Ia, q.5, a.4, ad 1.
[93] *Op cit.*, Ia IIae, q.27, a.1, ad 3.

for man may take pleasure also in things which are simply agreeable without being considered beautiful. Money, for instance, skill in trade, and a cool drink in hot weather are things which please, yet they are not considered to be beautiful. The beautiful pleases *when seen,* i.e., insofar as seen.[94] The pleasure experienced in the contemplation of the beautiful flows directly from the contemplation and not from the possession or usefulness of an object. Of course, the experience of the beautiful may be accompanied by pleasure derived from its possession, usefulness, etc., but it should not be identified with this pleasure—the sense of the beautiful is disinterested, i.e., it does not seek possession, but is satisfied with contemplation.

It is to be noted also that the words "when seen" do not primarily refer to sense perception. They refer in the first place to *intellectual intuition;* for only the intellect is capable of formally apprehending the conformity of an object with a cognitive power because conformity is a relation and therefore can be apprehended only by the intellect. Although the external senses, especially sight and hearing,[95] are used in the perception of material beauty, they perceive it only insofar as they are "tools" of the intellect, because of themselves they are not capable of formally perceiving the conformity of their object with a cognitive power.

---

[94] This should not be understood as if the pleasure experienced in the perception of beauty flows from the act of knowledge taken by itself, but in the sense that pleasure flows from the act of *knowing an object* which causes the experience of beauty.

[95] The so-called "lower senses" (smell, taste and touch) are not capable of perceiving beauty in their proper objects. However, the sense of touch is capable also of perceiving size and shape and thus may lead to the perception of beauty even if a person has been blind and deaf from birth.

106. *Relationship of the "Beautiful," the "True," and the "Good."* As was stated above, the "beautiful" is closely allied to the "true" and the "good." Both the *"true"* and the *"beautiful"* express a relationship of *conformity* with the intellect; both the *"good"* and the *"beautiful"* express *suitability* for the appetite. Yet the "beautiful" is not identical in concept with either the "true" or the "good." As regards the *"true,"* the "beautiful" *adds an element of pleasure* to the conformity, whereas the "true," as such, does not imply that pleasure is derived from it. On the contrary, the truth can be very unpleasant. Regarding the *"good,"* the "beautiful" expresses suitability for the appetite of the *intellect,* which comes to rest in its possession by contemplation, whereas the "good" expresses suitability for appetite in general.[96]

Is Every Being Beautiful?

107. It may seem rather rash to answer this question in the affirmative, for it appears to be an obvious fact of experience that many things are ugly. Yet St. Thomas does not hesitate to write: "There is nothing that does not participate of the beautiful and the good; for everything is beautiful and good according to its own form." [97] The reason for this statement is that every being has a form which is appropriate to it; now anything having an appropriate form pleases when seen. Therefore, every being is beautiful.

Obviously, there are certain *objections* against this view. In the first place, if every being is beautiful, the "beautiful" is *transcendental;* hence it should have been enumerated above together with the other transcendentals. The

[96] Cf. *Summa theol.,* Ia IIae, q. 27, a. 1, ad 3.
[97] *In Dionysium de divinis nominibus,* c. 4, lect. 5.

answer is that, although the "beautiful" is transcendental, it does not have to be enumerated with the "true," the "good," etc. because it is contained in the concept of the "good" inasmuch as the "beautiful" is the "good" in which the appetite of the intellect takes pleasure, and in the concept of the "true" inasmuch as the "beautiful" has a relation of conformity to the intellect.

Secondly, what about all those things which we judge to be *ugly?* We reply that, although "everything is beautiful according to its own form," the *human intellect is not always capable of perceiving this beauty.* This incapacity may be accounted for, partly by purely subjective reasons, partly by objective reasons, i.e., the very structure of the human intellect. For purely *subjective* reasons, such as the fashion of time or place, men may pre-establish more or less arbitrary norms of beauty and refuse to consider objects according to their own form. As a result, everything which does not agree with these pre-conceived ideas of beauty is judged to be ugly. Other reasons are more *objective* inasmuch as they flow from the nature of human knowledge. To appreciate beauty the intellect must *contemplate* an object, i.e., it must be able to come to rest in the vision of the thing; hence if anything prevents this contemplation, man cannot see the beauty of the object of his perception. Now there are certain reasons which may prevent our intellect from paying sufficient attention to the object and thus cause it *to become distracted.*

108. These reasons are the following:

a) If an object lacks a perfection, is *mutilated,* man's attention is more or less irresistibly drawn towards this defect, and as a result the intellect cannot come to rest in the contemplation of the perfections that remain in the object. The more striking the defect, the less the intellect is capable of refraining from considering it. For instance, if a beautiful face suffers the loss of its nose, the face is considered to be horribly ugly because we are prevented from paying attention to the beauty which remains in the undamaged part of the face.

b) Certain beings *remind us so much of others* that we can consider them only as caricatures of the latter. For instance, apes are generally held to be ugly, because they resemble man so much that upon seeing the face of an ape we unconsciously compare its face to that of man and conclude that an ape is ugly, whereas we should conclude merely that an ape would be an ugly human being. As Sully-Prudhomme remarks: "To know whether there are really ugly apes, one should be able to consult an ape." [98] On the other hand, when we consider the beauty of a racehorse, we are not reminded of the human form and therefore we may be able to find it beautiful.

c) Man is so *accustomed* to make objects that their beauty no longer strikes him; hence, again, such objects generally do not succeed in holding his attention long enough to allow contemplation of their beauty; for example, simple household objects such as spoons, pots, and pans. Yet when these objects are presented to him in a suitable setting so as to show forth their form with splendor, as is often done in advertisements, their beauty is sufficient to arrest man's attention.

109. *To be perceived by man,* beauty requires, as St. Thomas says, "three conditions, viz., in the first place,

[98] *l'Expression dans les Beaux Arts,* p 104, quoted by D Mercier in his work, *Métaphysique générale* (Louvain, 4th ed., 1904), p. 595.

integrity or perfection, for whatever is impaired is by the very fact ugly; secondly, due proportion or *harmony;* and thirdly, *clarity."* [99] The need for integrity should be clear from the foregoing. Proportion is required because whatever is disproportioned confuses and thus causes strain on the intellect whose nature it is to seek balance and unity; hence it cannot come to rest in things that are disproportioned. Proportion consists in *unity amid variety.* The more perfect the proportion is, the greater will be the beauty of the object. Clarity or splendor is required for the perception of beauty because without the compelling force of splendor the beauty of an object does not sufficiently attract the intellect to make it come to rest in contemplation.

110. A word remains to be said about the *definition of beauty*. It is far easier to appreciate beauty concretely than to define it because the perception of beauty comprises simultaneously objective and subjective elements. There are almost as many definitions as there are aestheticians who have attempted to analyze beauty. We may therefore restrict ourselves to two short definitions, the subjective definition of St. Thomas: "The beautiful is that which pleases when seen," and the objective definition of St. Augustine: beauty is the "splendor of order." [100]

Historical Notes

111. Professional treatises of beauty date from modern times. Ancient and medieval philosophers speak about beauty only incidentally.

The objectivity of beauty is denied by *Kant,* who re-

[99] *Summa theol.,* Ia, q.39, a.7.
[100] *De vera religione,* 41, 77.

duces all experience of beauty to the harmonious activity of the senses and the intellect. It is rejected also by idealistic and positivistic philosophers.

Certain modern philosophers confuse the beautiful with the delectable.

St. Thomas and *St. Augustine,* followed by most modern Thomists assert or defend that every being is beautiful.

SUMMARY

112. Beautiful is that which pleases when seen, i.e., that whose very contemplation pleases the intellect. The "beautiful" is closely allied to the "true" and the "good"; but it adds to the "true" an element of pleasure, and it differs from the "good" inasmuch as it is limited to the appetite of the intellect.

Every being is beautiful according to its own form because every being has an appropriate form; hence it pleases when seen. Nevertheless, not every being is considered to be beautiful because there may be reasons which prevent the intellect from coming to rest in the vision of the thing. The most important of these reasons which cause the intellect to become distracted are the following: any imperfection or mutilation attracts attention and thus prevents man from considering the perfection of an object; a thing may remind us so much of something else that it is considered only as a caricature; we are so accustomed to many things that we do not take the trouble to contemplate their beauty.

To strike us as beautiful an object must possess integrity, harmony, and clarity.

SUGGESTED READINGS

113. F. Van Steenberghen, *Ontology,* Wagner, 1952, pp. 46–69.
R. Garrigou-Lagrange, *God: His Existence and Nature,* Herder,

1949, vol. I, pp. 156–223 (principles of contradiction and identity).
J. Maritain, *A Preface to Metaphysics*, pp. 91–97 (principle of identity).
H. Renard, *The Philosophy of Being*, Bruce, 1952, pp. 172–177 (unity), pp. 39–44 (distinction).
R. J. McCall, "St. Thomas on Ontological Truth," in *The New Scholasticism*, 1938, pp. 9–29.
L. D. Keeler, *The Problem of Error From Plato to Kant*, Rome, 1934, pp. 83–111.
E. Smith, *The Goodness of Being in Thomistic Philosophy and its Contemporary Significance*, Catholic University of America Press, 1948.
V. H. Claire, "Whether Everything That is, is Good," in *Laval Théologique et Philosophique*, 1947, pp. 66–76; 177–194; 1949, pp. 119–140.
J. Maritain, *St. Thomas and the Problem of Evil (Aquinas Lecture, 1942)* Marquette University Press, 1943.
M. E. de Coursey, *The Theory of Evil in the Metaphysics of St. Thomas and its Contemporary Significance*, Catholic University of America Press, 1948.
G. B. Phelan, "The Concept of Beauty in St. Thomas," in *Aspects of the New Scholastic Philosophy*, New York, 1932.
C. J. O'Neill, "The Notion of Beauty in the Ethics of St. Thomas," in *The New Scholasticism*, 1940, pp. 346–378.

CHAPTER 3

Act and Potency

I. THE PROBLEM OF BECOMING

Statement of the Problem

✢✢✢ 114. When the ancient Greek philosophers set out to give a rational explanation of the world, they were faced almost immediately with a tremendous problem. They thought that before it would be possible to explain any particular phenomenon of change it would be necessary first to show that change in general is possible, i.e., intelligible. For if change *qua* change did not make sense, the very attempt to account for any particular change would be meaningless. To use a comparison, nobody in his right mind will ever attempt to construct a square circle because everybody is convinced that the whole idea of a square circle does not make sense. Hence, so reasoned the Greek philosophers, before we can explain any particular changes we shall first have to see whether change in general makes sense or not. The question was all the more urgent because sense experience seemed to offer many examples of changes. For instance, water was seen to freeze in winter and turn to vapor when heated; food was observed to change into living tissue in animals; animals themselves were born, flourished and died. Once the prob-

ACT AND POTENCY

lem of change in general had been solved, the Greeks were willing to examine particular changes, but first this most important fundamental problem had to be solved. Three basic answers were given to this problem.

The Answer of Parmenides

115. Parmenides of Elea [1] and the Eleatic school reasoned more or less in the following way:

A thing either is or is not. If it is, it is being; if it is not, it is non-being or nothing. Now when we say that a change takes place, that which comes to be, before the change either is or is not. If it is, it is being; if it is not, it is non-being. But we cannot say that before the change it is; for this would mean that it comes to be what it is already, that being comes to be being. Obviously a thing cannot come to be what it already is. On the other hand, it is equally impossible that what comes to be is not before the change; for this would mean that non-being comes to be, that non-being becomes being. But it is clear that non-being cannot come to be being. Hence we are forced to conclude that change or becoming is positively unintelligible [2] and therefore impossible. What, then, must we say about the so-called changes which we see happening all around us? Only one conclusion is possible: since change is impossible, our senses deceive us when they testify to the reality of change; for reason clearly shows that all change is a

[1] Cf. Aristotle, *Metaphysics*, bk. I, ch. 5 (986b 25 ff.); *Physics*, bk. I, ch. 3 (186a, 22 ff.). Cf. also St. Thomas' commentaries on these chapters.

[2] Positively unintelligible is that which is seen not to be possible; negatively unintelligible is that which is not seen to be possible. For example, a square circle is positively unintelligible, but a trip to the moon in one hour is negatively unintelligible because we do not yet see how it can be done.

contradiction in terms. Moreover, it follows that all reality is but one being. For whatever is different has to differ either by being or by non-being; now what differs by non-being or nothing is not different; while on the other hand things cannot differ by being because being is precisely that by which they are the same.

In this way, Parmenides was led to *static monism—monism*, because he admitted the existence of only one thing; *static*, because he denied that this one thing was subject to any change whatsoever.

The Answer of Heraclitus

116. Heraclitus (born about 530 B.C.), another Greek philosopher, went to the opposite extreme. He would have agreed with Parmenides that it is impossible to reconcile being with change, but thought that another conclusion should be drawn from it. Rather than deny the obvious testimony of the senses for the reality of change, he chose to deny the reality of being. According to him, reality is not being but becoming or change. Whatever seems to be is nothing but a deception, just as a stream may seem to be always the same, but in reality is always changing. His theory was aptly summarized in the famous formula πάντα ῥεῖ, "everything is in a state of flux."

Thus we see that, just as Parmenides, Heraclitus ended in *monism*. However, Heraclitus' monism is not of the static kind but *dynamic;* for the one that is is movement or becoming. Both forms of monism have found adherents even in modern times. For example, Spinoza's pantheism is static, whereas that of Schopenhauer is dynamic.

It is clear that both theories must lead to *skepticism* because they deny either that our sense experience is trustworthy in such a primary datum as the occurrence of change or that our intellect has any value at all.

The Answer of Aristotle

117. Other philosophers, such as Democritus (born about 460 B.C.), attempted a solution of the dilemma of Parmenides by denying that every type of change is unintelligible, but no solution was considered to be satisfactory before Aristotle solved the puzzle. With Parmenides, Aristotle maintained that being is real, and with Heraclitus, he asserted that change is real. The solution of the apparent contradiction he sees in the fact that a distinction has to be made in being itself. Being, he says, "is distinguished in respect of potency and complete reality," [3] or as it is usually expressed by scholastic philosophers, being is divided into being-in-act and being-in-potency. In other words, Aristotle admits that there is a middle ground, not between being and non-being, but between being-in-act and non-being, and this middle ground is called being-in-potency. "We say that potentially, for instance, a statue of Hermes is in the block of wood and the half-line is in the whole, because it might be separated out, and we call even the man who is not studying a man of science, if he is capable of studying." [4] Thus when we say that a thing comes to be, this does not mean that non-being becomes being, but merely that being-in-potency becomes being-in-act, and this does not imply any contradiction. Therefore, being and change are both intelligible, and there is no reason to reject the reality of either.

Aristotle's distinction between act and potency in real being furnished an immediate answer to the problem of becoming, but it has a wider application, as we shall see presently. However, let us first make sure that Aristotle's distinction is not a mere figment of his mind but object-

---

[3] *Metaphysics*, bk. IX, ch. 1; 1045b 34.
[4] *Op. cit.*, bk. IX, ch. 6; 1048a, 31.

ively justified. To do so, we must examine whether or not changes occur in reality.

The Objectivity of Change

118. In answering the question whether or not change is real, we should keep in mind that we accept and presuppose here as proved the epistemological viewpoint that there is an extramental world, and that objective knowledge of this world is possible for us. Once this viewpoint is accepted, observation makes it abundantly clear that changes do take place in reality. Bodies move from place to place, increase in size and shape; living things are born, grow, and die; man himself advances in skill and learning; etc. As a matter of fact, the occurrence of change is not only accepted as a datum of experience by most philosophers, but is also presupposed by experimental sciences, which endeavor to make particular changes intelligible. Hence the occurrence of change must be considered to be a primary datum of experience. In Aristotelian terms, before changing a thing is in-potency to that into which it changes, and after the change it is in-act with respect to that into which it changes. For example, cold water is hot-in-potency because it is capable of becoming what we call hot water, whereas what we call hot water is hot-in-act. Hence we may conclude that there is something in reality which corresponds to the concepts of act and potency.

II. THE PROBLEM OF LIMITATION

Statement of the Problem

119. Apart from the problem of change, there is another problem which has occupied the attention of philosophers

almost from the very beginning of philosophy in ancient Greece. It is called the problem of "the one and the many." Essentially, it is concerned with the question as to how it is possible to reconcile the unity of any given attribute or perfection with the multiplicity of things in which this perfection is found. The starting point of this problem lies in the primary datum of experience that there is a multiplication of perfections; e.g., there are many beings; many things that are good, beautiful, etc.; many plants, many men; etc. On the other hand, if the perfection or nature expressed by such terms as "being," "good," "man," etc., is taken by itself, it is not many but one. As St. Thomas expresses it: "Just as [a nature] is one as long as it is considered in itself, so also would it be one in reality if it subsisted or existed in itself.[5] Hence we face the problem how to explain the multiplication of perfections which in themselves are one.

The Answer of Plato

120. Plato (428–348 B.C.) tried to solve this problem with his theory of participation, which is intimately connected with his ultra-realistic teachings concerning the subsistence of ideas in a world of their own.[6] According to his view, there is a world of Ideas existing in themselves, separately from all intellects. In this world each nature or perfection exists in all its fullness, and this world of Ideas is the only "really" real world. Our halfreal world here below is but a faint image of the world of Ideas. Whatever perfections the things of this world have they

---

[5] *De substantiis separatis,* c. 6.

[6] Plato's main references to his theory of participation may be found in the following works: *Republic,* 480, 507b, 597c; *Philebus,* 16c; *Phaedo,* 102b, *Symposium,* 210d, ff.

derive by participation from the world of ideas. Accordingly, things of our world *are composed of two principles*, the finite and the infinite, one of which limits the perfection of the other and thus renders the multiplication of a perfection possible, because in the things of our world the perfection does not exist in its totality and exclusively.

From epistemological considerations it is clear that Plato confused the logical order of ideas with the ontological order of reality. Nevertheless his theory contains an important and true principle—namely, that *it is necessary to admit in the reality of our world a principle of limitation* if we want to explain why multiplication of a perfection is possible in it.

It would lead us too far afield to trace the development of Plato's theory among such NeoPlatonists as Plotinus, Proclus, and St. Augustine, who tried to correct its most obvious defects and vagueness. Suffice it to say that they succeeded neither in clearly distinguishing the order of ideas from the order of reality, nor in explaining the unity of a subject which receives many perfections by participation.[7] Therefore, it will be better to see at once how St. Thomas conceived the theory of participation.

The Answer of St. Thomas

121. For St. Thomas, participation is spoken of with respect to things which have a perfection, but not exclusively nor in its totality. For example, Peter has the perfection of "to be," but not totally, for his "to be" is limited to being Peter; nor exclusively, for other things, too, are. Hence Peter *is* not "to be," but merely participates in "to

[7] The interested reader may be referred to the articles of W. Norris Clarke quoted in no. 134, of which I have made a grateful use in the present problem.

be." As St. Thomas himself explains: "To participate is to receive, as it were, a part; and therefore when anything receives in a particular manner that which belongs to another in its totality, it is said to participate in it. Thus "man" is said to participate in "animal," because he does not possess the nature of "animal" in its universality; and likewise Socrates participates in "man." [8]

Elements of St. Thomas' Theory of Participation. 1) Participation implies a *superior source* which has the perfection without any limit, and *inferiors* which have the same perfection in a *limited* way and in *dependence* upon the superior source.

2) The *superior source,* which is the ultimate principle of the perfection, has the perfection by its very essence—it *is* the perfection. "That which totally is something does not participate in it, but is identified with it by its very essence." [9]

3) The *inferiors* have the perfection in question as received from the superior source; they *are not* the perfection, but merely *have* it. Hence the perfection which they have is received in them as in a subject which limits this perfection. "Whenever something is predicated of another by participation, there must needs be in this other, something other than that which is had by participation." [10] As a result, these inferiors *are composed of two principles,* viz., the perfection in which they participate, and a limiting subject.

4) The *ontological order* of things must be distinguished from the *logical order* of ideas. In both orders there can be question of participation, but the nature of this par-

[8] *In Boethium de hebdomadibus,* lect. 2.
[9] St. Thomas, *In I metaphysic.,* lect. 10, no. 154.
[10] St. Thomas, *Quodlibet.* 2, a.3.

ticipation will be in accordance with the order to which it refers. For instance, we may truthfully say that "man" participates in "animal" as a species participates in a genus. Such a participation is purely logical. As a result, the composition implied by such a logical participation will be purely *logical*, and the constituent parts will *not be really distinct* from one another. On the other hand, when we say that Peter participates in "to be," there is question of participation in the ontological order; therefore, the composition implied by it will be a *real composition of really distinct constituent principles*.[11]

III. SYNTHESIS OF ARISTOTLE'S THEORY OF POTENCY AND ACT WITH THE THEORY OF LIMITATION BY PARTICIPATION

122. In the foregoing pages we have seen two theories to explain two problems. With respect to the problem of change, there was the Aristotelian theory of act and potency. It explained the metaphysical structure of beings that are subject to change, but did not find any application outside the order of change. With respect to the problem of the one and many, there was the theory of participation, which explains the multiplication of a perfection by its reception into a limiting principle. Till the times of St. Thomas, both theories existed simultaneously and were used each in its respective order, but no philosophers had ever succeeded in finding a synthesis which would explain both the metaphysical structure of the mutable and the multiplication of perfection by limitation.

[11] The most important texts of St. Thomas concerning participation may be found in the following works: *In Boethium de hebdomadibus*, lect. 2, *In II de coelo et mundo*, lect. 18, no. 6, I *Contra gentes*, c. 32, *In librum de causis*, lect. 4; *Compend. theol.*, c. 68.

In his earlier works, St. Thomas himself does not seem to have realized the possibility of such a synthesis, but it appears in his writings from the *Summa Contra Gentes*.[12] This synthesis, which broadens the scope of the theory of act and potency beyond anything Aristotle ever dreamt of, forms the cornerstone of Thomistic philosophy and is contained in the simple principle: *act is not limited except by potency*.[13]

To arrive at this principle St. Thomas identified act with perfection, and potency with the principle of limitation. In his philosophy the function of potency is not merely to explain the possibility of change, but primarily to explain the multiplication of perfection by the reception of perfection in a limiting principle, and secondarily to explain the possibility of change.

Act Is Limited Only by Potency

123. The reason for this assertion is the following: the concept of act does not include any limitation; for act is perfection, whereas potency is limitation and therefore imperfection. Moreover, if act as act implied limitation, a pure act would be a contradiction in terms. For pure act excludes the possibility of higher perfection, whereas what is limited necessarily implies that a higher perfection is not impossible. Hence a pure act which is limited of itself would be a contradiction in terms.

However, the assertion that act is not limited in itself but only by potency should not be misunderstood. It does not mean that any act which exists in reality is without

---

[12] Cf. W. Norris Clarke, "The Limitation of Act by Potency" in *The New Scholasticism*, April 1952, pp. 167–194.

[13] Cf. I *Contra gentes*, cc. 28 and 43; *De potentia*, q. 1, a. 3; *Compend. theol.*, c. 17.

any limitation. Although act does not *include* limitation, it does not *exclude* it either. Hence the sense of the assertion is that if an act is found to be limited, it is not limited by itself but by the limiting principle in which it is received, i.e., by potency.

The objection has been raised that the perfection of a thing can be limited by its producing cause. Why, for instance, should it be impossible for God to limit the perfection which He wills to confer upon a thing? Even man himself is capable of determining how much perfection he is going to give to a thing. An architect, for example, can determine how much perfection this particular house is going to get. Hence act is not limited only by potency but also by its producing cause.

To this we may answer that the problem under consideration is not whether or not a producing agent is capable of limiting an act. Nobody, least of all St. Thomas,[14] wishes to deny that an agent can limit the perfection of an act. The question, however, is whether or not an agent can limit this perfection without putting any limit into the act. In other words, we are not concerned with the *extrinsic* principle of limitation but with its *intrinsic* principle, i.e., with that entity within the limited act which accounts for the limitation of the act. And with respect to this entity, Thomistic philosophers unanimously agree that it cannot be act itself but must be potency.

Potency Is Limited of Itself

124. The question may be raised as to what limits potency. To this question, we may answer that potency is limited of itself. By its very nature potency is a limited

[14] Cf. *De potentia*, q. 1, a. 3.

ACT AND POTENCY

receptive principle of perfection, a capacity for perfection. Nevertheless, in a certain sense potency may be said to be limited by the act to which it is ordered and which it receives—namely, in the sense that potencies are distinguished by the acts to which they are ordered. For instance, the potency of water to be heated is a potency to be heated and therefore limited by the act of heat; it is not a potency to become a lion. For this reason St. Thomas says that potencies are distinguished and diversified according to the act to which they refer.[15]

Corollaries of the Limitation of Act by Potency

125. A number of important conclusions follows immediately from the fact that act is limited only by potency. They are the following:

a) If any act exists which is not limited by potency, it is *infinite*. This is evident; for whatever is not limited is unlimited or infinite. Hence, such an act possesses at the highest level all the perfections proper to it. St. Thomas frequently illustrates this conclusion by saying that if, say, whiteness existed all by itself, i.e., without being received in a subject, it would have all the perfections of whiteness without any limitations whatsoever.[16]

b) If any act exists which is not limited by potency, it is *unique*. Two or more infinite acts in the same order are impossible. For such acts would either be different or not. If they are not different, then they are not two but one and the same. If they are different, one would have to have a

[15] Cf. St. Thomas, *In I sentent.*, d.12, q.1, a.1; *Summa theol.*, Ia, q.54, a.3, *De substantiis separatis*, c.5.
[16] Cf. St. Thomas, I *Contra gentes*, c.43; *De spirit. creaturis*, c.1; *Compend. theol.*, c.17.

ACT AND POTENCY

perfection which is lacking in the other; hence, this other would not be infinite but finite. Therefore, of necessity an infinite act will be unique in its own order.[17]

c) Anything whose act or perfection is limited is *composed* of two constituent principles, act and potency, which are proportionate to one another.

Potency and Act Are Really Distinct

126. The constituent principles of a thing which are called potency and act must be really distinct. For that which perfects cannot be really the same as that which is perfectible; otherwise the perfectible would give itself an act which it does not have, so that being would come from non-being. Moreover, if potency and act were not really distinct, that which limits and that which is limited would be really the same, so that act would limit itself.

From the real distinction of potency and act it follows that *nothing can be potency and act in the same respect* because this would imply that that which perfects is really the same as that which is perfected or perfectible. This assertion, however, does not mean that a higher degree of the same act cannot be received by a subject whose potency is already partially actualized. An intellect, for instance, which has already been actualized with respect to the knowledge of one thing can continue to acquire more knowledge and thus becomes more actualized. But that part of a potency which has become actualized is no longer potency. On the other hand, *in different respects* a thing may be potency and act at the same time. For instance, the power of speech may be considered as an act

---

[17] Cf. *In I sentent.* d.43, q.2, a.2; *In VIII physic.*, lect. 21; *De substantiis separatis*, c.6, *In librum de causis*, lect. 4; *Compend. theol.*, c.14.

insofar as it perfects man's nature, but insofar as it can be perfected by the act of speech it is a potency. Thus it is quite possible that what is an act in one order is a potency in a different order. It is even possible for an act to be unlimited in one order and limited in a different order (Cf. Chapts. 4, 5).

Potency and Act Enter Into a Real Composition

127. From the real distinction of potency and its act it follows that potency and act enter into a real composition. Hence, any limited being is a composite being. However, one should beware of conceiving this composition after the manner in which the physical parts of a thing constitute a whole. The body, wheels, motor, etc. of a motorcar are the physical parts which by their union constitute the whole called a car. Potency and act are parts which by their union constitute the whole called a limited act. The difference between these two types of composition is that the parts of a motorcar can exist separately as complete things (though not as motorcars); whereas potency and act, as a rule, cannot exist separately [18] because they are merely principles which by their union forms a complete whole. Hence, the real distinction between a potency and its act is not a distinction between two separate entities or beings, but a distinction between two principles of one and the same reality. Above, in no. 77, we have called this type of real distinction a *metaphysical* distinction.

The question may be raised as to *what keeps a potency and its act together*. The mere fact that such a question is raised shows that the nature of potency and act has not

[18] The only exception is the human soul, which can exist independently of the body because it is an act which surpasses the potency of the body.

been properly understood. It is impossible to conceive the union of two physical parts of a whole unless there is something which keeps them together. If I want to unite a number of pages into a book, I will have to use a ringbinder, glue, or some similar means. In this case, there is no question of a union between *principles* of one and the same thing which cannot have a separate existence, but of several things which are united by means of something else. In the union of act and potency, there is no need of any third thing to unite them. Potency and act are such that *by their very nature* they unite to become one thing. Those who look for an intermediate principle which unites potency to act seem to conceive them "as things which are actually diverse. . . . [But] potency and act somehow are one; for what is in potency comes to be in act. Hence there is no need to unite potency to act by means of some bond, as there is in the case of things which are altogether diverse.[19] This immediate union of potency and act is often expressed by the formula: potency and act unite because they are transcendentally related to one another.

In passing we may note here that potency and act are not univocal but *analogous* terms, whose meaning varies according to the problem to which they are applied. This analogous character should not be lost sight of when in subsequent pages metaphysical problems are solved by means of act and potency. Metaphysical problems are problems of being, and being is an analogous concept. Hence in each new problem the meaning of act and potency has to be adjusted and rendered determinate in a different manner according to the requirements of the problem under consideration.

[19] St. Thomas, *In VIII metaphysic.*, lect. 4, no. 1767.

ACT AND POTENCY

Potency and Act Adequately Divide Real Being

128. This assertion is true not merely if act and potency are taken in their Aristotelian sense as principles of change, but also in their more general Thomistic sense as perfection and limiting capacity for perfection.

With respect to *change,* real being is either subject to change or not. If it is not subject to change, it is a being without any potency, and we call it *pure act.* If it is subject to change, i.e., can become something-in-act, there are two possibilities. Either it is not yet something-in-act, but is capable of becoming something-in-act; or it is already something-in-act, but is still capable of becoming something else in-act. In the first case, it is *pure potency,* and in the second it is a *mixed act* or a *mixed potency.* Therefore, potency and act adequately divide being with respect to change.

With respect to *perfection,* real being is either finite or infinite in perfection. If it is infinite in perfection it is *pure act.* If its perfection is finite, it is composed of perfection and a capacity for perfection which limits the perfection, i.e., of two real constituent principles of being, called act and potency. Hence, such a composite being is a *mixed act* or a *mixed potency.* The limiting principle itself, as such, is without any perfection and thus is *pure potency.* Therefore, potency and act adequately divide real being with respect to perfection.

Definition of Act and Potency

129. In the foregoing no attempt has been made to give a strict definition of either act or potency. The reason is that a strict definition consists of a genus and a specific difference, and these cannot be found for the most pri-

mary principles of being. "The most fundamental notions cannot be defined because in the matter of definitions one cannot continue indefinitely." [20]

Nevertheless, *potency* may be described by means of its relationship to act as the *capacity for an act*. Act itself, however, cannot even be described in this way by means of a relationship to potency. For instance, it would not be correct to describe act as the actuation or fulfillment of a potency. For in doing so we should imply that every act is a fulfillment of a potency and therefore presupposes potency. While, as a matter of fact, it is true that most acts presuppose potency, this is not so because they are acts, but because they are limited acts. Act as act merely implies perfection, and not that this perfection is limited.

All we can do, therefore, to clarify the concept of act is give examples.[21] The act of "building" is in him who is building now; but the potency of "building" is in him who is not building now, although he is capable of it; the act of "heat" is in that which is hot now, but the potency of "heat" is in that which is not hot now, although it is capable of being hot; the act of "animality" is in that which is animal now, but the potency of "animality" is in that which is not animal now, although it is capable of becoming animal; etc.

Divisions of Act and Potency

130. *Act* may be either pure or mixed. An act is *pure* if it is without any potentiality. If an act is without any potentiality in any order whatsoever, it is *absolutely pure*.

[20] St. Thomas, *In IX metaphysic*, lect. 5, no. 1826.
[21] Cf. Aristotle, *Metaphysics*, bk. IX, ch. 6, 1048a, 35 ff., and also St. Thomas, *loc. cit.*, no. 1827.

Such an act is neither a co-principle united to a limiting potency nor in potency to any act of a superior order. Only God is a pure act in this sense, as we shall see in theodicy. A thing which is pure act in a certain order, while being potential with respect to a higher order, may be called a *relatively pure* act. A case in point is offered by Thomistic theology: a pure created spirit has an essence which is without any limitation in its own order, but this essence is in potency to the act of "to be." It should be clear that such a relatively pure act is, absolutely speaking, a *mixed* act, i.e., an act with an admixture of potency.

An act can be entitative or formal. By an *entitative* act we mean an act in the order of "to be," or existence. A *formal* act or form means an act in the order of essence. It specifies what a thing is. Such an act is, for example, the human soul, which makes man what he is.

A formal act may be either subsistent or non-subsistent. If it is *subsistent*, it is capable of existing all by itself, separately, whereas a *non-subsistent* form depends for its existence upon an intrinsic co-principle. An example of a subsistent form is the human soul, and of a non-subsistent form the soul of an irrational animal or plant.

A formal act which gives the first specification to a thing is called the *first act* or the *substantial form* of this thing; whereas a form which adds a secondary determination to a thing is called a *second act* or *accidental form*. The human soul, for instance, is the first act of man or his substantial form, whereas a man's weight, size, skill, etc., are second acts or accidental forms. Frequently, however, the terms "first act" and "second act" are used also in a different sense—namely, to indicate an *operative power* (first act), such as the power of sight, and its *operation* (second act);

ACT AND POTENCY

for such powers are related to their operation as the perfectible to that which perfects, although in relation to their subject they are perfections.[22]

Finally, we distinguish between *received* and *unreceived* acts, according as they enter into composition with a potency or not. An example of an unreceived act would be the essence of a pure created spirit, and of a received act the human or animal soul, which is received into the limiting potency of the body.

131. *Potency* may be either passive or active. By an *active* potency is meant a power of principle of action, such as the power of hearing. Since such a power in itself already confers a certain perfection upon its subject, it is an act with respect to its subject; hence it may also be called a first act, as we have seen above. A *passive* potency, which is the usual sense of the term "potency," is a receptive potency, i.e., a capacity or principle which can be acted upon.

Passive potency is either pure or mixed. A *pure* potency is a passive potency without any act, whereas a *mixed* potency is spoken of with respect to a subject which is already partly in-act but capable of further actualization. A mixed potency is the same as a mixed act viewed from the opposite respect. Prime matter, which is the potency for the first act or substantial form of a body, is pure potency, whereas secondary matter, i.e., any material substance capable of further modification, is an example of a mixed potency.

There are other divisions of potency, such as natural and obediential, but they need not concern us here.

Concerning the examples given above, it is to be noted

[22] Cf. *De potentia*, q. 1, a. 1.

ACT AND POTENCY

that in the course of the various sections of Thomistic philosophy we shall have to prove that they are correct. Any justification of their correctness at this point would entail long explanations, which would break the continuity of thought and therefore do more harm than good.

*Historical Notes

132. To the historical data offered in the course of this chapter little needs to be added. Since the principle that act is limited by potency only, is the cornerstone of Thomistic philosophy, it is obvious that it is unanimously accepted by all Thomists and equally unanimously rejected by all non-Thomistic philosophers. No one can call himself a Thomist without accepting this principle, and anyone who accepts it will, by sheer force of logic, embrace Thomistic metaphysics.

Scotus and *Suarez* assert that an act can be limited by its efficient cause. We have seen in what sense this assertion can be accepted. Scotus and Suarez deny that real act and potency must of necessity be really distinct.

Monistic and *phenomenalistic* philosophers, who deny that there are many things, obviously also deny that there is any real problem of multiplication and limitation.

SUMMARY

133. To the question whether change as such is intelligible, Parmenides answered in the negative because it would mean either that being comes to be being, or that non-being comes to be being. Hence he concluded that our senses deceive us when they testify to the reality of change. Reality is unchangeable and without any differentiation; for to be different things would have to differ by being; which is impossible, because being is that by which

they are the same. Thus Parmenides arrived at static monism.

Heraclitus also admitted that it is impossible to reconcile being and change. But rather than reject the reality of change, he chose to deny the reality of being and admitted that only change is real. Heraclitus was a dynamic monist.

Aristotle maintained that both being and change are real and intelligible. Distinguishing between being-in-act and being-in-potency, he showed that there is a middle ground between non-being and being-in-act. Change means the transition from being-in-potency to being-in-act, and thus there is no contradiction between change and being.

The reality of change is a primary datum of experience and cannot be denied without putting in jeopardy all science of the real. Hence, we may admit that act and potency are not mere figments of the mind, because only the theory of act and potency can give a satisfactory solution of the dilemma of Parmenides.

The problem of limitation is concerned with the following: whereas in itself a perfection does not imply any limitation, the particular things in which we see this perfection realized never have it without limitation. These things, therefore, *are* not this perfection, but merely *have* it, i.e., participate in it. Accordingly, whatever is limited must be composed of the perfection which is had by participation and a limiting principle. This composition will be logical or real according as the participation in question belongs to the logical or the real order.

St. Thomas made a synthesis of the theory of participation with that of potency and act by identifying act with perfection, and potency with the limiting principle. He thus arrived at the statement that act is limited only by potency. In Thomistic philosophy, therefore, potency is not merely a principle of the mutable, but also and especially of the finite.

Act cannot be limited of itself because act is perfection, and perfection as such does not imply imperfection or limitation. Hence if act is found to be limited, it is limited by potency. The producing cause of a thing may be considered as its limiting principle in the order of extrinsic causality. But no extrinsic cause can limit the perfection of a thing without putting a limit into it, and this intrinsic limit is potency. Potency itself is limited of its very nature; for potency is conceived as a limited capacity for perfection or act.

Since act is limited only by potency, it follows that:
a) Any act which is not limited by potency is infinite;
b) Any act which is not limited by potency is unique;
c) Anything whose act is limited is composed of potency and act.

Potency and act are really distinct because the perfectible cannot be really the same as that which perfects; otherwise a thing would perfect itself, i.e., give itself an act it does not have. Hence, nothing can be in potency and act in the same respect, but it is possible for a thing to be act in one respect and potency in another.

Potency and act enter into a real composition because they are really distinct. However, this composition should not be conceived as a physical composition of complete things or beings, but as the metaphysical composition of principles of one and the same thing. Such principles need not be united by means of a common bond, but are united and kept together by their very nature.

Potency and act adequately divide real being both with respect to change and perfection. The immutable and the infinite will be pure act; the mutable and the finite will be composed of act and potency.

Neither act nor potency can be properly defined. Potency, however, may be described by means of its relationship to act as a capacity for act or perfection. Act itself can be clarified only by examples.

Potency and act are analogous concepts and their meaning varies according to the problem to which they are applied.

Act can be pure or mixed, subsistent or non-subsistent, substantial or accidental, received or unreceived, entitative or formal. Potency is either passive or active. Passive potency is either pure or mixed.

SUGGESTED READINGS

134. H. Renard, *The Philosophy of Being*, pp. 17–25.
F. Van Steenberghen, *Ontology*, pp. 70–117.
W. N. Clarke, "The Limitation of Act by Potency," in *The New Scholasticism*, 1952, pp. 167–194.
——— "The Meaning of Participation in St. Thomas," in *Proceedings of the American Catholic Philosophical Association*, 1952, pp. 147–157.
W. Van Roo, "Act and Potency," in *The Modern Schoolman*, 1940, pp. 1–5.

PART TWO

The Philosophy of Finite Being

THIS PART is divided into three sections. The first section deals with the nature of finite being in general; the second with its supreme classes; the third with the causes of finite being.

SECTION I

The Nature of Finite Being

THIS SECTION is divided into three chapters. First, we shall consider two problems of actual being—the problem of multiplication of "to be" itself; and secondly, the problem of multiplication of essence. Both problems will be solved by means of the Thomistic principle that act is limited by potency only. In the third chapter we shall consider one problem of possible being—namely, the ultimate foundation of possible being.

CHAPTER 4

Multiplication of "To Be"

✣✣✣ 135. It is a primary datum of experience that of *many* things we can truthfully say that they really *are*. I am, this desk is, the sun is, etc. In other words, the perfection or the act of "to be" is multiplied. Now, as we have seen in the preceding chapter, wherever there is multiplication there is limitation; and wherever there is limitation, there is potency. Hence, if "to be" is multiplied it must be received in a potency, so that any finite being is composed of a limited "to be" and a principle of limitation as its potency. This potency to "to be" is called *essence*, and the act of "to be" may be called *existence*. St. Thomas, however, rarely, if at all, speaks of existence; and with him we prefer to indicate existence simply as "to be," or the act of "to be." For the sake of a better understanding of the present problem let us examine essence and "to be" more in detail.

Essence and "To Be"

136. As we have seen in no. 19, the concept of being is "that whose act it is 'to be.'" This description implies two things in the subject which is called a being—namely, the reference of this subject to the act of "to be" and the act of "to be" itself. The reference to the act of "to be" is

called the "essence," and the act by which the subject *is* is called existence or "to be." A strict definition of essence is impossible, because essence does not have a genus; hence we shall have to be satisfied with a description. The usual description of *essence* is *"that by which a thing is what it is."* For instance, the essence of water is that by which water is water and not gold or a lion; the essence of man is that by which man is man and not an angel or a cow.

There are a few other terms which are approximately equivalent to essence. They are nature and quiddity. While the reality indicated by these terms is the same, the term *nature* is used in preference to essence whenever we mean the essence insofar as it is a principle or terminus of activity.[1] For example, rather than "essence" we use "nature" in sentences such as: To be capable of speech or subject to suffering is proper to man's nature. The term *quiddity* is synonomous with essence. It is derived from the Latin *quid* (what), and indicates that essence answers the question as to what a thing is.

137. *In its own order* any essence is a perfection or act. That, for example, by which man is man, or that by which water is water, expresses a certain perfection or act. *In the order of "to be,"* however, essence does not express any act.[2] Of itself, it does not imply actual "to be," but merely something which is capable of becoming in the order of "to be"; something which has a capacity or potency for the act of "to be." This is the reason why it is possible to

[1] Cf. St. Thomas, *De ente et essentia,* c. 1. As to how substance is compared to essence and nature, see Chapt. VIII.

[2] Unless the essence is identified with "to be" itself, as is the case with the Infinite Being, God.

know an essence without knowing whether or not it exists in reality.[3] Thus it is clear that an essence is conceived as a potency for "to be." This potency limits "to be," because any particular essence is a capacity for a definite act of "to be." For instance, the essence of water is limited in its capacity for "to be" to the reception of the act of "to be" water, and not gold or steel; the essence of man is limited in its capacity to the act of "to be" as man, and not as an angel or a lion.

138. *"To be"* itself cannot be defined in the strict sense; for a definition always expresses *what* a thing is; whereas "to be" does not answer the question *what* a thing is, but *whether* it is. However, we may describe "to be" as *"that by which a thing is."* It is scarcely necessary to point out that "to be" is a perfection, an act. It is not merely an act; it is the greatest, the most perfect of all acts, for without "to be" no other act is. St. Thomas calls it "the perfection of perfections"[4] because it is the actuality of all acts.

The Multiplication of "To Be" Can Be Explained Only by the Reception of "To Be" in a Limiting Essence

139. After the foregoing the reason for this assertion should be clear. The multiplication of an act can be explained only by its limitation. Limitation can be explained only by potency. Hence if the act of "to be" is multiplied it must be received in a limiting potency. Now, the potency which limits the act of "to be" is called "essence." Hence the multiplication of "to be" can be explained only

[3] Cf. *De ente et essentia*, c.5.
[4] *De potentia*, q.7, a.2, ad 9.

by the reception of "to be" in a limiting essence.[5] Thus it follows that any finite being is composed of potency (essence) and act ("to be").

"To Be" and Its Limiting Essence Are Really Distinct

140. This assertion follows at once from the fact that "to be" and its limiting essence are related to one another as real act and real potency, for real act and real potency are really distinct, as we have seen in no. 128. Hence, we could dismiss this question without further discussion as an immediate corollary of the theory of potency and act. Historical reasons, however, compel us to examine the question more carefully. From the thirteenth century on, the real distinction of essence and "to be" has been the object of endless and often bitter disputes. Thomistic philosophers consider it the fundamental truth of all Christian philosophy, because it shows the ultimate basis of the difference between God and creatures. God is pure "to be"; hence, He is infinite, unique, and simple. Creatures, on the other hand, are not pure "to be"; hence, they are finite, many, and composite. Other philosophers, however, deny that any serious consequences follow if the real distinction of essence and "to be" in a finite being is denied. For this reason, we must examine the question more carefully and see whether the Thomistic position is justified.

Distinctions Admitted by All

141. Let us first see what is *not* the point under discussion. With regard to this we may safely say that all agree in the following points:

[5] Cf. St. Thomas, *Summa theol.*, Ia, q.3, a.4 and q.75, a.5, ad 4; II *Contra gentes*, c.52.

a) There is *no real distinction* between the essence and the "to be" if "to be" is unlimited. In the Infinite Being the "to be" is the very essence itself; the Infinite Being is pure "to be" and therefore without any real composition and distinction.

b) There is a *real* (negative) *distinction* between a *possible* essence and *actual* "to be." Obviously, a possible man is not really the same as an actually existing man. Hence, the problem is limited to the essence and the "to be" of actually existing essences. In other words, we consider INDIVIDUAL essences, say, the essence of this man or that cat, and ask ourselves whether or not the essence of this man is really distinct from his "to be."

c) There is *some kind of a distinction* between the essence and the "to be" of an *actually existing essence*. The question, however, is whether this distinction is logical or real.

What Is Not Implied by the Real Distinction

142. To prevent other misunderstandings we should keep in mind also the following points:

1) In Thomistic philosophy real distinction is not the same as *separability*. While it is true that things which can be separated or are separate, are also really distinct, one should beware of converting this statement into: Things that are really distinct can be separated. Essence and its "to be" are not complete beings, but merely principles of being which by their union form one being. They *are* not separately, but the composite of essence and "to be" *is*. It is necessary to stress this difference between real distinction and separability because in the past there have been authors who identified them.

2) From the foregoing it follows that the union of es-

sence and its "to be" should not be conceived as a union of two beings, but merely as the *union of two principles of one and the same being*. An essence without a "to be" would not exist, and a "to be" without an essence would be unintelligible. Hence, that which exists is neither the essence alone nor the "to be" alone, but the essence existing through its "to be."

3) Although the essence is real, it does not have any *actuality* in the order of "to be" independently of its "to be." Whatever actuality an essence has in the order of "to be" comes to it from its "to be." Hence its reality is merely a real capacity for "to be."

Proof of the Real Distinction

143. Above, in no. 140, we have seen that a proof of the real distinction between the essence and the "to be" in any finite being can easily be derived from the Thomistic theory of act and potency. St. Thomas offers many other proofs which are based upon this theory.[6] There is one proof, however, which is independent of act and potency. It is the following:

"Whatever is not of the concept of an essence or quiddity is something which comes to it from without, and enters into composition with the essence because no essence can be understood without those elements which are part of the essence. Now every essence or quiddity can be understood without anything being understood of its "to be." For I can understand what a man is or a phoenix without knowing whether they have a "to be" in reality. Hence, it is clear that "to be" is different from the essence or quiddity, unless perhaps there exists a thing whose quiddity is its very "to be." And this thing can only be unique and

[6] Cf. *De ente et essentia*, c.5; II *Contra gentes*, c.52.

first. . . . Hence it must needs be that in every other thing, apart from this thing, its "to be" and its quiddity i.e., its nature or form, are different." [7]

Or, to say the same in a short form, the concept of an essence includes everything which is really identical with the essence. Now the essence of a finite being does not include "to be." Therefore, "to be" is not really identical with this essence.

*The *objection* has been raised that this argument is similar to the ontological argument for the existence of God, and therefore, this argument, too, must be held to be invalid, because it passes from the logical to the ontological order. This objection, however, is not to the point. In the ontological argument one concludes that God exists in reality because God's essence includes "to be" in its definition; whereas in this argument we do not conclude that finite beings exist in reality, but merely that if they exist, their essence is not their "to be."

A Finite Essence and Its "To Be" Enter Into a Real Composition

144. This assertion follows immediately from the fact that a finite essence is a real potency for "to be," and that "to be" is its act. For a real potency and its act enter into a real composition, as we have seen in no. 129.

Concerning the question as to what unites an essence and its "to be," the answer is the same as that given for the union of potency and act in general. An essence and its "to be" do not need to be united by means of a third intrinsic constituent principle which acts as a common bond, but by their very nature they unite to become one

---

[7] *De ente et essentia,* c. 5.

being. They are, as it is called, transcendentally related to one another.

Importance of the Real Distinction

145. How important a role is played by the real distinction of essence and "to be" in finite beings and their real identity in Infinite Being may be gauged by a few of its applications.[8]

The division of all beings into pure act and composites of act and potency is based upon the fact that finite beings *are* not by their very nature, whereas Infinite Being *is* by its very nature. Without real composition of essence and "to be" there could be no contingent beings. Without real composition of essence and "to be" there could be no real diversity of perfections in beings. From the identity of essence and "to be" in God it follows that God is simple, all-perfect, immutable, unique, etc.

The proofs for the existence of God lead to a Being whose essence is its "to be."

The creation of the world is proved from the fact that outside God everything is composed of essence and "to be" and therefore requires a composer.

From the distinction of essence and "to be" in finite beings follows the distinction of substance and power, substance and action, because action follows being.

Because of its real composition in the order of "to be," a finite being needs to be preserved in its "to be."

Because of its real potentiality in the order of "to be," a finite being is potential also in the line of action, and thus needs to be moved to act as well as to "to be."

---

[8] Cf. N. del Prado, *De veritate fundamentali philosophiae christianae*, Fribourg, 1911.

There are scores of other problems which find their solution in the application of the real distinction between essence and "to be" in a finite being, as will become clear throughout the course of philosophy.

Historical Notes

146. The Greek philosophers were concerned with essences; hence one would look in vain for the discussion of real distinction in ancient Greek philosophy. *Aristotle's* theory of potency and act offered a basis for this distinction; but he did not apply his theory to the order of "to be." *Plato's* theory of participation contained a suggestion of the distinction, but it remained a mere suggestion. This suggestion, however, was developed by such Neoplatonists as *Plotinus*, who affirmed that all beings except God are composed. *St. Augustine* (354–430) distinguished between being by essence and being by participation and thus may be quoted as in favor of the real distinction. Similar distinctions were made by the *Pseudo-areopagite* and *Hilary*. *Boethius* distinguished between "to be" and "what is," although it is doubtful at least whether his "to be" had any existential meaning.[9]

Alfarabi and *Avicenna*, two medieval Arabian philosophers, clearly held for the real distinction, but Avicenna conceives "to be" as an accident. It is found also in the medieval Jewish philosopher *Moses Maimonides*.

William of Auvergne seems to have introduced it into the philosophy of the West. It was accepted by *Bonaventure*, *Albert the Great*, and *Thomas Aquinas*. Extensive historical research as well as a study of his works leaves no doubt that St. Thomas taught the real distinction. Any

[9] Cf. M. D. Roland-Gosselin, *Le "de ente et essentia" de St. Thomas d'Aquin* (Paris. 1948), pp. 142 ff.

denial of this can be based only upon complete ignorance of his times and his works. Needness to say, it is unanimously accepted by all Thomistic philosophers.

Aegidius the Roman (Giles of Rome) admitted the separability of essence and "to be."

The real distinction is denied by *Scotus, Suarez,* and the *nominalists.* The reason for this denial is that they do not admit the need for an intrinsic principle of limitation. *Scotus* asserts that essence and "to be" in a finite being are distinct by his formal distinction, which is actual on the part of the thing. *Suarez* and his school admitted only a virtual distinction. In recent years, however, the number of Jesuit philosophers who still follow Suarez in this matter has been reduced almost to the vanishing point, at least outside Spain and South America. Among outstanding Jesuit philosophers who teach the real distinction we may name *Billot, Schiffini, Remer, Mattiussi, de la Taille, Boyer,* and *Renard.*

Outside scholastic schools of philosophy, *Descartes, Spinoza,* and *Hegel* are quoted for the real distinction.

A purely logical distinction was defended by *de Benedictis.*

SUMMARY

147. It is a primary datum of experience that many things are. Hence, "to be" is multiplied. Now the multiplication of an infinite perfection is not possible; hence only one being can be infinite; all others must be finite. Since no act is finite or limited by itself, it follows that the perfection of "to be" in finite beings is limited by a receiving potency, which is called the essence of the finite being.

Essence may be described as that by which a thing is what it is; whereas "to be" is that by which a thing is. In its own order an essence is a perfection or an act; but in the order of "to be" the essence of a finite being is a mere capacity for the act of "to be."

Since the multiplication of "to be" can be explained only by the reception of "to be" in a limiting potency, it is clear that finite beings are composed of act and potency in the order of "to be." This composition is called the composition of "to be" and essence. "To be" and its limiting essence are really distinct because they are real act and real potency, and real act and potency are really distinct. Moreover, the concept of an essence includes everything which is really identical with this essence; but the concept of the essence of a finite being does not include "to be"; otherwise the finite being would have to exist of necessity. Hence the "to be" of a finite being is really distinct from its essence.

The real distinction of essence and "to be" in a finite being does not mean that they can be separated. Separation is possible only between complete beings; but essence and "to be" are not beings but only principles of being, which by their union constitute one being. A separate essence would not exist, and a "to be" without an essence is altogether unintelligible.

The importance of the real distinction lies in the fact that it makes clear in what ultimately consists the difference between God, pure act, and creatures, which are composites of act and potency.

SUGGESTED READINGS

148. H. Renard, *The Philosophy of Being*, pp. 46–62.
P. Coffey, *Ontology*, Smith, 1938, pp. 74–115.
W. M. Walton, "Being, Essence and Existence for St. Thomas Aquinas," in *Review of Metaphysics*, 1950, pp. 339–365.

H. Carpenter, "A Note on the Fundamental Principle of Thomism," in *Dominican Studies*, 1949, pp. 30–37.

Louis de Raeymaeker, *The Philosophy of Being*, Herder, 1954, Ch. VI, pp. 99–155.

CHAPTER 5

Multiplication of Essence

✤✤✤ 149. Experience attests that many beings belong to the same species, i.e., possess the same specific essence. Experimental sciences, as a matter of fact, are based upon this presupposition. For instance, there are many men, many brute animals, many plants. Even though we do not always know exactly where the dividing line must be drawn between different species, this much is certain: Concrete reality possesses a definite nature or essence, and this essence is multiplied, or, at least can be multiplied in a number of individual essences. Hence, reality reveals itself to the mind as possessing a species-individual structure.[1] Once again we are faced with a problem of multiplication. This time, however, the problem does not lie in the line of "to be," the existential line, but in the line of essences themselves. Thus the problem is: How is it possible for a specific essence to be multiplied in individuals. To this problem we may attach another: What makes an individual an individual? It is clear that the answer to the second question will depend upon the answer to the first. As we shall see at once, it is again the Thomistic theory of act and potency which furnishes the answer.

[1] Cf. Andrew G. Van Melsen, *The Philosophy of Nature*, pp. 115 ff.

I. HOW CAN AN ESSENCE BE MULTIPLIED?

The Multiplication of a Specific Essence Can Be Explained Only by the Reception of the Specific Perfection in a Limiting Potency

150. The proof [2] of this assertion is as follows:

From the fact that many beings have the same specific essence it follows that they participate in this essence in a limited way.[3] For either this essence is had in a limited way or in an unlimited way. Now it is impossible that many things have the same specific essence in an unlimited way. Therefore, they participate in it in a limited way. Now, a specific essence is a perfection, an act; and act is limited only by potency. Hence, the multiplication of a specific essence is possible only if the specific perfection is received in a limiting potency.

That we must exclude two or more infinite or unlimited acts of the same specific essence is clear from the following: An essence is an act. Now, two unlimited acts would either be different or not. If they were not different, they would not be two but one. If they are different, one must have something which the other does not have, so that

[2] Cf. St. Thomas, In II sentent., d.3, q.1, a.4; II *Contra gentes*, c.93 (second proof); *In III de anima*, lect. 8, no. 706.

[3] Like all metaphysical concepts, the notion of limitation by participation is analogous in its application to various orders. In the preceding chapter, there was question of participation in a perfection ("to be") which exists as something unique and infinite in the order of reality. Here the question is one of limitation of a perfection (a specific essence) which exists as infinite and unique only in the intellect. Nevertheless, the problem of the multiplication of specific essences does not belong to the purely logical order because the specific essence is limited in concrete realizations which exist in the order of reality.

this other is not unlimited but limited. Hence, two unlimited acts of the same specific essence are impossible.

The name of the act of a specific essence is *form*, and that of its limiting potency is *matter*. The theory of act and potency as applied to the order of specific essences is called *hylomorphism*—a name which is derived from the Greek words for matter (ὕλη) and form (μορφή).

Matter and Form

151. In Thomistic philosophy *matter* as a principle of a specific essence is conceived as a real potency for the act of essence. Of itself, matter has no determination whatsoever, but is pure potency. As Aristotle expresses it, matter "is of itself neither a particular thing, nor of a particular quantity, nor otherwise positively characterized."[4] Whatever perfection an essence has in its own order does not come from its potential principle, matter, but from its actual constituent principle, the form which is united to the potential principle. Hence, it should be obvious that matter, as a potential principle of essence, does not, and cannot exist all by itself.[5] For, if it did exist separately, it would have the act of "to be" and thus would not be pure potency. It is to be noted, however, that what we call matter in ordinary language, for instance, stone, wood, iron, etc., philosophically speaking, is not matter in the sense in which the term is used here. Stone, etc., is what philosophers call "*secondary matter*," i.e., a compound of matter in the above sense, and a substantial form which is capable of further determination. To distinguish this secondary matter from matter which is the principle of limi-

[4] *Metaphysics*, bk. VII, ch. 3; 1029a, 23.
[5] Cf. *Summa theol.*, Ia, q.7, a.2, ad 3.

tation of specific perfection in the substantial line, we may call the latter prime or *primary matter*.

Form is the actual constituent principle of the limited specific essence of the individual thing. Together with the potential principle which it actuates it constitutes the limited essence. Hence, whatever perfection is found in the essence of an individual thing comes from this form.

Matter and Form Are Really Distinct and Enter Into a Real Composition

152. This assertion follows immediately from the fact that matter and form are related to one another as potency is to act. For, potency and act are really distinct and enter into a real composition, as we have seen in nos. 126 and 127.

If the question is raised as to *what unites matter and form*, the answer is the same as that given regarding potency and act in general: There is no need for a third intrinsic principle which binds matter and form together. As St. Thomas says: "Form is united to matter without any intermediary. For it is by its very essence that it belongs to a form to be the act of such a body, and not by means of anything else. Hence there is nothing which makes a unified thing of matter and form, save the agent which reduces the potency to act, as Aristotle proves in VIII *Metaphysics*.[3] For, matter and form are related to one another as potency is to act." [7] "To look for the cause of a thing is like looking for the cause of the unity of that thing; for insofar as any thing is, it is one, and potency and act somehow are one, because what is in potency comes

[6] *Metaphysics*, bk. VII, ch. 6; 1045b, 21.
[7] II *Contra gentes*, c. 71.

to be in act. Thus, there is no need to unite potency and act by means of a common bond, as there is in the case of things which are altogether diverse. Hence, any cause which causes the union of what is composed of potency and act does so by causing the passage from potency to act." [8]

It is to be noted that the *agent* which reduces a thing from potency to act, or causes the union of potency and act, is not an intrinsic constituent principle of the thing but its *extrinsic* efficient or producing cause. Hence, there is no third intrinsic constituent principle which unites matter and form, but they are united by their very nature. In other words, they are transcendentally related to one another.

From the fact that matter and form unite by their very nature as the constituent principles of the same thing, it follows that they enter into a *perfect union* or are perfectly unified.

There Is No Limitation of Form Without Matter

153. An immediate conclusion of this theory of matter and form is that any form which exists without being received in a potency will possess all the perfections proper to this form, without any limit, so that no multiplication of this form is possible.[9] Such a form is said to be individual of itself. Reason alone, however, cannot prove the existence of such forms. If their existence is admitted upon theological grounds, it follows according to the Thomistic theory that such forms cannot be multiplied within the same species. Hence, each one of these forms will be unique and infinite in its own species.

[8] *In VIII metaphysic*, lect. 4, no. 1767.
[9] Cf. St. Thomas, II *Contra gentes*, c. 93 and elsewhere.

This brief consideration of hylomorphism suffices for our purpose. A more detailed study and the solution of the many difficulties which can be raised against it belongs to the section of metaphysics which is called the philosophy of nature, or cosmology.[10]

II. THE PRINCIPLE OF INDIVIDUATION

154. Now that we have solved the first question—what makes the multiplication of a specific essence in individuals possible—we must face the second question: What makes an individual essence THIS individual essence and no other? From the foregoing it should be clear that we are concerned only with individuation within a species; in other words, only with the individuation of corporeal essences, since only corporeal essences can be multiplied within the same species. This second question is called the problem of the principle of individuation. Before attempting to solve this rather obscure problem, let us first analyze the concept of individual and, state what we mean by the principle of individuation.

The Concept of Individual

155. The individual may be defined as that "which is undivided in itself but divided from everything else."[11] By *"undivided in itself"* is meant that it is not divided further by any differences whether formal or material. Hence, an individual cannot be divided and multiplied and still retain its identity. It would be inconceivable, for instance, that Peter Jones would be at the same time *this man* and *that other man*. Individuality cannot be common

[10] Cf., for instance, Andrew G. van Melsen, *The Philosophy of Nature*, ch. 4.
[11] *Summa theol.*, Ia, q. 29, a. 4.

to many; therefore, the individual is said to be *incommunicable*.

The second part of the definition, "*divided from everything else*," indicates that the individual is *distinct* from every other individual in the same species.

Therefore, the concept of individual implies two things —incommunicability and distinction.

The Concept of "Principle of Individuation"

156. To avoid confusion about the meaning of the principle of individuation the following should be kept in mind:

a) By the principle of individuation one could mean that by which we *know* or recognize an individual. This is what the ancients used to call the individuating notes, which are expressed in the following jingle:

Form, figure, place, time, ancestry, fatherland and name
Are seven things which together never are the same.

Nowadays we could make sure of an individual by his fingerprints, noseprint, or other such more advanced means. However, in metaphysics we are not concerned with the principle of *cognition* of individuals.

b) The *efficient* cause which produces individuals may be called a principle of individuation. Again note that this is not the principle which concerns us here. For, the efficient cause is the *extrinsic* principle of individuation, whereas we are concerned with the *intrinsic* principle.

c) By the *intrinsic* principle of individuation we mean that entity within the individual which accounts for the fact that this individual is this individual and no other. Even the intrinsic principle of individuation may be understood in two manners. We may answer the question why Peter is Peter and no one else, by saying that Peter is

Peter by his whole individual essence. Of course, there can be no argument about it. But we might as well have answered that Peter is Peter by his "Peterness." In fact, if the question is understood in this way, it does not make much sense. The answer will indicate the immediate or *formal* principle of individuation, and such a principle will always have to be the essence of the thing. Hence, the answer is not very illuminating because it does not tell us anything new.

What we are really interested in is this: Why does Peter have this individual essence and no other? Or, why does Peter have this body and this soul, and not John's body and Michael's soul? Taken in this sense our question is concerned with the *fundamental* principle or the *root* of individuation, and it is in this sense that we must attempt to answer it.

Matter Is the Principle of Individuation

157. At first sight it is clear that the fundamental principle of individuation must be an *intrinsic* constituent principle of the individual essence, because the fundamental principle is an intrinsic principle. Now, an individual essence is composed of two constituent principles, matter and form. The *form*, however, *cannot be the ultimate root of individuation* because of itself any form is common, and thus can be found in several.[12] If, for instance, Peter would be this man because he has the form of man, every man would be Peter, because every man has the form of man. Moreover, individuation within a species implies multiplication, and therefore also limitation. Form, however, of itself does not imply any limitation; hence,

[12] St. Thomas, *Quodlibet.* 7, a. 3.

again, we arrive at the conclusion that the form of an individual cannot be the ultimate root of individuation.

For the same reasons we must exclude the possibility that the fundamental principle of individuation would be an *additional form,* or a combination of additional forms added to the compound of matter and form. For, of itself any formal principle is communicable to many, and thus cannot be the ultimate basis of incommunicability. "No matter how many forms are joined together, no definite assignation of this singular thing will result, save accidentally inasmuch as the collection of these forms happens to be found only in one thing." [13] Moreover, if such an additional formal principle belonged to the essence, it would cause an essential difference, a new species, and not a purely individual difference within the same species. On the other hand, if it did not belong to the essence, it could not cause the individuation of this essence from within, but, at most, would be something by which this essence could be recognized.

Hence, by exclusion, it follows that the root of individuation must be found in matter.[14]

How Matter Is the Principle of Individuation

158. We must now see how matter can be the root of individuation. As will be recalled, individuality implies two things—incommunicability and distinction. Hence the root of individuation has to account for both these characteristics of the individual. It is easy to see how matter

[13] St. Thomas, *In VII metaphysic*, lect. 15, no. 1626.

[14] The root of individuation cannot be the "to be" of the corporeal thing, for that which comes to be is precisely the individual corporeal thing; hence "to be" presupposes the individuation of the corporeal essence.

can be a principle which explains why an essence is *incommunicable*. For, matter is the potency in which the form is received; and once received by matter the form is rendered incommunicable because matter is purely receptive, and therefore incommunicable. Hence, matter alone suffices to explain why an individual is incommunicable.[15]

Matter alone, however, cannot explain why an individual is *distinct* from every other individual. For, of itself matter is purely potential, indistinct and indeterminate; hence, it cannot be a principle of distinction.[16] Only matter which is distinct can make a form distinct. We have therefore to find a principle which can make matter distinct. This principle is found in *quantity*. For, quantity implies extension, and whatever is extended has position, so that its parts can be distinguished according to their position. That quantity is really a principle of distinction can be seen in mathematics. Mathematics considers only quantity; yet mathematical figures of the same species, such as two lines of the same dimensions, are distinguished by their position. Hence, quantity is a principle of distinction and therefore capable of making matter distinct from every other matter.[17]

The function attributed to quantity in the explanation of individuation merely consists in *conditioning matter* for its role of making the essence distinct from every other essence in the same species. The principle of individuation is really matter and not quantity; for the principle of individuation must be an essential co-principle, and quantity does not belong to the essence of matter. But the principle

[15] Cf. *Summa theol.*, Ia, q.3, a.2, ad 3; IIIa, q.77, a.2.
[16] Cf. St. Thomas, *In Boethium de trinitate*, q.IV, a.2.
[17] Cf. IV *Contra gentes*, c.65.

of individuation is not matter taken by itself, but *matter made distinct by quantity*. Quantity, then, is not a direct co-principle of individuation, but a principle which "marks" matter, so as to make it possible for matter to fulfill its role as the principle of individuation. For this reason St. Thomas says that the principle of individuation is "matter marked by quantity," [18] i.e., matter made distinct by quantity.

Matter Made Distinct by Quantity

159. Quantity insofar as it makes matter distinct and capable of assuming its role as the principle of individuation, should not be understood as the *actual* quantity possessed by an individual body. For, actual quantity is an accident, and as such is not prior to the body which is to be individuated, but presupposes it as its subject of inhesion.

Hence, we must understand quantity in the formula, "matter made distinct by quantity," as radical quantity, i.e., as *the requirement of matter to have quantity*. In scholastic terminology, this requirement of matter to have quantity is often referred to as the transcendental relation of matter to quantity. By its very nature matter requires quantity, because it is the potential principle of a body, and it is proper to a body to be quantified; hence matter is transcendentally (essentially) related to quantity.

*160. This explanation, however, does not bring us to the end of our difficulties. Two problems remain to be solved. In the first place, it is not sufficient to say that matter has a requirement for quantity. If matter requires

---

[18] Cf *In IV sentent.*, d.12, q.1, a.1; *In Boethium de trinitate*, q.IV a.2.

quantity by its very nature, it cannot serve as a principle of distinction, for it has this requirement in Peter as well as in John. To be a principle of distinction, matter will have to have a requirement for *this* quantity rather than *that*. Now it would seem that matter cannot have a requirement for one determinate quantity in preference to another, because such a requirement would imply a determination, and matter is supposed to be purely potential. Secondly, even granted that matter has a requirement for *this* quantity rather than *that*, what is the reason that matter has such a requirement?

Regarding the first question—*how matter can require this quantity and remain purely potential*—the answer is that the requirement of this quantity rather than that does not take away the pure potentiality of matter. All it does is *limit the potentiality of matter in a negative way*. Hence, matter remains purely potential; but this potency is limited to a form accompanied by a certain determinate quantity. Although in metaphysical questions hardly any correct comparison is possible, perhaps it may be permissible to illustrate the point in this way. An empty one pint glass is fully in potency to the reception of water; yet its potency or capacity for water is limited to the reception of water having a volume of one pint. So also, matter is fully in potency to the reception of a form; but insofar as matter requires a form accompanied by a certain determinate quantity and no other, its potency is limited to the reception of a form with *this* quantity and no other.

*161. This brings us to the second point: *What is the reason why matter has a requirement for this determinate quantity and no other?* Before answering the question, let us first consider why matter is never in immediate potency

MULTIPLICATION OF ESSENCE

to just any and every form. As we have seen in no. 151, matter is pure potency, and therefore never exists separately; hence, it is found only together with the material form of which it is a co-principle. Now, any material form is accompanied by certain qualities which predispose matter to the reception of certain forms in preference to others. In other words, matter changes more easily to certain forms than to others. So, for instance, it is easier to change matter which has a form of water into matter having the forms of hydrogen and oxygen than to change it into matter having the form of, say, lead; although absolutely speaking, even this change is not impossible. Thus we see that although of itself matter is purely potential with respect to all forms, only certain potentialities of matter, as existing under a given form, are capable of immediate actuation; whereas other potentialities can be actualized only after a process of intermediary changes.

Something similar applies to the problem under consideration. Matter always exists under a certain determinate quantity, because matter is always actuated by a certain material form which has a determinate quantity. Hence, when a new form comes to actuate matter there are certain predispositions in the matter which make this matter capable of immediate actuation only by a form with a determinate quantity, corresponding to the quantity of the preceding form. This does not mean that the quantity of the receding form becomes the quantity of the succeeding form, but merely that the succeeding form will have to be a form whose quantity extends the body so as to make it occupy the same position as previously occupied by the preceding body. In this way matter may be said to have a transcendental requirement for this determinate quantity and no other, and to individuate the new body. Once this body is individuated it remains distinct from every other body, because by reason of its quantity it occupies a definite position different from that of any other body.

A last remark: In the foregoing explanations we have endeavored to show why matter can act as the fundamental principle of individuation. It should be kept in mind that this principle merely indicates the *root* of individuation; it does not and cannot account *adequately* for the distinctions between individuals. Our answer, therefore, does not mean that Peter differs from Paul merely because Peter is here and Paul is there. Individuals belonging to the same species participate in the same essence in a different and limited way, and thus the perfection of this essence reveals itself differently in each individual. Accordingly, the "essence"—if we may use this term—of the individual lies "formally" in the particular manner in which it participates in the common nature. However, considerations of this type do not refer to the fundamental principle of individuation but to the formal principle.

*Individuation of Unreceived Forms and Pure "To Be"

162. The question may be raised how an *unreceived form,* i.e., an act of essence which is not received in any potential principle, is individuated. Obviously, such a form cannot be individuated by matter or quantity, since it does not have any matter or quantity. As St. Thomas says, such a form "is not individuated by matter, but of itself; because such a form is naturally incapable of being received in any matter; hence it is not subject to multiplication or to predication of many." [19] Accordingly, in such forms "the individual does not add any reality to the spe-

[19] *Quodlibet.* 2, a.4.

cific nature because in such forms the essence itself is the subsistent individual itself. . . . Nevertheless, [individuation] adds something conceptual to it, namely, not to be able to exist in many." [20]

Regarding *pure "to be"*—which in theodicy will be identified with God—"this 'to be' does not allow the addition of any difference, for it would no longer be pure 'to be' but a 'to be' plus a certain form. Still less is it capable of receiving the addition of matter; for otherwise it would no longer be subsistent 'to be' but a material 'to be.' " [21] Thus "no addition at all can be made to it; consequently, it is by its very purity that it is distinct from every other 'to be.' " [22]

*Historical Notes

163. Concerning the theory of matter and form *Plato* distinguished between matter and form, but it is *Aristotle* who must be considered to be the author of the theory of hylomorphism. Among the earlier Christian philosophers *St. Augustine* held a theory of matter and form, but the importance of hylomorphism was not realized before the Middle Ages. Scholastic philosophers unanimously adopted Aristotle's theory although they differed in their interpretation of it. The pure potentiality of matter was denied by *Duns Scotus*, but defended by *St. Thomas* and the Thomists in general. The position of *Suarez* is somewhat ambiguous, since he calls matter pure potency but attributes a kind of actual existence to it. The necessity of an intrinsic principle of limitation was denied by *Albert the Great*, the *nominalists* and *Suarez*.

[20] St. Thomas, *De spiritualibus creaturis*, a.5, ad 9.
[21] St. Thomas, *De ente et essentia*, c.5.
[22] *Ibid*

Regarding the principle of individuation, *Duns Scotus* sought the solution in adding to the specific nature the form of "thisness," which, he says, is formally distinct from the specific nature but actual on the part of the thing. The *nominalists*, true to their principles, denied that there is any basis for a problem of individuation. *Suarez* held that an essence is individual by its very entity. As we have seen above, this answer is correct but unsatisfactory, because it does not explain how this entity is this entity and no other. *Plato* and *Aristotle* appealed to matter. *St. Thomas* developed Aristotle's theory by adding to matter the qualification "marked by quantity." While the entire Thomistic school admits this formula, there is a difference of opinion about its interpretation, and even about the sense which St. Thomas ultimately intended to give to it. *Sylvester of Ferrara* (1474–1528), followed nowadays by *Boyer* and *Renard*, explain this quantity as the actual quantity of a body; whereas *Cajetan* (1469–1534) and more recently *Remer*, *Gredt*, and *Phillips* explain it as the transcendental relation of matter to quantity.

Other philosophers, such as *Rosmini* (1797–1855), have tried to explain individuation by means of existence.

SUMMARY

164. The multiplication of a specific essence can be explained only by the reception of the specific perfection in a limiting potency, since without being received in a potency the perfection would be unlimited and therefore unique. The act of the specific essence is called the form, and its limiting potency matter. This theory is known as hylomorphism. Of itself matter has no perfection whatsoever, but is pure potency. Hence, it cannot exist separately, but only insofar as actuated by a form, which is

the actual constituent principle of the specific essence.

Matter and form are really distinct because they are real potency and real act. They are united without any intermediary because they are essentially ordered to one another as constituent principles of one and the same essence. Hence their union is perfect.

No form can be limited without matter; hence the multiplication of pure, immaterial form is impossible.

By individual we mean that which is undivided in itself and divided from everything else. Hence an individual is incommunicable and distinct. When we inquire here about the principle of individuation, we do not mean that by which the individual is recognized as an individual, nor the extrinsic cause which produces individuals; but the intrinsic constituent principle of individuation. The formal or immediate principle of individuation is, of course, the individual essence itself. But the question we are interested in is: Why does this individual have this essence and no other? The answer to this question will indicate the fundamental principle, or the root of individuation.

The solution of this problem cannot be that the form itself is this principle, because of itself any form is communicable. For the same reason the root of individuation cannot be a combination of forms. Neither can the root be found in the "to be"; for that which comes to be is precisely the individual essence. Hence, the root of individuation must be found in matter.

Of itself matter can explain why a form becomes incommunicable; matter is the ultimate receiving substratum of all forms, while not being subject to reception by anything else. But matter alone cannot make an individual distinct from every other individual, because of itself matter is indistinct. A principle of distinction may be found in quantity, because quantity implies extension and therefore position; hence, whatever is quantified is distinct by position. Accordingly, matter made distinct by quantity is capable of individuating an essence. Quantity itself is not a direct co-principle of individuation, but merely conditions matter to fulfill its role as the principle of individuation. The phrase, "matter made distinct by quantity," means matter insofar as it has a requirement for quantity. As a potential principle of a body matter is transcendentally related to quantity, because it is proper to a body to be quantified.

*Regarding the question how matter can have a requirement for this quantity rather than that and still remain purely potential, the answer is that this requirement does not determine matter in any positive way, but merely limits its capacity to a form with this quantity and no other. Hence, matter will still be purely potential. The reason why matter may have a requirement for this determinate quantity is that matter never exists without a determinate quantity, since it is always informed by a form with a determinate quantity; hence, matter is predisposed to the reception of a new form having a quantity corresponding to the quantity of the original compound of matter and form in preference to others which are not accompanied by this determinate quantity.

*Unreceived forms are individuated of themselves, because they are naturally not capable of being received in any matter. Hence, in such forms the individual is only conceptually different from the species. Pure "to be" is distinct from every other "to be" by the very purity of its "to be," to which no addition at all is possible.

SUGGESTED READINGS

165. Andrew G. Van Melsen, *The Philosophy of Nature*, pp. 107–125 (hylomorphism).
F. Renoirte, *Cosmology*, Wagner, 1950, pp. 212–239 (critique of various starting points).
H. Renard, *The Philosophy of Being*, pp. 62–70 (hylomorphism).
R. J. Slavin, *The Philosophical Basis for Individual Differences According to St. Thomas Aquinas*, Catholic University of America Press, 1936.
J. B. Wall, "The Mind of St. Thomas on the Principle of Individuation" in *The Modern Schoolman*, 1940–1941, pp. 41 ff.
Louis de Raeymaeker, *The Philosophy of Being*, Herder, 1954, Ch. VI, pp. 155–169.

* CHAPTER 6

Possible Being

✠✠✠ In the two preceding chapters we have considered actual real being and its limitations. In the present chapter we shall consider possible real being or, as it is frequently called, being in objective potency.

The Concepts of Possible Being and Possibility [1]

166. In the first chapter we have seen that a being is anything which has a reference to "to be," or existence. Such a reference may be actual or merely possible. It is actual if it has a "to be" in the realm of reality, outside the intellect; and possible if it can have such a "to be." In the first case we speak of *actual* being; in the second, of *possible* being.[2] Possible being must not be confused with potency. As we have seen in the preceding chapters, potency is an intrinsic constituent principle of existing but limited beings; hence, potency is an actual being, for it exists through its act. In other words, "actual" here is not taken in opposition to "potential," but to "possible."

"Possible being" may be understood in a stricter and in a wider sense. In a strict sense, a possible being is a being

---

[1] Cf. St. Thomas, *Summa theol*, Ia, q.25, a.3.
[2] We abstract from the division of logical being into actual and possible.

which was not, is not, and will not be, but can receive existence in the order of reality. This is what is called *pure possible* being. In a wider sense, by prescinding from its existence in the order of reality, we may call any finite being a possible being. Unless it is mentioned specifically we shall use the term "possible" in the sense of the pure possible.

A Possible Is Not the Same as Nothing. Possible beings are capable of receiving "to be" in the order of objective reality, whereas nothing is not capable of such an existence. Secondly, possibles differ from one another because their concepts are concepts of different possible realities. Thirdly, possibles are conceived as something positive, whereas nothing is negative in concept.

A Possible Is Not the Same as a Logical Being. A possible is a being which can become existent in the order of reality, whereas a logical being can have existence only in the intellect.

167. *Possibility* is twofold, extrinsic and intrinsic. By *extrinsic* or relative possibility is meant that a thing has a reference to "to be" because there is a cause capable of producing it.[3] For example, a marble statue is extrinsically possible insofar as there is a sculptor capable of carving it. The *intrinsic* or absolute possibility of a thing means that the thing itself does not contain any self-contradictory elements. For instance, a mountain of gold

[3] A threefold relative possibility may be distinguished. *Metaphysically* possible is whatever is capable of actualization by the omnipotence of God, which extends to everything which is absolutely possible. *Physically* possible is whatever is capable of actualization by causes belonging to the order of nature. *Morally* possible is whatever is capable of actualization without great difficulty.

is intrinsically possible, because "mountain" does not contradict "gold"; but a square circle is intrinsically impossible, because "square" contradicts "circle."

Concerning possible being, there is one problem which we must consider here, namely: What is the ultimate foundation or reason why certain things are possible and others impossible? In accordance with the distinction which we have made between intrinsic and extrinsic possibility, this question may be divided into two parts, viz., 1) what is the ultimate foundation of extrinsic possibility? and 2) what is the ultimate foundation of intrinsic possibility? Although we do not intend to develop here proofs for the existence of God, we shall see that the solution of this problem postulates the existence of a Pure Act, or God.

The Ultimate Foundation of Extrinsic Possibility Can Be Found Only in a Being Whose Essence Is Its "To Be"

168. By extrinsic possibility we mean that a thing has a reference to "to be" because there is a cause capable of producing it. It is true that an *immediate* foundation for such a reference can be found in any existing thing which is capable of producing something, since such a thing is a cause. However, beings whose essence is not their "to be" cannot be the *ultimate* foundation of extrinsic possibility. Anything whose essence is not its "to be" belongs to the order of possibles in a wider sense; hence it itself is something which has passed from the order of possibility to the order of actuality. Now, it is obvious that nothing can cause itself to pass from the order of possibles to the order of actuality, because nothing can give itself what it does not have. Hence, the ultimate foundation of extrinsic pos-

sibility can be found only in a being whose essence is its "to be." Consequently, unless we admit the existence of such a being it will be impossible to assign any ultimate foundation to extrinsic possibility.[4]

Regarding the question under what aspect the Pure Act or God, who is the being whose essence is its "to be," is the ultimate foundation of extrinsic possibility, the answer is that God is this foundation under the aspect of *omnipotence*. When we consider God insofar as He can make possible beings become actual beings, we consider His power, or omnipotence. This power extends to everything which is intrinsically possible. "The divine "to be," upon which the divine power is based, is infinite and not limited to any genus of being, but possesses in itself the perfection of all being. Hence, whatever can have the nature of being is contained under the absolutely possibles, with respect to which God is called omnipotent."[5]

The Ultimate Foundation of Intrinsic Possibility Can Be Found Only in a Being Whose Essence Is Its "To Be"

169. Before proving this assertion, let us first see why we cannot ultimately base intrinsic possibility upon contingent reality. It is true that contingent beings furnish an *immediate* explanation for possible beings. When, for example, we derive from observation the concepts of "mountain" and "gold," our intellect perceives that these concepts are compatible, and can be united into one concept whose component parts do not contradict one another. Hence, we can base the possible "mountain of gold" upon the contingent realities from which we have ab-

[4] Cf. St. Thomas, I *Contra gentes*, c. 16.
[5] *Summa theol.*, Ia, q. 25, a. 3.

stracted the concepts of "mountain" and "gold." However, this foundation of intrinsic possibility *cannot be ultimate*,[6] for the following reasons:

a) The possibles remain possible even if we suppose the whole universe non-existent. Hence, their possibility cannot have as its ultimate foundation the existence of our contingent universe.

b) The possibles reveal themselves to the intellect as necessarily, eternally, and immutably possible; whereas the reality of the universe is contingent, temporal, and mutable. Man, for instance, is a being whose non-existence is possible; a being which exists only for a time, and then is corrupted; yet, if man exists he possesses of necessity, regardless of time and place, the essence contained in the concept of the possible "man." Hence the possibles cannot be ultimately founded upon contingent reality.

c) Contingent reality is limited to a certain number, whereas no limit can be assigned to the possibles. For instance, the total number of men who actually exist or have existed is, say, five billions; but it is impossible to assign a number beyond which no other human being would be possible. Hence, again, the possibles cannot ultimately be founded upon contingent reality.

We must now prove that the *ultimate* foundation of intrinsic possibility can be found only in a being whose essence is its "to be." This proof is as follows:

A thing is possible if it can have a "to be" in actuality. Now, it is clear that whatever can have a "to be" in actuality can participate in, i.e., receive in a limited way, the nature of that which is "to be" itself. But whatever participates in a nature depends upon that which *is* this

[6] Cf. D. Mercier, *Métaphysique générale*, no. 23.

nature, for whatever has a perfection in a limited way depends upon that which by its very nature is this perfection.[7] Therefore, it follows that the possibles have their ultimate foundation in that whose essence or nature is "to be."

170. The question may be asked *under what aspect* the Pure Act, whose essence is "to be," is the ultimate foundation of all possibles.

In the first place it should be clear that the Pure Act cannot be the ultimate foundation under the aspect of *power*. For otherwise either God, who is the Pure Act, could create impossible things, such as square circles and irrational rational beings; or His power would be limited so that He would not be the Pure Act.[8] Hence, as St. Thomas remarks, "it is better to say that such things cannot be done than that God cannot do them."[9]

Secondly, God's *will* cannot be the ultimate foundation of intrinsic possibility. For the will acts upon an object as proposed by the intellect; now the intellect can propose only an object which is intelligible, i.e., possible; hence the will presupposes the possibility of the object and therefore cannot be its ultimate foundation. Moreover, if God's will were the ultimate foundation of intrinsic possibility, two and two would be four because God wills it to be four, and for no other reason; hence, God could also will it to be five, could will man not to be man, being to be nothing. This would mean the end of all certitude.

Thirdly, God's *essence* is the ultimate foundation of all

[7] Cf. St. Thomas, *Compend. theol.,* c. 67.
[8] Cf. *De potentia,* q 1, a.3.
[9] *Summa theol.,* Ia, q. 25, a. 3.

intrinsic possibility.[10] God's essence can be imitated in a limited way by participation. As a matter of fact, God's essence is imitated in a limited way by those possibles which actually exist in reality; for, to a greater or lesser extent, these possibles participate in the perfection of God's essence.

However, if God's essence is taken by itself, it offers no foundation for the distinction between this and that possible. The basis for this distinction is provided by God's essence *as understood by the divine intellect*. The divine intellect "sees" the different ways in which the divine essence is imitable by participation in a limited way. Thus, the divine essence as understood by the divine intellect is the exemplary cause, i.e., the model according to which all reality is made or can be made.[11] Hence, although the possibles have their ultimate foundation in the divine essence, it is the divine intellect which makes them formally distinct as possibles.[12] This is the reason why St. Thomas says that God's essence is the exemplary cause of all things "not insofar as it is essence, but insofar as it is understood" by the divine intellect.[13]

What Kind of a "To Be" Do the Possibles Have?

171. It should be clear that a pure possible does not have any *actual* reference to "to be," since otherwise it would not be a pure possible but a possible in a wider sense, or an actually existing possible. The only kind of reference to "to be" which can be attributed to pure pos-

---
[10] Cf. *Ibid.*, q. 15, a. 2.
[11] Cf. *De veritate*, q. 3, a. 1.
[12] *Ibid.*, a. 2, *Summa theol.*, Ia, q. 45, a. 3.
[13] *De veritate*, q. 3, a. 2.

sibles is a possible reference to "to be," i.e., pure possibles exist insofar as the divine *essence* can be imitated in a limited manner by participation; insofar as they are objects of the divine *intellect* which "sees" that the divine essence can be imitated in this or that limited manner; and insofar as the divine *omnipotence* can make pure possibles actual beings.

Historical Notes

172. The ancient Greek school of philosophy at *Megara* denied, according to Aristotle, that apart from the actual anything else is possible. Likewise, the *fatalists,* who claim that everything happens of necessity.

The *nominalists* identified the possibles with nothing.

Some *Scotists,* such as *Herrera,* attributed to the possibles a kind of "to be" which was neither real nor logical, but somewhere in between—whatever this may mean. *Henry of Ghent* thought that the possibles had a "to be" of essence.

Protagoras held that intrinsic possibility is based upon God's will.

Occam based all possibility upon God's power.

According to *Descartes* intrinsic possibility is based upon God's will. "Because God willed the three angles of a triangle to be of necessity equal to two right angles; therefore, indeed, it is true and cannot be otherwise." [14]

Scholastic philosophers in general base intrinsic possibility upon God's essence, but they are divided on the question whether the mere analytic consideration of the possibles leads to the existence of God, or the possibles can be based upon God only after His existence has been proved by other arguments. The second view is held, for

[14] *Réponses aux sixièmes objections,* ed. Cousin, vol. II, p. 353.

instance, by *Mercier*. All philosophers who admit the existence of God and distinguish the possible from nothing base extrinsic possibility on God's omnipotence.

SUMMARY

173. A possible, in the strict sense of a pure possible, is something which was not, is not, and will not be, but can receive existence in the order of actuality. In a wider sense any finite being is a possible. A pure possible is not the same as a logical being, because it can become existent in the order of reality. Pure possibles are not nothing, because they are capable of existence, distinct from one another, and conceived in a positive manner.

Extrinsic or relative possibility means that a thing has a reference to existence because there is a cause capable of producing it. Intrinsic or absolute possibility means that the concept of a thing does not contain any contradictory elements.

The ultimate foundation of extrinsic possibility can only be a being whose essence is its "to be." Any other being is something which has passed from the order of pure possibility to the order of existing reality, and therefore needs a foundation outside itself. Since the consideration of extrinsic possibility is concerned with producing causes, and God is said to produce by means of His power, it is clear that all extrinsic possibility is ultimately based upon God's power or omnipotence.

Contingent reality cannot be the ultimate foundation of intrinsic possibility because possibles remain possible, even if we suppose the whole universe non-existent. Moreover, contingent reality is contingent, temporal, and mutable, whereas the possibles are necessarily, eternally, and immutably possible. Besides, contingent reality is limited to a certain number, whereas no such limit can be assigned to the possibles.

The ultimate foundation of intrinsic possibility is found only in the being whose essence is its "to be." For possibles can have a "to be" in reality, i.e., they can participate in the nature of that which is "to be" itself. Now, whatever participates in "to be" depends upon that which is "to be" itself; in other words, the possibles find their foundation in the Pure Act. Pure Act is the ultimate foundation of intrinsic possibility, not under the aspect of power (for otherwise either God would not be all-powerful or the impossible would be possible), nor under the aspect of will (for the will follows the intellect and therefore presupposes that the object of the intellect is intelligible, i.e., possible); but under the aspect of essence, namely, insofar as this essence can be imitated in a limited way by participation. This divine essence, taken as understood by the divine intellect, offers the models according to which the divine essence can be imitated. Thus, it is the divine intellect which makes the possibles formally distinct.

Pure possibles do not have any actual reference to "to be"; for otherwise they would actually exist. Their reference is purely possible, namely, insofar as the divine essence can be imitated in a limited way by participation; insofar as the divine intellect "sees" the modes in which this imitation is possible; and insofar as the divine power can make such pure possibles become actual beings.

SUGGESTED READINGS

174. P. Coffey, *Ontology*, pp. 74–115.
H. Renard, *The Philosophy of Being*, pp. 108–112.
Louis de Raeymaeker, *The Philosophy of Being*, Ch. V, pp. 88–98.

SECTION II

The Supreme Classes of Finite Being

THIS SECTION is divided into five chapters. First, we shall consider the supreme classes of finite being in general, and their derivation from the concept of being. The second chapter of this section will consider the necessity of distinguishing between substance and accidents. It will be followed by a study of supposit and person. In the second last chapter we shall speak about accidents in general. The last chapter is dedicated to the category of relation.

CHAPTER 7

The Categories in General

The Meaning of the Term "Category"

✤✤✤ 175. It will be recalled from logic that there are supreme classes of direct universals—and therefore also of reality—which are called *predicaments* or *categories*. Each of these categories expresses a *special* mode of being. These modes of being should be distinguished from the transcendentals. As we have seen in no. 52, our intellect obtains all its concepts by adding to being the expression of a mode of being, which the concept of being itself does not formally express. If such a mode of being is *general*, i.e., consequent upon every being, it is called a transcendental mode of being. But it may also happen that the expressed mode of being is a *special* mode which is not consequent upon every being, but expresses a determinate and invariable manner in which a thing is related to its "to be." [1] Such a mode of being will be found only in those beings which are related to their "to be" in accordance with this determinate and invariable relationship. For instance, "substance" expresses that a being is related to its "to be" in such a way that the being can exist in itself. Hence, substance is not a general mode of being but the

[1] Cf. St. Thomas, *De veritate*, q. 1, a. 1.

mode of being of a special class of beings. It applies to all beings in this class in a formally univocal way.[2] By categories, then, we mean the supreme modes of being which express a univocal relationship to "to be." By the word "supreme" we mean that these modes cannot be reduced to any more general mode which applies to them univocally.

The Number of Categories

176. The question as to the number of categories may be formulated in the following way: which modes of being determine being in such a way that they do not have a common genus?

Aristotle enumerates ten categories. They are: substance, quantity, quality, relation, action, passion, place, time, posture and habitus.[3] But nowhere in his extant works does he show how he arrived at this number. In his commentaries on Aristotle's *Physics* and *Metaphysics,* St. Thomas[4] shows how by a logical analysis the ten categories can be derived from the relation between subject

---

[2] We say that *formally* such a term applies in a univocal way. There may still be analogy in a broader sense of the term, so-called analogy "according to 'to be' but not according to intention" (*In I Sentent.,* d.19, q.5, a.2, ad 1). By this expression is meant that the character expressed by a generic term is always formally the same, so that things having this character will be classified under the same genus. At the same time, however, this character is realized according to varying degrees of perfection in different inferiors of the genus (Cf. *Summa theol.,* Ia, q.4, a.3), e.g., all animals equally belong to the genus of animal, but some animals are more perfect than others. Cajetan calls this type of analogy in a wider sense "analogy of inequality" (*De nominum analogia,* c.1).

[3] Aristotle, *Categories,* ch. 4; 1b 25.

[4] *In V metaphysic.,* lect. 9, no. 889, *In III physic.,* lect. 5, no. 15.

and predicate. However, it is also possible to derive them by a metaphysical analysis from the concept of being.[5] It is this analysis which we shall follow in this chapter. The schema on p. 174 shows how it is done.

*No Category Is a Purely Extrinsic Denomination

177. Concerning the last six categories, which are derived from an extrinsic principle according to which a substance is modified and therefore also denominated, it is to be noted that these categories do not consist in purely extrinsic denominations, such as to be seen, to be desired, etc. Purely extrinsic denominations do not express any special mode of being of the thing which is, say, seen, desired, etc., and thus they do not add any reality to it. The last six categories are not purely extrinsic because they add something to substance; for example, to be acting, to be acted upon, to be in a certain place. However, in adding this reality to a substance they depend upon something outside this substance, not merely as a terminus to which they refer the substance, but as a source from which the substance receives a new mode of being. For instance, passion or reaction confers upon a substance a mode of being which is named with reference to an agent which acts upon the substance; e.g., being cut, being driven.[6]

Categories Have No Common Genus

178. *Being* itself, as we have seen in no. 31, is not a genus. Neither is *accident* with reference to quantity, quality, etc. For a genus is contracted to a species by the addition of a difference not contained in the genus. For instance, to the genus "animal" we can add the difference

[5] Cf. J. Gredt, *Elementa philosophiae*, vol. I, no. 715.
[6] Cf. John of St. Thomas, *Ars logica*, II, 14, 5.

CATEGORIES IN GENERAL

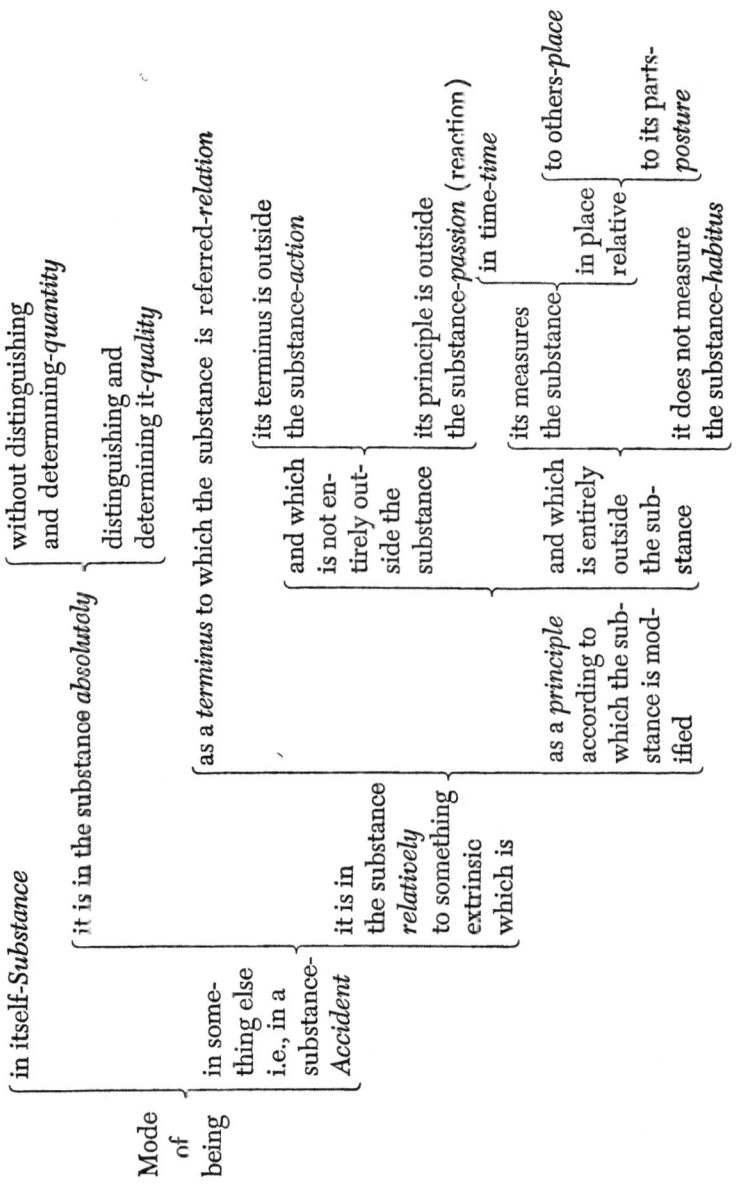

Mode of being
- in itself-*Substance*
- in something else i.e., in a substance-*Accident* — it is in the substance *absolutely*
  - without distinguishing and determining-*quantity*
  - distinguishing and determining it-*quality*
- it is in the substance *relatively* to something extrinsic which is
  - as a *terminus* to which the substance is referred-*relation*
    - and which is not entirely outside the substance
      - its terminus is outside the substance-*action*
      - its principle is outside the substance-*passion* (reaction)
  - as a *principle* according to which the substance is modified
    - and which is entirely outside the substance
      - in time-*time*
      - its measures the substance
        - in place relative
          - to others-*place*
          - to its parts-*posture*
      - it does not measure the substance-*habitus*

"rational" to obtain the species "man," and the genus "animal" does not actually contain the specific difference "rational" by which it is contracted to the species "man." But we cannot add to "accident," say, "to be heavy," as something which is not actually contained in it, for "to be heavy" itself is an accident and therefore actually (although only implicitly) contained in the concept of accident.

It is to be noted that the ten categories are supreme classes of *real finite being*. They do not merely classify logical beings nor do they contain the Infinite Being. The supreme classes of logical beings are negation and relation (cf. no. 48). The Infinite Being is not a genus because it contains all perfections and therefore cannot be contracted by any added specific difference. The Infinite Being is not contained in a genus; for whatever is in a genus is composed of that genus and a differentiating element [7] whereas the Infinite Being is without any real composition. Hence only real finite beings can be classified in the categories.

After these brief considerations of the categories in general we must now turn our attention to some of the categories in particular. Because most categories are found only in corporeal beings and therefore will be considered in the philosophy of nature, we shall limit ourselves to a study of substance, accidents in general, and relation.

*Historical Notes

179. Before Aristotle, a few attempts had been made to give a general classification of reality. The *Pythagoreans*

[7] This logical composition presupposes a real composition in the subject because otherwise it would be impossible to conceive this subject by two concepts in such a way that one does not implicitly contain the other.

(6th cent. B.C.) enumerated ten pairs of opposites, such as light-darkness, one-many, good-evil, etc. The *Platonists* divided all things into five classes, viz., being, rest, motion, same, and other. The Stoics admitted only four classes.

The division given by *Aristotle* has become the classical division accepted by scholastic philosophers, although there is much disagreement about its value. *Hoenen, Daric*, and others claim that the last six categories are purely extrinsic denominations, whereas most others admit that they are real accidents and distinct from substance by a real (modal) distinction.

In the philosophies of *Kant, Hegel,* and *Stuart Mill* there is also a division into categories. But the Kantian categories are classifications of judgments, the Hegelian categories are forms of thought which are dynamic processes of being, and Mill's categories are classes of feelings.

Many modern philosophers, especially in Germany, show a pronounced interest for the problem of the categories, e.g. *N. Hartmann.*

SUMMARY

180. By a category we mean a supreme mode of being, i.e., a mode in which an essence can be related to "to be" which cannot be reduced to a common genus. Categories are distinct from transcendentals, which apply to being in general, insofar as each of them applies only to a special class of being. The ten Aristotelian categories are substance, quantity, quality, relation, action, passion, time, place, posture, and habitus. No category is a purely extrinsic denomination, but in the last six categories the name given to the category is derived from something extrinsic which modifies the substance.

The last nine categories are accidents, but "accident"

CATEGORIES IN GENERAL

itself is not a genus because it actually contains the differences of its inferiors. The categories classify only real finite beings. The Infinite Being does not belong to any genus because it is not composed of a genus and a difference.

SUGGESTED READING

181. M. Scheu, *The Categories of Being According to Aristotle and St. Thomas,* Catholic University of America Press, 1944.

CHAPTER 8

Substance

I. THE NECESSITY OF DISTINGUISHING BETWEEN SUBSTANCE AND ACCIDENTS

✲✲✲ 182. It is a primary datum of experience that in finite beings there is a kind of multiplicity even within the confines of the individual being. Remaining the individual it is, the finite being shows itself to be *manifold in the order of activity,* i.e., it can undergo changes without becoming an altogether different individual. For instance, a small seedling will grow up into a tall tree, drop its leaves periodically, bring forth flowers and fruit; yet it remains the same tree. A baby will grow up and increase not only in size and age, but also in skill, knowledge, etc; yet internal consciousness reveals to each one of us that we are still the same Ego as five, ten, or twenty years ago. Hence, we face the problem to explain how it is possible for a being to change without becoming altogether different. As in the questions of multiplicity in the order of "to be" and in the order of specific essence, the answer will again be supplied by the theory of act and potency.

A Being Which Is Subject to Change While Remaining the Same Individual Is Composed of Potency and Act in the Order of Activity

183. When a change takes place in a being in such a way that this change does not modify the thing in its individual essence, it merely adds a secondary determination. It gives a *new mode of being,* but does not take away the first or essential mode of being which the thing possessed prior to the change. Now in order to receive a new mode of being, to become existent in a new mode, that which receives this new mode must be in *potency* to this new mode of being, and the new mode of being itself is compared to the receiving potency as an *act.*

Hence in addition to the composition of potency and act in the order of "to be," and the composition of potency and act in the order of essence if the essence is limited, we must admit in finite beings a real composition in the order of activity.[1] The act in this order is called *"accident"* because it is a mode of being which accedes to an already existing subject, and the potential principle which remains primarily the same throughout the change by which the new mode of being is acquired is called the *"substance."*

If we wish to present a formal argument [2] to prove that a finite being is composed of act and potency in the order of activity, we may proceed as follows: If in a finite being action were really identical with the subject of the action, the subject would be pure act, and therefore its own "to

---

[1] The order of activity should be understood in a wider sense so as to include not only actions but also any secondary changes and modifications resulting from being acted upon.

[2] Cf. St. Thomas, *Summa theol.,* Ia, q. 54, a. 1.

be."³ But a finite being is not pure act nor its own "to be." Therefore, in it action is not really identical with the subject. Accordingly, the subject must be conceived as in potency to action, so that a finite being will be composed of potency and act in the order of activity.⁴

From the foregoing it is clear that the real composition of potency and act in the order of activity cannot be understood without the composition of potency and act in the order of "to be." For, if a being has no real composition in the order of "to be," it is pure act and therefore cannot be in potency to any further determination.⁵

Union of Substance and Accidents

184. If this new composition of act and potency is compared to that of essence and "to be" and that of matter and form, it will be noticed that all these compositions are compositions of principles which are related to one another as potency and act. However, the composition of substance and accidents differs from the others in one important respect. The union of essence and "to be" makes

---

³ For, as an act, action is ultimate and therefore cannot be in potency to anything, hence if not limited by a subject which is in potency to it, action would be pure act.

⁴ Two other arguments for the composition of finite beings of potency and act may be presented as follows: If the action of a finite being were really identical with its subject, the finite being would always be exercising all its actions. But finite beings do not always exercise all their actions. Therefore, their action is really distinct from its subject (Cf. *Summa theol.*, Ia, q.77, a.1).

Every finite being has its "to be" from the Infinite Being; hence it has a real relation of dependence to this Infinite Being. But a real relation is an accident. Therefore, finite beings are composed of substance and accident (Cf. *Quodlibet.* 7, a.10, ad 4).

⁵ Cf. *Quodlibet.* 7, a.7, c and ad 1.

a thing really existent, gives the first "to be" to the thing; but when an existing thing acquires a new mode of being without losing its first mode of being, it does not get a first "to be," but only a secondary "to be." When, for example, a bare tree gets leaves, it retains its "to be a tree," but acquires in addition the secondary mode of being, "to be leaved." When a man becomes skilled in mechanics, he retains his first mode of being, "to be a man," but acquires in addition the secondary mode of being, "to be skilled in mechanics." Thus, while the union of essence and "to be" results in a being which is perfectly unified or "one," the union of the primary and secondary modes of being *does not result in a being which is perfectly unified.*

Likewise, the union of matter and form results in an essence which is perfectly unified and exists by one "to be." But the composition of the primary and secondary modes of being is a union of principles *possessing their own essence and their own "to be."* [6] It would be inconceivable that, for instance, whiteness would have the "to be" of man and thus exist as man.

II. THE CONCEPT OF SUBSTANCE

185. From the foregoing considerations we may conclude that finite beings are composed of a relatively permanent principle which remains primarily the same throughout secondary changes, and secondary principles which may come and go without producing a change in the primary mode of being. The relatively permanent principle was called "substance," and secondary principles are called "accidents." There is, however, far more to the con-

---

[6] Cf. *Summa theol.*, IIIa, q. 17, a. 2. We shall come back upon this point in Chapter Nine.

cept of substance than appears directly from this relationship. We must, therefore, examine this concept in greater detail.

How the Concept Is Acquired

The concept of substance may be acquired from the analysis of *external experience.* Our external senses reveal to us, say, an unripe orange as a concrete whole which is extended in space, green-colored, of a spherical shape, sour, etc., but they are unable to distinguish between, on the one hand, extension, shape, color, flavor, etc.; and, on the other hand, that which is extended, shaped, colored, flavored, etc. They can also perceive that in the process of ripening the concrete whole which was first small, green, etc., increases in size and becomes orange, sweet, etc. When the external senses perceive this, the intellect may endeavor to find a rational explanation of this process on the level of being. Thus it conceives the qualities which may come and go as determinations which affect something that is underneath these changes and modified by them. The difference between the determinations and their subject is expressed by the terms "accidents" and "substance." Thus our intellect acquires at the same time the concepts of substance and accidents as corresponding to a reality existing in the extramental world.

The concept of substance may be acquired also from the analysis of our *internal intellectual activity.* We are conscious that in our acts of knowing our own Ego, which first did not think about a certain subject, e.g., electricity, now thinks about it. Hence, again, the acts of thinking are conceived as transitory affections or determinations of a more permanent Ego. This leads us to conceive them as accidental determinations of the substance of our Ego.

The Existence of Substance

186. When a relatively permanent reality is compared to its transitory determinations, the intellect perceives that the latter are real, no doubt, but not capable of existing in themselves. For instance, running, being blue, being struck, etc., are perceived by the intellect as incapable of existence except in a subject which is running, blue, struck, etc. But is the reality in which these transitory determinations exist capable of existing in itself? If so, then its nature is different from that of the transitory determinations or accidents, which cannot exist in themselves. If not, then it presupposes something else which can exist in itself, and therefore differs in nature from the accidents. In either case we are led to the existence of substance.

If we wish to present a formal proof for the existence of substance, we may argue as follows:

If there is any reality at all, it will exist either in itself or in another. If it exists in itself, it is a substance. If it does not exist in itself but in another, this other exists either in itself or in another. But we cannot continue this series to infinity because an actually infinite series is impossible and does not explain anything. Therefore, substance exists.

Definition of Substance

187. From the foregoing we may draw two conclusions concerning substance:

a) It is the *subject*, the substratum, in which accidents inhere. The term "substance" can express this function, for it is derived from the Latin *"substo,"* I stand under, I support.

b) It *exists in itself* and does not need to inhere in another.[7]

Now which of these two is the primary reality of the substance, to support accidents or to exist in itself? While we are willing to admit that *psychologically* "to support accidents" is prior to "to exist in itself," i.e., that we arrive at the knowledge of substance through its function of supporting accidents, it should be clear that *ontologically,* or in the order of reality, "to exist in itself" is prior to "to support accidents." For in order to act as a support of something else a thing must be capable of supporting itself, i.e., it must exist in itself. If a thing is of such a nature that it can exist in itself, it will be able to act as a support of others. Hence to be a subject or a support of accidents is a property which flows from such a nature if there are accidents to be supported. Accordingly, the proper definition of "substance" should not express the function of supporting but the nature which is such that it can exist in itself. Thus we arrive at the traditional definition of substance as *"that to whose nature is due a "to be" in itself and not in another."* [8]

Concerning this definition, it is to be noted that we do not define substance as "a being existing in itself," but as "that to whose nature is due a "to be" in itself." By using the first formula we would make "to be" the essence of substance and thus we would identify the essence and "to be" of substance.[9]

As *compared with the term "essence,"* substance has a more restricted meaning. We may speak about the essence of an accident and about the essence of a substance, but

[7] Cf St. Thomas, *De potentia,* q.9, a.1.
[8] Cf *Summa theol.,* IIIa, q.77, a.1, ad 2.
[9] *Ibid.*

SUBSTANCE

generally we do not speak about the substance of an accident.[10] If, however, we limit the use of essence to that of substantial beings, both terms, "essence" and "substance," indicate one and the same reality, although from a different point of view. By "essence" we indicate *what a reality is*, whereas by "substance" we indicate the *mode of being* of this reality.

A last remark. From the foregoing considerations it should be clear that in *philosophy* the meaning of the term "substance" is entirely different from that in *physical science*. In physical science "substance" is a subdivision of matter, i.e., of bodies, and applies to those classes of bodies which under the same conditions have the same physical and chemical properties. The substance of physical science is opposed to "mixture," which term indicates bodies with variable physical and chemical properties. In philosophy "substance" is opposed to "accident" and applies to any being to whose nature is due a "to be" in itself.

Is God a Substance?

188. The question may be asked whether the concept of substance is applicable only to finite beings or also to the Infinite Being, God.

In the first place, it is evident that the Infinite Being does not belong to the *category* "substance." For whatever belongs to a category belongs to a genus; hence is composed of a genus and a specific difference. Accordingly, the absolute simplicity of the Infinite Being excludes it from being placed in the category "substance."

Secondly, the Infinite Being cannot be modified and determined by accidents. As a Pure Act, it is without any

---

[10] Moralists, however, speak about the substance of an action.

potentiality; hence it cannot be a substance in the sense of acting as a *support* of accidents.

Thirdly, as we have seen above, the function of supporting accidents is not the essence of substance but a property which flows from this essence under certain conditions. If a being exists in itself and is at the same time subject to accidental modifications, then the substance can assume the function of acting as a support. If, however, a being cannot have any accidents, as is the case with the Infinite Being, but exists in itself, it is a substance in a true and proper sense; for it possesses that which is primarily implied by the concept of substance. Hence, insofar as the concept of substance expresses *"to be in itself"* God is a substance.[11]

Fourthly, the concept of substance insofar as it is applicable to God does not have exactly the same meaning as when it is applied to finite beings. While in a finite being the essence to which is due a "to be" in itself is really distinct from this "to be," in the Pure Act the essence is only logically distinct from the "to be." In other words, the concept of substance as predicated of finite beings and the Infinite Being is *analogous*. As the nature of a finite substance is proportioned to its "to be," so also is the nature of the Infinite Substance proportioned to its "to be."

Meaning of the Term "To Be in Itself"

189. "To be in itself" is not merely a negation of existence in another, but expresses the positive perfection of *independence* in being. Independence in being, however,

---

[11] The term "substance" is derived from the most striking function which a substance exercises, viz., to act as a support of accidents. However, one should beware of making the etymology of a word the ultimate criterion of its meaning (cf. the etymology of "pontiff").

may be either absolute or merely relative. By *absolute* (intrinsic and extrinsic) independence in being is meant that a thing does not depend upon anything else in any way whatsoever—it exists not only *in* itself, but also *of* itself. Such absolute independence, of course, can be found only in the Pure Act. Hence if absolute independence in being were required of a substance, only God could be called a substance. But independence may be taken also in a *relative* sense, i.e., as merely intrinsic independence, which is had when a being exists *in* itself, but not *of* itself. It is in this sense that substances are said to be independent in being.

A Misconception

190. Much of the modern opposition to the concept of substance is based upon a misunderstanding of its true nature—a misunderstanding for which perhaps the scholastic philosophers of the seventeenth century are most to blame. When we say that a substance *"supports"* accidents or that accidents *"inhere"* in the substance, these metaphorical expressions might convey the impression that the substance is like a pincushion into which pins are stuck, or like an inert piece of rock in the middle of a stream to which things cling precariously. Nothing is further from the truth. The true relation between substance and accidents was shown in the first part of this chapter—the substance is a determinable element, a *potency*, which is determined by accidents as its *acts*. Now when a potency acquires a new act, it becomes something. Hence a substance is not an inert, unchanging support but a dynamic reality. Every time a new accident inheres in the substance, the substance itself is modified. Such accidental modifications take place continuously, so that the sub-

stance is continuously "becoming" something. Moreover, the substance is really identical with the essence, and the essence is, in a way, the active principle of its proper accidents, which emanate from it "by a kind of natural resultance."[12] Thirdly, the reality which is the substance is identical with the nature or essence of a thing, which is the primary principle of all activity of this thing; therefore, the reality which is the substance is also the principle of all activity exercised by this thing.[13] Lastly, the activity of a finite being, especially if it is of an intellectual nature, gives meaning to its existence and tends to make it overcome as far as possible the limitation inherent to being finite.[14] If this dynamic character of substance had been sufficiently stressed in the seventeenth and eighteenth centuries, much of the subsequent confusion might perhaps have been avoided.

*Division of Substance

191. As we have seen above in no. 188, by an analogous division substance may be divided into *finite* and *infinite* substance. By a further analogous division, finite substance may be divided into complete and incomplete substance. An *incomplete* substance is one whose nature must be united to another substantial co-principle. Matter and

[12] *Summa theol.*, Ia, q.77, a.6, c, ad 2 and ad 3. Cf. also *De ente et essentia*, c.7, *Summa theol*, Ia, q.77, a.1.

[13] We say the "reality which is the substance" and not simply "the substance." Substance and nature are really the same reality, but with respect to activity this reality is spoken of as "nature" and not as "substance."

[14] We say "especially if it is of an intellectual nature" because by knowing, the intellect becomes the object known. The limitation of being finite is overcome to the highest possible degree when a finite intellect knows the Pure Act of "to be" as it is in itself.

form by their union form one substantial essence; hence they are substantial co-principles or incomplete substances. A *complete* substance is one whose nature does not have to be united to another substantial co-principle; for instance, the substances of a cat, a tree, a man. Substances may be incomplete in substantiality, or complete in substantiality but incomplete in specific perfection. A substance which is *incomplete in substantiality* cannot exist without being united to its substantial co-principle. Such are primary matter and purely material substantial forms. A substance which is *incomplete in specific perfection* but complete in substantiality can exist in itself, but cannot exercise all its functions without being united to its substantial co-principle. The human soul, as we shall see in rational psychology, is the only example of this type of substance. It can exist independently of the body, but without the body it cannot exercise all its functions, such as nutrition and sensation.

Another important division of substance is that into primary and secondary substance. In Aristotelian and Thomistic philosophy *primary* substance means the individual substance, i.e., that which ontologically is the subject of accidents and logically the subject of predicates. Primary substance itself has no subject, whether logically or ontologically, but is the subject. *Secondary* substance is that which, although ontologically it does not have a subject, nevertheless has a subject in the logical order of attribution. In other words, secondary substance refers to the universal ideas (genus and species) under which individual substances are classified. This division also is rather analogous than univocal.[15]

[15] Cf. *De potentia*, q.9, a.2, ad 6.

SUBSTANCE

The essential division of finite substance has been studied in logic; hence there is no need to explain it here again. We shall simply recall it in the schematic division given below.

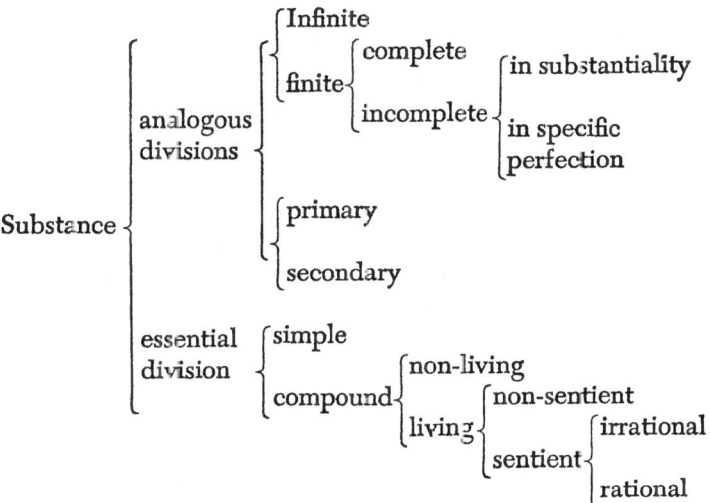

*Historical Notes
Modern Philosophy and Substance

192. Many modern philosophers, imbued with phenomenalistic theories of knowledge, reject the traditional distinction of substance and accidents. They claim that what Aristotle and the Scholastics call "substance" is a mental fiction whose reality cannot be proved and which, even if its existence is admitted, must forever remain unknown and unknowable because it does not fall under the observation of our senses. One could draw up quite an impressive list of modern philosophers who more or less reason in this way, such as *Hume, Berkeley, Stuart Mill,*

Spencer, Kant, Paulsen, etc., and oppose them to all the past and present masters of Aristotelian and scholastic philosophy, and to common sense itself. Must we admit that these modern thinkers lack philosophical perspicacity, or that *Aristotle, Averroes, St. Thomas, Scotus, Suarez, Cajetan*, etc., were simply victims of their own silly imagination? As Mercier [16] remarks, there must have been misunderstandings and many arguments beside the point. These misunderstandings may perhaps be cleared by investigating how the opposition against the traditional view came into existence.

When *Descartes* (1596–1650) revolted against the degenerate scholasticism of his time and founded "The New Philosophy" along mathematical lines, he exaggerated the dualism of mind and matter to such an extent as to deny cognitional communication between body and soul. According to him, mind and matter work in close union, in the sense that the mind on the occasion of certain bodily movements produces ideas of things belonging to the extramental world. Hence these ideas are innate inasmuch as they are not derived from sense knowledge. Although Descartes himself did not deny the existence of both material and immaterial substances, his theory led to doubt about the validity of our innate ideas. *John Locke* (1632–1704) showed that Descartes' theory of innate ideas was false, but unfortunately he explained knowledge as the perception of ideas (which for him included also sense perception) and not of extramental objects. Thus he was led to the conclusion that we do not know and cannot know anything about the reality of substance except that it is conceived as a support of accidents. *George Berkeley* (1685–1753) went a step farther and denied that there

---

[16] *Métaphysique générale*, no. 138.

was any need for a *real* support of accidents which are merely ideas in our mind. Thus he arrived at the conclusion that only spiritual substances, God and the human mind, exist. Whereupon *David Hume* (1711-1776) added the last straw and claimed that there is no need either for a real support of mental phenomena, i.e., of ideas or states of consciousness as he called them. So the conclusion followed that there are no substances at all, whether material or immaterial, which act as supports of phenomena.

193. It is to be noted that these phenomenalists did not reject the concept of substance as posited by St. Thomas—that to whose nature is due a "to be" in itself—but the concept which we also have rejected above, namely, that a substance is a mere inert support to which accidents fasten themselves. As a matter of fact, by claiming that our concept of substance agrees with everything that can possibly be conceived, *Hume* seems to substantialize all accidents rather than deny all substances.[17] But later phenomenalists, especially *Huxley*, interpreted Hume as if he denied all substance, while perhaps he should rather be understood as a keen critic of Descartes' theory of knowledge. Even such a confirmed phenomenalist as *Stuart Mill* (1807-1873), who reduced the body to a "permanent possibility of sensations," and the mind to "a series of actual and possible states," admits that "there is a bond of some sort among all the parts of the series, which makes me say that they were feelings of a person who was the same person throughout, and this bond, to me, constitutes my Ego,"[18] and thus, as someone wittily remarked, opens a trapdoor in his own philosophy.

[17] Cf. *A Treatise on Human Nature*, part 4, par. 2 and 5.
[18] *Notes to Analysis*, II, 175.

The Real Issue

194. The real issue at stake between the phenomenalists and traditional philosophy is not the existence of substances but our *knowledge* of them. When Hume reasons that substance is nothing but a name by which we recall a collection of conjoined phenomena, he labors under the false impression that substance and accidents, *as such,* must be objects of sense knowledge. Hence it was natural for him to argue: If I enumerate all phenomena (sense perceptible accidents) of a thing, there will be nothing left to which we can attribute the function of acting as a support of these phenomena; therefore, there is no such support. However, our external senses reveal to us directly neither substance nor accidents as such, but only this or that concrete whole which impresses itself upon the senses as, say, fragrant, soft, warm, etc. It is the intellect which interprets these sense impressions and abstracts from them the concepts of accident as existing in something else, and of substance as existing in itself and supporting accidents.

The phenomenalists are right when they claim that sense experience itself does not teach us anything about the nature of substance; for we do not directly perceive substances with our senses; but they deny or forget that we have the power to analyze the data of sense experience with our intellect, and thus to arrive at an abstract but valid knowledge of substance.

Kant and Substance

195. Thoroughly alarmed by the conclusions of Berkeley and Hume, *Emmanuel Kant* (1724–1804) wanted to restore the human intellect to its rightful place. Against the phenomenalists, he maintained that our knowledge is

not limited to mere sense experience, but contains also a subjective element. Our intellect seeks unity, and therefore is bound to perceive the contingent phenomena of experience according to certain *innate mind-forms,* which he called "categories." These categories are purely subjective and do not reveal to us anything about the nature of things as they are outside the mind. Now our reason postulates a permanent subject for a succession of phenomena, and this subject is the substance. Therefore, we must admit, in strict logic, the existence of substance as a principle which unites phenomena *in the mind.* In this manner Kant reduced substance to an *a priori,* subjective, category of the mind. It would lead us too far afield to examine here Kant's theory critically. It is done in epistemology.

Erroneous Definitions of Substance

196. *Descartes* defined substance as "a thing which exists in such a way that it does not need any other thing to exist." [19] Realizing that this definition could apply only to God, he conceded that substances are also those things "which require only God's concourse to exist."

Spinoza took over Descartes's definition, and explaining it in a pantheistic sense recognized only one substance: "By substance I understand that which is in itself and is conceived by itself; in other words, that whose concept does not need the concept of any other thing from which it must be formed." [20]

Leibnitz defined substance as "independent power of action." While it is true that substance really is the principle of activity in a being, this definition at best describes substance by one of its properties.

[19] *Principia philosophica,* I, no. 51.
[20] *Ethica,* I, def. 3.

SUMMARY

197. It is a primary datum of experience that even within the confines of the individual finite being there is multiplicity with respect to activity, i.e., the finite being can act and undergo change without becoming essentially different. This datum of experience can be explained only if we admit that the finite being is composed of potency and act in the order of activity, i.e., that it is in potency to secondary determinations which actualize it by giving it secondary modes of being, without taking away its primary mode of being. For, if the action of a finite being were really the same as its subject, the finite being would be pure act, because action is an act and therefore limited only by a receiving potency.

The real composition of finite beings in the order of activity, which is called the composition of substance and accidents, presupposes the composition of act and potency in the order of "to be"; for a being which is not composed of act and potency in the order of "to be" is pure act and therefore without any potency whatsoever.

The union of substance and accidents differs from the union of essence and "to be" and that of matter and form in this that it does not terminate in a perfectly unified being, because both substance and accidents have their own mode of being; hence they do not exist by one and the same "to be."

The concept of substance is acquired from the intellectual analysis of sense experience. The concrete whole perceived by the senses is examined by the intellect, which distinguishes in this whole a relatively permanent principle that exists in itself but is in potency to further determination, and these determinations themselves which actualize the finite being in a secondary way, but do not exist in themselves.

The existence of substance is clear to anyone who admits that there is any reality at all. For such a reality either exists in itself or not. If it does not exist in itself, it presupposes reality which exists in itself.

Thus substance is known not only as a substratum or support of accidents, but also as a thing which exists in itself. Its function as a substratum of accidents is psychologically prior, but ontologically "to exist in itself" is prior, because in order to act as a support a thing must not need to be supported, which is the same as to exist in itself. Hence the definition of substance is not "that which supports accidents," but "that to whose nature is due a "to be" in itself."

*The Infinite Being, God, does not belong to the category "substance"; for whatever belongs to a category belongs to a genus. Neither can the Infinite Being act as a support of accidents because it is not in potency to any accidental determination. However, insofar as the Infinite Being exists in itself, the definition of substance applies to it. Hence it is a substance in a true and proper sense. Nevertheless, it is not a substance in exactly the same (univocal) sense as finite beings, but in an analogous sense, because a different mode of "to be" is due to its nature.

"To be in itself" does not merely deny the existence in another; it indicates the positive perfection of independence in being. Relative or intrinsic independence is sufficient to make a thing a substance. Only in God do we find absolute (intrinsic and extrinsic) independence.

It is a misconception to conceive substance as a mere inert substratum of accidents. The relationship of substance and accidents as potency and act shows that we are here in the dynamic order. It is the substance which becomes something when a new accident determines it. If an accident is a property, the substance, in a way, is even the active principle of this accident. Moreover, the reality which is the substance is the primary principle of all activity. Hence a substance is not inert but something dynamic.

Primary substance means individual substance, which is the subject of accidents in the ontological order and of predicates in the logical order. Secondary substance is universal substance, under which individual substances are classified.

SUGGESTED READINGS

198. R. Markus, "Substance, Cause and Cognition in Thomist Thought," in *The New Scholasticism*, 1947, pp. 438–448.

F. S. Moseley, "The Restoration of the Concept of Substance to Science," in *The New Scholasticism*, 1936, pp. 1–17.

A. Marc, "Being and Action," in *The Modern Schoolman*, 1950–1951, pp. 175–190.

H. Renard, *The Philosophy of Being*, pp. 70–77, 199–215.

Louis de Raeymaeker, *The Philosophy of Being*, Ch. VII, pp. 170–194.

*CHAPTER 9

Supposit and Person

✳✳✳ The problem which we are going to consider in this chapter owes its origin to the data of revelation, inasmuch as attention was first drawn to it by religious truths. According to revelation there are two natures in Christ, but only one person. Hence it follows that there must be a difference between person (supposit) and nature.

Although this problem is brought to our attention by revelation, it is obvious that, as philosophers, we are not going to appeal to revelation for its solution, but shall consider the matter from the purely natural viewpoint of reason.

Meaning of the Terms "Supposit" and "Person"

199. In the previous chapter we have seen that primary substance is individual substance. Normally [1] the individual substances of a human nature are human *persons*. But we do not call individual substances of a non-rational nature "persons." In ordinary language there is no term to indicate on the non-rational level what person expresses on the rational level. Philosophers, however, have coined a special term and speak of *"supposit"* or *"hypostasis."* A

---
[1] The only exception is the individual substance of the human nature of Christ, which is not a supposit.

supposit or hypostasis is in the non-rational order what person is in the rational order. However, these two terms are used also in a wider or generic sense to indicate not only non-rational supposits but also persons or rational supposits. It is in this more generic sense that the terms are used here.

In general, supposit means a complete, independent being. As such, it is not attributed to anything else, but is itself the ultimate subject of all predicates, operations, and "to be" itself. As St. Thomas expresses it: "It is to the hypostasis alone that are attributed the operations and natural properties and whatever else belongs to the nature taken concretely; for example, we say that this man reasons, is capable of laughter, and is a rational animal. And likewise, this man is said to be a supposit because he is 'supposed to' (underlies) whatever belongs to man and receives its predicates." [2] Hence the supposit exists as a being in its own right; it is entirely incommunicable and autonomous. It may be defined as a *subsistent, individual, and complete substance* or nature.[3]

This definition excludes from the supposit all *communicability*.[4] Hence:

a) The *secondary* substance is not a supposit because it is universal and therefore communicable to individual substances. The word "individual" in the definition excludes from the supposit the communicability of secondary substance;

[2] *Summa theol.*, IIIa, q.2, a.3.

[3] Cf. Cajetan, *In Summa theol. comment.*, in Ia, q.3, a.3.

[4] Individuality implies incommunicability insofar as a form received in matter is rendered incommunicable to any other potency. In the present question, we are not merely concerned with the incommunicability of a coprinciple of essence, but with the incommunicability of the whole being.

b) The *integral parts* of a whole, such as the arms or legs of a human body, are not supposits because they communicate with the body. Likewise, the *essential parts*, matter and form, body and soul, are not supposits because they communicate with one another. This kind of communicability is excluded from the supposit by the word "complete."

c) *Accidents* are not supposits because they communicate with the substance in which they inhere. They are excluded by the word "substance" in the definition.

d) An *individual complete substance* or nature is not a supposit because it does not absolutely exclude the possibility of being assumed by a supposit which has already an individual complete nature. Hence "subsistent" is added to the definition. This last kind of incommunicability is the only one which distinguishes the complete individual substance from the supposit.

200. The perfection by which the individual complete substance becomes a supposit is called *"subsistence"* or, in the case of a rational supposit, *"personality."* This perfection renders the individual complete substance, entirely incommunicable and intrinsically self-sufficient.[5] In the order of activity this self-sufficient being is also the ultimate principle which acts, and to which all actions are ultimately attributed.[6] The nature is the ultimate principle *through which* or by which activity is exercised, but the supposit is the ultimate principle *which* exercises the activity. For instance, this person, Peter, is the ultimate principle *which* exercises *through* his rational nature the

---

[5] Extrinsically, the supposit may remain dependent upon an efficient cause.

[6] Cf. *Summa theol.*, Ia, q.75, a.2, ad 2.

act of thinking; this supposit, Fido, is the ultimate principle *which* performs *through* its canine nature the act of barking. Hence the axiom: "Actions belong to the supposits."

Subsistence adds to individuality *autonomy of independence*. This autonomy of independence is an analogous concept and increases the higher we climb on the scale of beings. While on the lowest grade of being hardly any difference between the individual and the supposit is discernible, precisely because there is very little independence, this independence becomes more and more striking as we climb higher on the scale of beings. Minerals, for example, can merely exist in themselves and act upon others in virtue of inherent powers; plants, in addition, have an intrinsic principle of growth and reproduction; to whatever self-sufficiency a plant has animals add the power of guiding themselves by means of sensation in their activity; man surpasses animals in autonomy because he has also the power to determine for himself for which purpose he is going to act. Thus subsistence adds to individuality an increasing degree of self-sufficiency.

Individual Substance or Nature and Supposit Are Really Distinct

201. To quote the words of St. Thomas: "In every thing to which can accede something which does not belong to the concept of its nature, the thing itself and its essence, i.e., the supposit and the nature, are distinct. For, in the meaning of the nature is included only that which belongs to the essence of the species, whereas the supposit has not only what belongs to the essence of the species but also whatever else accedes to this essence. Hence, the supposit is signified by the whole, but the nature or quiddity [is

signified only] as the formal part. Now, in God alone no accident can be found added to the essence because His "to be" is His essence, as has been said; hence in God supposit and nature are entirely the same. But in an angel [i.e., an unreceived subsistent form] the supposit is not entirely the same [as the nature] because something accedes to it which does not belong to the concept of its essence. For the "to be" itself [7] of an angel is in addition to the essence or nature; and other things [acts of intellect and will] accede to it, which belong to the supposit but not to the nature." [8]

Putting this argument in a *formal* way, we may say:

The supposit and nature are really distinct in any being to which something can be added which does not belong to its very nature. Now, in any finite being at least "to be" itself does not belong to its very nature. Therefore, it follows that in every finite being supposit and nature are really distinct.

However, this real distinction should not be understood as if the supposit were one thing and the nature another thing. The distinction is not adequate but inadequate, inasmuch as the supposit includes the individual nature and adds a reality to it.[9]

The Nature of Subsistence or Personality

202. We come now to the question concerning what this reality is which subsistence adds to the complete individual substance.

---

[7] "To be" cannot be called an accident in the strict sense. It is accidental to the nature in a broader sense, namely, inasmuch as it does not belong to the essence.

[8] *Quodlibet.* 2, a. 4.

[9] Cf. *Ibid., Sed contra est.*

In the first place, it should be clear that subsistence does not add *a mere negation* of communicability to the individual substance. For subsistence makes a thing independent in its being from any subject of inhesion and any substantial co-principle. Although independence is a negative term, it expresses the positive perfection of autonomy or self-sufficiency. Hence that which causes this positive perfection cannot be entirely negative.

Secondly, subsistence is *not the same as the existence* or the "to be" of the individual substance. In the opinion of Billot [10] and others, subsistence must be identified with actual existence. This view offers an easy argument for the real distinction of substance and subsistence; for, if subsistence is the same as "to be," and "to be" is really distinct from essence or substance, it is evident that subsistence and substance are really distinct. However, there is one great difficulty in this view, and that is the fact that actual existence does not confer any new perfection upon a thing, but merely *actualizes* whatever real perfection there is in an individual essence. As St. Thomas says: "To be" is the actuality of all acts and therefore the perfection of all perfections." [11] For, "to be" is that by which a thing is placed outside the order of possibles and made actual. Now that which is made actual by the "to be" is precisely the supposit, the subject of the "to be." Hence, "to be" presupposes subsistence or, as St. Thomas says: " 'To be' itself does not form part of the concept of the supposit." [12] Moreover, "to be" is a contingent attribute of any finite being. If subsistence were really the same as "to be," it

[10] *De verbo incarnato* (Rome: 1892), p. 66.
[11] *De potentia*, q 7, a 2, ad 9.
[12] *Quodlibet.* 2, a.4, ad 2.

would seem to follow that finite supposits are their own "to be," which is impossible.

203. Hence most Thomists say that subsistence is *the ultimate perfection which terminates the individual substance in the order of essence*. This is the opinion of the majority of Thomistic philosophers, who conceive subsistence as a positive perfection which terminates or closes the individual nature by adding to it the ultimate perfection and making it the subject which can receive "to be" and accidents.[13] They argue as follows:

A corporeal substance is composed of really distinct principles, matter and form. Now "to be" merely actualizes whatever is real; hence if the really distinct principles of a substance were not united into one subject prior to their union with "to be," it would seem that the "to be" would fall upon each of these principles separately, so that a unified whole would not result. The function, then, of subsistence is to unite these principles into one closed subject which can become the unique recipient of "to be."

Moreover, they argue, if the individual substance or nature were not terminated or closed prior to receiving "to be" and accidents, there would seem to be no reason why the "to be" and the accidents would not penetrate into the essence of the substance. Subsistence, therefore, is the ultimate perfection in the essential line of the substance and really distinct, not only from the "to be" of this substance, but also from the individual substance itself. As we have previously mentioned, the distinction of subsistence from the individual substance is real but not adequate—it is the distinction between a thing and its ter-

[13] Cf. Cajetan, *In IIIa Summa theol. comment.*, comm. 2.

minus. For this reason subsistence is called a *substantial mode*.

Consciousness and Personality

204. After *Descartes* many philosophers have defined personality as self-consciousness. "Since consciousness," says *Locke*, "always accompanies thinking, in it alone consists personal identity."[14] This conception of personality has been taken over by many modern psychologists. For instance, when as a result of a mental disturbance a person develops consciousness of two or more series of his acts as belonging to different persons, they speak of a "split personality." Perhaps this concept of personality may suffice for all of the practical purposes of non-philosophical psychology because, as a matter of fact, self-consciousness is found only in persons; yet it does not suffice as a metaphysical concept. For consciousness is an act, whereas a person is the subject which is conscious of itself. Moreover, as an act, consciousness proceeds from nature as its ultimate principle, and nature is not the same as person. While we can readily admit that consciousness arises from the specific element in the rational supposit, we should avoid the mistake of making it the essence itself of personality.

Historical Notes

205. According to an opinion put forward by *Duns Scotus*, subsistence consists in something negative, namely, the negation of communicability. This opinion is closely connected with Scotus' view of individuality. Because he conceived individuation as a positive perfection added to the specific nature, there was no need for him to add

[14] *Essay on Human Understanding*, bk. II, ch. 27, sect. 9.

another positive perfection to make the individual autonomous. All he needed to do was to add incommunicability.

Suarez explained subsistence as a substantial mode which completes the individual substance. Since he did not admit the real distinction of essence and "to be" in finite beings, his substantial mode differs from that proposed in no. 202 in this, that it comes to the substance after the "to be." It is difficult to see how such a mode could be substantial because it accedes to a substance which is already actualized by "to be."

Cajetan explained subsistence by a substantial mode which is the ultimate perfection in the essential line of the individual substance. Most Thomists, such as *Mercier, del Prado* and *Phillips,* follow his explanation, although not a few prefer to identify subsistence with existence; for example, *Capreolus, Billot,* and *Renard.* Both schools of thought claim to be the faithful exponents of St. Thomas, in whose works there are indeed texts favorable to both views.[15] However, when St. Thomas proves the real distinction of subsistence and individual substance, he never uses the argument: Subsistence is identical with "to be," and "to be" in a finite being is really distinct from essence or substance; therefore, subsistence and substance are really distinct. This is all the more remarkable because the real distinction of essence and "to be" plays such an important role in St. Thomas' philosophy. Hence we should be inclined to say that he did not identify subsistence with existence.

[15] If favor of the identity of subsistence and existence are quoted: *Summa theol*, Ia, q.29, a.3; IIIa, q.19, a.1, ad 4; *De veritate,* q.21, a.10; against it: *Summa theol.,* Ia, q.50, a.2, ad 3; IIIa, q.17, a.2, ad 1; *Quodlibet.* 2, a.4.

SUMMARY

206. In general, supposit means a complete, independent being. It is the ultimate subject of whatever belongs to a nature taken concretely, and thus is autonomous. It may be defined as a subsistent, individual, and complete substance or nature. A person is a supposit of a rational nature.

The perfection which makes the individual complete substance a supposit is called subsistence or, in the case of a rational nature, personality. It makes the individual an entirely incommunicable, intrinsically self-sufficient being. The self-sufficiency which subsistence adds to the individual is analogous and becomes more and more pronounced the higher we ascend on the scale of beings.

The individual nature and the supposit are really distinct in finite beings because it is possible to add to the finite being something which does not belong to its nature. For, at least the "to be" is in addition to the nature. Hence the individual nature or substance and the supposit are really distinct, although only by an inadequate real distinction.

Regarding the nature of the perfection which subsistence adds to the individual substance, it should be clear that subsistence is not purely negative because it makes a finite being intrinsically independent. Neither is subsistence to be identified with "to be," because "to be" merely actualizes whatever is real in a thing; hence "to be" presupposes the supposit as its subject. Subsistence is the ultimate perfection in the essential line of the essence. Its function is to close the essence so that the "to be" will fall upon a unified and closed whole. Hence, subsistence is called a substantial mode, which is distinguished from the substance it terminates as the terminus of a thing is distinguished from the thing itself.

Self-consciousness cannot be considered to be an adequate metaphysical definition of personality because self-consciousness is an act, whereas a person is a subject.

SUGGESTED READINGS

207. R. P. Phillips, *Modern Thomistic Philosophy*, vol. 2, pp. 213-222.

G. Duggan, "The Teaching of St. Thomas Regarding the Formal Constitutive of Human Personality," in *The New Scholasticism*, 1941, pp. 318-348.

Louis de Raeymaeker, *The Philosophy of Being*, Ch. VIII, pp. 240-250.

CHAPTER 10

Accidents in General

✥✥✥ Several questions concerning accidents in general have already been treated in the foregoing chapters; it will be sufficient to give here a few additional points.

Definition and Division of Accidents

208. As will be recalled from logic, we must distinguish between predicable and predicamental accidents. At present we are not concerned with *predicable* accidents, which are opposed to essence and property and belong to the logical order, but only with *predicamental* or *categorical* accidents, which are opposed to substance and belong to the ontological order.

The predicamental accident is defined as *that to whose nature is due a "to be" in another as in a subject.* Concerning this definition the following are to be noted:

a) Just as we did not define substance as "that which exists in itself," but as "that to whose nature is due a "to be" in itself," because "to be" is not of the essence of any finite substance, so also the predicamental accident is not defined as "that which is in another," but as "that *to whose nature is due* a "to be" in another," because "to be" is not of the nature of any finite being.[1]

[1] Cf. St. Thomas, *In IV sentent*, d.12, q.1, a.1, *Summa theol.*, IIIa, q.77, a.1, ad 2.

b) The words *"as in a subject"* are added to the definition to indicate the manner in which accidents are in another. They are not in another as a part is in the whole (a limb in the body), nor as the contents in the container (water in a glass), nor as a substantial form is in matter and gives it its first "to be," but as a form is in a subject to which it gives a further determination.

c) Because accidents are such that to their nature is due a "to be" in another, they are by their very nature *imperfect* beings. As St. Thomas remarks, they should be called "something belonging to being," rather than "being."[2] Hence we do not say that accidents, say, whiteness, come to be, but rather that their subject becomes white.[3] However, this imperfection of accidents should not be conceived as if the essence of an accident were incomplete and in need of an essential co-principle. It is a complete essence, but one which lacks independence, and therefore has to inhere in a subject.[4]

209. Regarding the *division* of accidents, as has been explained in no. 178, by an analogous division they are divided into nine categories. Of these one is *relative*, relation, because it belongs to its subject only insofar as this

[2] *Summa theol.*, Ia IIae, q.110, a.2, ad 3.
[3] *Ibid.*
[4] Cf. St. Thomas, *In I sentent.*, d.8, q.4, a.2. Note that *actual* inherence is not of the essence of an accident. The definition merely implies that the essence is such as to have a requirement for inherence. Hence the definition does not exclude the possibility that an accident would exist without actually inhering in a subject, although such an accident would retain its requirement of inherence. Revelation offers an example of accidents existing without actually inhering in the Holy Eucharist, in which the accidents of bread and wine continue to exist without their subject.

subject has a respect to something else; for example, paternity belongs to a man with respect to his son. All the other categories are absolute, not in the sense that they are independent of their subject, but insofar as in themselves they add a new reality to a subject.

Accidents are also divided into *intrinsic* and *extrinsic* accidents according as they inhere in the subject of which they are called accidents, or inhere in one subject and modify another which is denominated by them. Examples of intrinsic accidents are quantity and quality, and of extrinsic accidents, time and place.

Beside these, there is sometimes question of *modal* accidents, by which are meant further determinations of accidents. For instance, shape is a modal accident of extension, which it determines, and pitch is a modal accident which determines sound. Modal accidents affect directly the accident which they determine, and indirectly the subject in which this accident inheres.

The Reality of Accidents

210. That there are real accidents which are really distinct from their subject is unanimously accepted by all scholastic philosophers and follows immediately from what we have seen in nos. 182 ff. If there are changes which do not result in a new substance, such changes take place in a subject which loses or acquires a perfection that does not belong to its substantial essence, but is a secondary determination of this substance. Now, if a perfection can be lost without a change in the essence of its subject, it follows that this perfection is really distinct from the subject, i.e., from the substance.

Accidents Have Their Own "To Be"

211. Some Thomistic philosophers do not think that real accidents have their own "to be," and admit that they

exist by the same "to be" as the substance itself. However, as St. Thomas remarks, "in Socrates there is one "to be" insofar as he is white, and another "to be" insofar as he is a man. . . . To be white is a "to be" of Socrates, not insofar as he is Socrates, but insofar as he is white. Hence there is nothing to prevent the multiplication of this kind of "to be" in one hypostasis or person; for the "to be" by which Socrates is white is other than the "to be" by which he is a musician." [5] Keeping in mind that "to be" merely actualizes whatever is real, we should have no difficulty in accepting the view that each accident has its own "to be." For the act of existence or "to be" is proportioned to the potency whose act it is; now the "to be" of the substance is not proportioned to the essence of accidents, nor is the essence of one accident proportioned to the "to be" of another. Hence it is necessary to admit for every accident a "to be" of its own which is proportioned to its essence or nature.

The *objection* to this view is that it seems to militate against the unity of the individual substance. If substance and accidents each have their own "to be," they may conceivably exist close together, but they would not, so it seems, form a unit. To this, we may answer that both substance and accidents are abstractions of reality. The reality is the concrete individual whole, which is composed of substance and accidents. It is this whole which "becomes" something when a new perfection is acquired by the substance. Hence the "to be" of each accident is really a "to be" of the concrete individual whole. Moreover, as we have explained in nos. 182 ff., substance and accidents are related to one another as potency to act. Now potency and act by their union become one. Although this union of substance and accidents does not result in a perfectly uni-

---

[5] *Summa theol.*, IIIa, q. 17, a. 2 Cf. Also IV *Contra gentes*, c. 14.

fied being, nevertheless there is real, though imperfect, unity.[6] Were we to require perfect, substantial unity for the composite of substance and accidents, it would be impossible to explain accidental change. Any change in that case would be a change of a substantial unity as such.

Individuation of Accidents

212. Since accidents are related to their subject as act is related to potency, an accidental form received in the potency of an individual substance is rendered *this* individual accident by the very fact that it is a determination of this individual substance. However, the accident of quantity may be said to be individuated also by itself, inasmuch as its nature implies position, as has been explained in no. 158.

From the fact that accidents are individuated by the subject in which they inhere we may draw the conclusion that accidents do not remain individually the same when their subject is corrupted, i.e., when a substantial change takes place.

*Historical Notes

213. *Descartes* denied that there are any real absolute accidents which are really distinct from the substance. He identified spiritual substance with thought, and material substance with quantity, and explained all other accidents as relations.

St. Thomas, Suarez and scholastic philosophers in general, with few exceptions, such as *Mercier*,[7] admit that accidents have their own "to be."

[6] Cf. *De ente et essentia,* c.7; *Summa theol.,* Ia, q.76, a.3; II *Contra gentes,* c 5.

[7] *Métaphysique générale,* no. 157.

SUMMARY

214. A predicamental accident is that to whose nature is due a "to be" in another as in a subject. By their very nature accidents are imperfect beings, in the sense that they lack independence and have to exist in something else.

By an analogous division accidents are divided into nine categories. Of these, relation is relative, and all the others are absolute. Accidents may be intrinsic or extrinsic according as they determine and denominate the subject in which they inhere or another subject. A modal accident is a further determination of an accident.

Accidents are really distinct from the substance in which they inhere because they can be lost without a change in the essence of the substance. They have their own "to be." For "to be" must be proportioned to the essence which is in potency to it; now the "to be" of the substance is not proportioned to the nature of an accident. Hence, the unity of substance and accidents is not perfect because each of the components has its own "to be."

Accidents are individuated by the individual substance in which they are received. Hence they cannot remain individually the same when their subject is corrupted through substantial change.

SUGGESTED READINGS

215. P. Coffey, *Ontology*, pp. 207-251.
J. S. Albertson, "The *Esse* of Accidents According to St. Thomas," in *The Modern Schoolman*, 1953, pp. 265-278.
Francis E. McMahon and James Albertson, "The Esse of Accidents: a Discussion," *Ibidem*, 1954, pp. 125-132.

CHAPTER 11

Relations

✣✣✣ 216. Relations occupy a very important place in philosophy because the various beings which form the universe are not entirely isolated from one another, but every being has certain relations to others. For example, a man has relations of dependence to the First Cause and to his parents; of causality to his descendants, of specific identity to other human beings; of equality to all beings having the same size, weight, etc. Moreover, in science man is forever engaged in a search for the relationships existing between various objects. Lastly, the question of relation has great importance for theology, which conceives the divine persons in God as subsistent relations.

The Nature of Relation

217. Relation consists in the order between things. "The essence of every relation," says Aristotle, "is to be *to another*." [1] "For instance, the term 'superior' is explained by reference to something else, for it is superiority over something else that is meant. . . . Again, that which is said to be similar must be similar to something else." [2] Hence it is clear that three things are necessary in order that a

[1] *Topics*, bk. VI, ch. 8, 146b, 3.
[2] *Categories*, ch. 7; 6a, 37.

relation may arise—namely, a *subject* which has a reference, a *term* to which the subject is referred, and a *foundation* or reason why the subject has a reference to the term. For example, if Peter has a relation of equality to Paul, Peter is the subject, Paul is the term, and their height is the foundation of the relation of equality.

Relation, as Such, Does Not Imply Anything Real. Relation "differs from the other genera in this that the latter by their very nature imply that they are something [real [3]], as for instance, quantity implies something real. . . . But relation does not imply anything real in its very nature; hence there are relations which do not exist in the order of reality but only in the logical order, which does not happen in the other genera."[4] For this reason relation is not only a class in the division of real being, but also in that of logical being (cf. no. 48).

Relation, as Such, Does Not Imply Any Imperfection. The essence of a relation merely implies a respect to another. It does not imply that this respect is something accidental.[5]

Transcendental and Predicamental Relations

218. By a *transcendental* or essential relation is meant the essence of something absolute, insofar as it implies an order to something else. For example, body and soul are something absolute, yet by their very nature they are related to one another. So also, the power of reproduction is transcendentally related to the production of offspring. We have seen other examples of transcendental relations

[3] Cf. *Quodlibet* 1, a.2.
[4] *Quodlibet.* 9, a 4. Cf. *Summa theol.*, Ia, q.28, a.1.
[5] Cf. *In I sentent.*, d.8, q.4, a.3. In theology, the divine Persons are conceived as subsistent relations.

in potency and act and its applications, such as essence and "to be," matter and form, substance and accident. Transcendentally related things are related to one another *by their very nature,* i.e., not by means of an accident added to their nature, but immediately by themselves. Hence, such relations are not really distinct from the subject and term which are transcendentally related but identical with them. Because of this real identity with some absolute reality, *transcendental relations are always real.* For the same reason they can exist or continue to exist even when the term to which they refer does not exist, provided of course that the absolute reality with which they are identified can exist separately. For instance, when the human body dies, the human soul continues to exist, and is still transcendentally related to this body.

A *predicamental* or categorical relation is an accident whose whole being consists in its reference to another. It constitutes the category of relation and is also called accidental relation in opposition to essential relation. Like the "to be" of the other accidents, its "to be" is a "to be" in another. However, whereas in the other accidents "their proper nature is taken by comparison to their subject . . . the proper nature of relation . . . is taken by comparison with something outside the subject." [6] Hence a predicamental relation depends not only upon its subject, but also upon the term to which it refers this subject; it is not only *"in* another" but also *"to* another." For this reason, St. Thomas calls the predicamental relation the "weakest of all beings." [7]

It is to be noted that the definition of predicamental relation is this: "an accident whose whole being consists

[6] *Summa theol,* Ia, q.28, a.2. Cf. *De potentia,* q.7, a.9 ad 7.
[7] *De potentia,* q.7, a.9.

in its reference to another." For, as Aristotle remarks, "such terms as 'head' and 'hand' are *defined* with reference to that of which the things indicated are parts. . . . But the fact that a thing is defined with reference to something else does not make it essentially relative." [8] To be truly relative a thing must not only be defined with reference to something else, but its very *being* must be relative. Therefore, 'head' and 'hand' are not relations, but terms such as 'father' and 'son' express true relations because, formally speaking, 'father' implies nothing but a reference to 'son,' and 'son' merely expresses a relation to 'father.'

Conditions Required for a Predicamental Relation

219. Four conditions must be fulfilled before a predicamental relation can arise. They are the following:

1) There must be a *real subject*. This is evident because a real relation can refer only a real subject to a term.

2) There must be a *real term* because a real relation exists independently of the mind; hence it cannot refer the subject to something which exists only in the mind.

3) There must be a *real foundation,* for if the foundation does not exist outside the mind, it is clear that the relation cannot exist independently of the mind.[9]

---

[8] *Categories*, ch. 7; 8a, 27.
[9] The foundation of a predicamental relation may be either action and passion (causality) or quantity (in a transcendental sense, i.e., the perfection of a thing), because the foundation of a relation either exercises a positive influence upon the "to be" of a thing or not. Quantity gives rise to the relationships of identity and distinction, equality and inequality, similarity and dissimilarity. Causality gives rise to the relationships of the four genera of causes (efficient, final, material, and formal intrinsic) insofar as it is not a measure, and to the relationship of the measure and the measurable according to being and truth, which is called the relationship of formal extrinsic

4) The subject must be *really distinct* from the term; otherwise either the subject or the term would exist only in the mind; hence there could be no question of a relationship independently of the mind.

A predicamental relation is called *mutual* or bilateral if to the real relation of the subject to the term there corresponds a real relation of the term to the subject. Otherwise the relation is *non-mutual* or unilateral. For example, to the real relation of father to son (a relation of paternity) there corresponds in the son a real relation to the father (a relation of filiation); hence these relations are mutual. But while there is a real relation of the intellect to the thing known, because in knowing the intellect depends upon the thing known, the relation of the thing known to the intellect is purely logical, because by becoming known a thing does not change; hence, the real relation of the intellect to the thing known is non-mutual. Likewise, the relation of the creature to the Creator is real in the creature but logical in the Creator.

Existence of Predicamental Relations

220. The *proof* for the existence of predicamental relations is simple and was indicated at the beginning of this chapter. Independently of the consideration of the mind there exists order in the universe. Now, this order consists in real relations. Therefore, real or predicamental relations exist.[10] The *major* premise is clear from experience. Even if no one considers the universe, the various beings in it are ordered to one another, as is clear from the relationships of cause and effect, similarity, equality, etc. Hence

causality. Relations of the measure and the measurable are non-mutual Cf. St. Thomas, *In V metaphysic.*, lect. 17, nos. 1001 ff.

[10] Cf. *De potentia*, q. 7, a. 9.

there is real order in the universe. The *minor* premise also is evident; for order means relations, and real order means real relations.

Those philosophers who deny the reality of relation seem to confuse our knowledge of relations with relations themselves. Relations do not exist independently of the mind *for us*, in the sense that we do not know them independently of the mind. But this does not mean that relations do not at all exist when our mind does not consider them.

Distinction of Predicamental Relations from Their Subject, Term, and Foundation

221. This question offers more difficulty; especially has the real distinction of predicamental relations from their foundation caused differences of opinion.

Predicamental relations are *really distinct from their subject* because the subject and the relation are related to one another as real potency and act, as has been shown in chapter VIII. Moreover, things which can be separated are really distinct. Now predicamental relations can be separated from their subject; for instance, a man will acquire a relation of paternity by an act of reproduction and lose it by the death of his offspring.[11]

Predicamental relations are *really distinct from their term*. For the subject and the term of a predicamental relation are really distinct; the relation is a determination of the subject; hence it follows that the relation is really distinct from the term.

Predicamental relations are *really distinct from their foundation*. For otherwise there could be no question of a real relation, because the foundation of a relation is always

[11] Cf. *In I sentent.*, d. 21, q. 1, a. 2.

something absolute,[12] whereas the relation itself is totally relative. Hence, either there are no real relations or they are really distinct from their foundation.[13] Moreover, sometimes it is possible to separate the relation from its foundation. For example, between identical twins there is a real relation of similarity based upon their physiognomy. The death of one will destroy this similarity, but its foundation, this particular physiognomy, will remain in the survivor.

* Multiplication of Relation

222. Relations are multiplied *specifically* by the specific diversity of their foundations and terms. It should be clear that a specifically different *foundation* will give rise to a specifically different relationship. No one will claim, for instance, that the relations of paternity and equality are essentially the same. Likewise, if the *terms* to which a relation refers are specifically different, the relationship itself will be specifically different.[14] For instance, the same foundation of whiteness will give rise to a relation of similarity to a white object and to the specifically different relation of dissimilarity to a green object.

Relations are multiplied *numerically* according to the multiplication of their *subjects,* so that in one subject there

[12] One real relation cannot be the foundation of another real relation because a relation needs to be supported by something more perfect in being than itself. Moreover, if a relation could give rise to another real relation, this relation again could give rise to a third, and so on to infinity.

[13] Cf. *De potentia,* q.7, a.9.

[14] We mean specifically distinct *insofar as they are terms.* Hence whiteness does not give rise to specifically distinct relations with respect to a white man and a white cat.

can be only one relation of paternity, equality, similarity, etc. The reason is that an accident is individuated by its subject of inherence; hence there cannot be two specifically the same accidents in one and the same individual subject. However, one and the same numerical relation may refer its subject to several terms; for instance, one man can be related to ten children by one relation of paternity.[15]

A Misconception

223. The reluctance of many philosophers to admit the real distinction of the predicamental relation from its foundation seems to flow from a misunderstanding of its true nature. If relations are real and really distinct from their foundation, so they seem to reason, they surely are very strange entities, having nothing absolute and merely pointing to something else. How can we represent such things in our mind? As a kind of gossamer web linking every creature to all other creatures by innumerable threads, possessing a higher degree of elasticity than the best grade of bubble-gum, so that they can stretch and shrink with every move of every correlated being without becoming hopelessly entangled in one another?

The answer is that we should beware of using our imagination in metaphysical problems. Just as any effort to imagine what potency and act, essence and "to be," substance and accident, look like if taken by themselves can end only in disaster, so also any effort to draw a mental picture of real relations. Our imagination can properly represent only a concrete whole; substance, accident, potency, act, relation, etc., are not concrete wholes but real-

[15] Cf. *Quodlibet.* 1, a.2.

ities which our intellects abstract from our sense images. Their intellectual representation is not a representation of the whole reality as it exists in nature, but a representation of real co-principles, which together with other co-principles form the concrete whole existing in nature. If we have to deny real relations because we cannot imagine what they look like, then, for the same reason, we must deny the validity of all other abstract concepts of reality, and thus we should have to give up all attempts towards a rational conception of the universe. Moreover, the analogy of being should not be lost sight of. Every category is a class of being *sui generis*, in the strictest possible sense of the term; hence, no category can be properly represented by a being belonging to a different category. Our mind, however, has a persistent tendency to think in univocal terms and to reduce everything to univocation, and therefore tries to conceive relations as if they were something absolute. As philosophers, we must react against this tendency and keep in mind that being is analogous.

*Historical Notes

224. The *Stoics*, the *nominalists* (*Occam*), and many *positivists* admit logical relations, but deny the existence of real relations.

According to *Kant*, relation is a category of the mind without objective value.

With *Aristotle*, scholastic philosophers in general admit the reality of predicamental relations. Some, however, as *Schiffini*, explain their reality by the reality of their term, while others, such as *Suarez*, identify real predicamental relation with its foundation. *St. Thomas* and *Duns Scotus* defend the reality of predicamental relations and their distinction from their foundation.

SUMMARY

225. The essence of every relation is to be to another. Hence, for every relation there is needed a subject, a term and a foundation, or reason why the subject is related to the term. Relation, *qua* relation, does not imply anything real; hence logical relations are possible. Relation, *qua* relation, does not imply any imperfection because it merely indicates a respect to something without implying that this respect exists by inherence.

A transcendental relation is the essence of something absolute, insofar as it implies an order to something else. Hence, transcendentally related things are related immediately by themselves, and not by an added relation. So, because a transcendental relation is identical with an absolute reality, it is always real.

A predicamental relation is an accident whose whole being consists in its reference to something else. It is the weakest of all beings, because it depends for its existence not only upon the subject in which it is, but also upon the term to which it refers.

A predicamental relation can arise only if there is a real subject, a real term, which is really distinct from the subject, and a real foundation. If the relation is real in both subject and term, it is called mutual; otherwise it will be non-mutual.

The existence of predicamental relations is clear from the fact that independently of the mind there exists order in the universe.

Predicamental relations are really distinct from their subject because they are related to it as real act is to real potency. Moreover, they can be separated from it. They are really distinct from their term because they are determinations of a subject which is really distinct from the term. They are really distinct from their foundation because the foundation is always absolute, whereas the relation is totally relative. Moreover, sometimes they can be separated from their foundation.

*Relations are multiplied specifically by the specific multiplication of their foundation and terms. Hence, if either the foundations or the terms are specifically different, the relations resulting from these foundations or referring to these terms will be specifically different. Relations are multiplied numerically according to the numerical multiplication of their subject. However, numerically one and the same relation may refer its subject to several terms.

When studying the nature of real predicamental relations we should keep in mind that all our philosophical concepts are abstractions from reality and therefore cannot be represented as such by our imagination. Moreover, relation is a being *sui generis;* hence its nature cannot be studied properly by means of comparison to other genera of being.

SUGGESTED READINGS

226. N. D. Ginsburg, "Metaphysical Relations and St. Thomas Aquinas," in *The New Scholasticism*, 1941, pp. 238–254.

C. G. Kossel, "Principles of St. Thomas' Distinction Between the *Esse* and *Ratio* of Relation," in *The Modern Schoolman*, 1945–1946, pp. 19–36 and 93–107.

C. G. Kossel, "St. Thomas' Theory of the Causes of Relation," in *The Modern Schoolman*, 1945–1946, pp. 151–172.

SECTION III

The Causes of Finite Being

THIS SECTION consists of four chapters, the first of which considers causes in general; the second, efficient causality; the third, final causality; and the fourth, the mutual relationship of causes.

CHAPTER 12

Causes in General

✲✲✲ 227. "Knowledge is the object of our inquiry and we do not think that we know a thing till we understand the 'why' of it." [1] Our study of finite beings in general would not be complete if we neglected to inquire into their causes. For if there are beings whose essence is not "to be," inevitably the question will arise as to why they are at all. It is the concept of cause which answers the question why a thing is.[2]

I. THE CONCEPT OF CAUSE

228. With St. Thomas we may say that a cause is "that upon which something else follows of necessity," [3] understanding this, of course, in the sense of "as a result of its influence." But in order to determine the meaning of "cause" more accurately, it is best to compare the concept of cause to other more or less cognate concepts.

Cause and Principle

A principle is "that from which something proceeds in any way whatsoever." [4] This definition implies two things,

---
[1] Aristotle, *Physics*, bk. II, ch. 2; 194b 17.
[2] Cf. Aristotle, *op cit* , ch. 7; 198a 33.
[3] *In V metaphysic* , lect. 1, no. 749.
[4] *Summa theol.*, Ia, q.33, a.1.

viz., that the principle is prior to that which proceeds from it, and that there is a special connection between what is called the principle and that which proceeds from it, in virtue of which the former is the principle of the latter. Let us examine these two conditions.

Priority may be in the order of time or merely in the order of nature. We speak of a priority *of time* when one thing has existence before the other; for instance, Napoleon was prior in time to Stalin; and parents, *qua* human beings, are prior in time to their children. A priority *of nature* means that the nature of one thing is such that it presupposes the nature of the other, even though in the order of time both things are simultaneous. For example, when water is produced from hydrogen and oxygen, both the substance of water and certain accidental qualities, such as being of a certain temperature, colorless, liquid, etc., come into existence at the same time. Nevertheless, we say that the substance of water is prior in nature to the accidents because the nature of the accidents presupposes the nature of the substance as their subject of inhesion. Likewise, a cause, *qua* cause, is prior to its effect by a mere priority of nature, although materially a cause may be prior in time to its effect. By this is meant that something which is going to become the cause of a certain effect may exist prior to the actual exercise of its causality.[5]

The *special connection* between a principle and that which proceeds from it may be in the logical or in the ontological order. It is *logical* if one thing proceeds from another according to the working of the intellect; for ex-

---

[5] Apart from these two types of priority, there is still a third type, so-called priority of origin, which is used in theology to explain the dogma of the Holy Trinity.

ample, the conclusion of a syllogism proceeds from the premises, which therefore may be called its logical principle. The connection is *ontological* when in reality one thing proceeds from another; for instance, an effect from a cause.

An ontological principle either *exercises influence* upon the "to be" of that which proceeds from it, or not. A point, for example, is the principle at which a line begins, but does not exercise any influence upon the "to be" of the line.[6] When, however, a father begets a son, he exercises influence upon the "to be" of his son. We do not call a point the cause of a line, but a father is the (partial) cause of his son.

Hence, when compared to principle, the concept of cause is seen to have a more restricted meaning, for a cause is an ontological principle which exercises an influence upon the "to be" of a thing.

Cause and Condition

229. By a condition, in the strict sense of the term, we mean something which does not exercise any positive influence upon the "to be" of the effect, but is a prerequisite for the action of the cause. For example, a connection with a source of electricity is a prerequisite for the incandescence of an electric bulb. The connection does not make the bulb glow, but merely enables electricity to reach the bulb and to produce there incandescence. Hence, a condition differs from a cause in this that its influence is not positive, but purely *dispositive,* insofar as it removes obstacles which prevent the cause from acting. The difference between cause and condition may be illustrated by

---

[6] Cf. *De potentia,* q. 10, a. 1, ad 9.

the following example. A stone of fifty pounds is firmly held in place by the suction of mud in a swamp. My efforts to lift it are in vain. A friend comes to help me. Together we lift the stone. Both of us exercise *positive* influence upon the effect, viz., the change in position of the stone. If, however, my friend limits himself to the removal of the mud around the stone and leaves the rest to me, he would not exercise any positive influence upon the change of position, but his action would remove the obstacle which prevents me from lifting the stone; hence it would be *dispositive*.

Cause and Occasion

230. By an occasion we mean a favorable opportunity for a free cause to exercise its causality. An occasion exercises positive influence insofar as it helps to induce a free agent to produce an effect. A free cause, however, can exercise its causality even when there is no favorable opportunity. Hence occasion differs from condition insofar as its influence is positive and not merely dispositive; from cause, insofar as its influence is not necessary for the production of the effect and is limited to free causes.

Cause and Sufficient Reason of Being

231. By the sufficient reason of being of a thing we mean that which can give an adequate explanation for the "to be" of a thing. It differs from cause inasmuch as the sufficient reason does *not* have to be *really distinct* from the thing whose "to be" is explained by it, whereas the cause of a thing is always *really distinct* from it; [7]

---

[7] This real distinction is *adequate* with respect to extrinsic causes (the efficient and the final cause), but *inadequate* with respect to intrinsic causes (matter and form). For matter and form are related

otherwise, the thing would be the cause of itself. Hence, it is absolutely true that every being has a sufficient reason of being, but it is not true that every being is caused. If the essence of a thing is really identical with its "to be," this essence is the sufficient reason for its "to be"; but if an essence is really distinct from its "to be," the sufficient reason for its "to be" must be found outside the essence. Hence a cause is a sufficient reason for the "to be" of something else.[8]

From all these considerations we may derive the conclusion that a cause is an *ontological principle which exercises a positive influence upon the "to be" of something else.*

II. THE EXISTENCE OF CAUSES

232. We must now see whether or not the concept of cause corresponds to objective reality. The reason for this investigation should be clear. In the chapter concerning substance we have already taken issue with phenomenalism because it denies the objective reality of substances. In the present problem phenomenalists, such as Hume and Stuart Mill, claim that we can know only what can be perceived by the senses, and since the senses are not able to see the causal connections between things, they assert that our concept of cause is a figment of the mind without any objective value. Upon perceiving regular successions of phenomena we merely imagine that there is a causal connection. Against them and others who hold similar views, we claim that the concept of cause has objective value.

---

to the composite of matter and form as parts are related to the whole, and the whole, "properly speaking, is not its parts but something constituted by the parts " St. Thomas, *In III sentent*, d.2, q.1, a.3.

[8] Cf. nos. 232 and 237 ff.

This assertion is established by the following *metaphysical proof:* If the "to be" of a thing is distinct from its essence, this "to be" must come either from some external agent or from the essential principles of the thing itself. Now, it is impossible that the "to be" of a being come from the sole essential principles of the thing; for no finite essence which is not its "to be" can be the sufficient reason of its own "to be." Therefore, any thing whose "to be" is distinct from its essence must have its "to be" from another.[9] Now, to give "to be" to something else is to exercise true causality. Hence, the concept of cause corresponds to objective reality.

Thus we see that it is the real distinction between essence and "to be" in finite beings which leads us to the conclusion that the concept of cause has objective value. As St. Thomas expresses it very succinctly, "by the very fact that a thing is a being by participation it follows that it is caused by another." [10]

A *confirmation* of this metaphysical proof may be taken from our own internal and external experience. We are conscious that we are the cause of acts of intellect and will, and that changes are made in other things by our actions. Our intellect, for instance, perceives that the motions of our organs of speech and the sounds that follow these motions are not merely a succession of disconnected phenomena. The only rational explanation it can give of these phenomena is that the sounds are produced by these motions. Likewise, when external experience shows us, first,

---

[9] Cf. *Summa theol.*, Ia, q.3, a.4 and *De ente et essentia*, c.5. Strictly speaking, this argument merely establishes that "cause" is a concept having objective value, and not which beings are true causes. The extension of the concept "cause" will be studied in subsequent pages.

[10] *Summa theol.*, Ia, q.44, a.1, ad 1.

a man driving his fist into somebody's eye and, secondly, this eye black and swollen, our intellect clearly perceives that there is some connection. While we can agree with phenomenalism that our senses can perceive only the succession of phenomena and not their causal connection, we cannot agree that our knowledge is limited to the senses, but must allow our intellect to give a rational interpretation to these sensations.

III. GENERA OF CAUSES

233. Aristotle enumerated four genera of causes. "Cause means: (1) that from which, as immanent material, a thing comes into being, e.g., the bronze is the cause of the statue, and the silver of the saucer; (2) the form or pattern, i.e., the definition of the essence, and the classes which include this; (3) that from which the change, or resting from change first begins; e.g., the father is the cause of the child, and in general the maker a cause of the thing made; (4) the end, i.e., that for the sake of which a thing is done; e.g., health is the cause of walking. To the question: 'Why does one walk?' we say, 'That one may be healthy'; and in speaking thus we think we have given the cause." [11] These four causes are called respectively the material, the formal, the efficient, and the final cause.

234. The *material cause* is "that from which something is made." [12] Primary matter is the material cause of a corporeal substance, and secondary matter, such as marble, is the material cause of a secondary or accidental determination of a body.

[11] *Metaphysics,* bk. V, ch. 2; 1013a, 24 ff. Cf. *Ibid.,* by. I, ch. 3; 983a, 26 ff. and *Physics,* bk II, ch. 3; 194b, 23 ff.
[12] *In* V *metaphysic.,* lect. 2, no. 763.

The *formal cause* "is compared to the thing in two ways. In one way, as the *intrinsic* form of the thing, and this is called the species. In another way, as *extrinsic* to the thing, as that to the likeness of which the thing is said to be made, and in this sense it is called the exemplar," [18] model, or exemplary cause of the thing.

Both the material and the formal intrinsic cause are internal or intrinsic causes. We have studied them to a certain extent in previous chapters. They will be considered more in detail in the philosophy of nature. Concerning the exemplary cause, see the Appendix at the end of chapter XIV.

235. The *efficient cause* is the first principle of change in the order of execution.[14] The order of execution is taken in opposition to the order of intention, which belongs to final causality. The term "first" should be understood as first in the order of execution as compared to the other genera of causes, and not in the sense that only the first cause of everything, God, can be called an efficient cause, as we shall see in the next chapter.

Efficient causes are either principal or instrumental causes.[15] A *principal* cause acts in virtue of its own power, e.g., in virtue of his own power a man eats, walks, etc. If a principal cause is absolutely independent of everything else in the exercise of its causality it is called *primary* cause; otherwise it is a *secondary* cause. Apart from the Pure Act or God, all other causes are dependent in the exercise of their causality and therefore secondary causes, as we shall see in the next chapter. An *instrumental* cause

[13] *Ibid*, no. 764.
[14] Change is to be taken in a wide sense so as to include even the transition from non-existence to existence.
[15] Cf. *Summa theol.*, IIIa, q. 62, a. 1.

CAUSES IN GENERAL

acts insofar as it is moved by a principal cause; for instance, a pen writes insofar as it is moved by the writer. The correctness of this division will be shown in the second and third parts of the next chapter.

236. The *final cause,* purpose or end is "that for the sake of which something is done"; [16] e.g., a student will come to school for the sake of attending a lecture. The final cause is first in the order of intention because it induces the agent to act. We may distinguish *"the end for which"* i.e., that for whose benefit a thing is done, and *"the end which,"* or the object intended. The end which is intended may be *immediate* or *ultimate* according as it is subordinated to another end or not. For example, if a man works hard to send his son to college, the son is the end for which, and "to send to college" is the immediate end which is intended; the ultimate end intended by the father in this particular line would be to give his son a better preparation for life, or something similar.

We may also distinguish the end of the act and the end of the agent. The *end of the act* is the end towards which the act naturally tends, whereas the end of the agent is the end which the agent has in mind in performing the act. For example, the end of the act of healing is the restoration of health, but the end of the agent (the physician) may be to make money.

237. The *correctness of the division* of causes into these genera may be shown as follows: There are as many genera of causes as there are general modes of exercising a positive influence upon the "to be" of a thing. Now a cause can exercise such an influence in the following manners:

[16] *In V metaphysic.,* lect. 2, no. 771.

a) by its action, which gives us the efficient cause;

b) as that which receives the "to be," which is the material cause;

c) as that which determines the material cause, either from within or from without, which gives us the formal intrinsic cause and the exemplary cause;

d) as that which moves the agent to act, which gives us the final cause.

It is to be noted that we distinguish here different genera of causes and not different species. Taken in a formal sense, the concept of cause is analogous to the different genera, and predicated of them by analogy of proportionality. It is important to keep in mind this analogous character of causes when there is question of other than efficient causality. Because efficient causality is most striking, man is naturally inclined to think about it immediately when he hears the term "cause." Thus he will be tempted to conceive all causes after the manner of efficient causes as if all causes work in the same way as efficient causes. Such a procedure is totally wrong. No genus of causality can be reduced to any other genus; each of them has to be conceived in its own way. Failure to do so can end only in a misconception of the causality of non-efficient causes and lead to their denial or complete neglect.

*Historical Notes

238. The ancient *skeptics* denied the reality of causes, for cause is relative to effect, and according to them all relations are purely logical.

As we have seen above, the *phenomenalists* deny the objectivity of the concept of cause and consider it to be a figment of the mind which is based upon the invariable

CAUSES IN GENERAL

succession of phenomena. The falsity of this position is clear not only from the foregoing but also from the fact that we do not conclude to causality wherever there is an invariable succession of phenomena.

Kant distinguished causality from invariable succession, but considered it a category of the mind, the objective value of which is unknowable.

Scholastic philosophers unanimously admit the reality of causes. So also *Descartes, Leibnitz,* and many others.

Exemplary causality was introduced into scholastic philosophy under the influence of neoplatonic philosophy. Aristotle himself distinguished only four genera of causes.

SUMMARY

239. The fact that there are beings whose essence is not their "to be" leads to the question of why such beings are at all. It is the concept of cause which answers the question why a thing is. Cause differs from principle inasmuch as a cause is an ontological principle which exercises influence upon the "to be" of a thing. It differs from condition inasmuch as the influence of a cause is always positive, whereas the influence of a condition is merely dispositive, insofar as it removes the obstacles which may prevent the cause from acting. Cause differs from sufficient reason inasmuch as a cause is always really distinct from its effect, whereas a sufficient reason may be identical with that whose sufficient reason it is.

The objectivity of the concept of cause is evident from the fact that there are beings whose essence is not their "to be." Their existence cannot find a sufficient reason in their essence; hence this reason must be found outside this essence. Now a sufficient reason for the "to be" of a thing which is found outside this thing is a cause.

CAUSES IN GENERAL

Aristotle distinguished four genera of causes, viz., the material cause, the formal cause, the efficient cause, and the final cause. In addition, we speak of the exemplary cause, which is the model, to the likeness of which a thing is made.

The efficient cause is either principal, if it acts in virtue of its own power, or instrumental, if it acts insofar as moved by another cause. A principal cause is either primary or secondary according as it is independent in the exercise of its causality or not.

Regarding final causes, we may distinguish the end which is intended, and the end for which something is done. Moreover, we distinguish the end of the act, i.e., that to which the action naturally tends, and the end of the agent, i.e., the end the agent has in mind in acting.

SUGGESTED READINGS

240. I. Thomas, "Deduction of the Four Causes," in *Dominican Studies*, 1949, pp. 309–317.

P. Coffey, *Ontology*, pp. 357–380.

Louis de Raeymaeker, *The Philosophy of Being*, Ch. X, pp. 268–270 (cause, condition, reason, and principle).

CHAPTER 13

Efficient Causality

✥✥✥ 241. In some of the preceding chapters we have studied the ultimate reasons which explain why finite beings are intrinsically possible and can undergo change. Our conclusion was that both the intrinsic possibility or intelligibility and the mutability of a finite being postulate its composition of act and potency. But we did not consider then the ultimate reasons why such beings, whose essence is not their "to be," *are* and *do* change. It is evident that there must be something which gives an adequate explanation for the fact of their existence and change. The search for this explanation leads us to the so-called principle of (efficient) causality.

I. THE PRINCIPLE OF CAUSALITY

242. Regarding the first question, *why finite beings are*, although their essence is not "to be," the answer has already been given in the proof for the existence of causes. Since the "to be" of a finite being cannot be adequately explained by its essence, the sufficient reason for this "to be" can be found only in something which is extrinsic to this essence, i.e., in an efficient cause. Hence it follows that every being whose essence is not its "to be" has an

efficient cause. In other words, *every contingent being has a cause.*

Concerning the second question, *why finite beings do change,* it should be noted that a thing which is capable of changing is in potency to an act. Change or motion is conceived as a transition from potency to act. Now nothing can be moved from potency to act except by a being in act. As St. Thomas states it: "Whatever is in motion is moved by another, for nothing can be moved unless it be in potency to that to which it is moved, whereas a thing moves insofar as it is in act. For motion is nothing but the reduction of something from potency to act. Now, nothing can be reduced from potency to act except by something which is already in act. For instance, what is actually hot, as fire, makes wood, which is potentially hot, actually hot and thereby moves and changes it. Now it is impossible for one and the same thing to be simultaneously in act and in potency under the same respect. . . . For what is actually hot cannot be simultaneously potentially hot, but is simultaneously potentially cold. Therefore, it is impossible that under the same respect and in the same way a thing should be both mover and moved, i.e., that it should move itself. Hence, *whatever is in motion is moved by another.*[1] Or, to say the same in a short form, motion means the transition from potency to act. Now, what is in potency to an act cannot move itself to this act, because nothing can give itself what it does not have. Therefore, it is moved to this act by another.

Formulas of the Principle of Causality

243. From the foregoing it is clear that both the existence and the change of finite beings lead to the admission

[1] *Summa theol.,* Ia, q. 2, a. 3.

of the principle of causality. Both conclusions, *every contingent being has a cause,* and, *whatever is in motion is moved by another,*[2] are formulas of this principle. Besides these two, there are other formulas to express the same principle. Let us examine a few of them.

Every effect has a cause. This is the most popular formula. The term "effect" should not be understood in its usual sense as "that which has been caused," but as "that which comes to be existent," for otherwise the formula would be a mere tautology and not a principle.

The formula of St. Thomas *"whatever comes to be has a cause"* [3] is not open to a tautological interpretation and therefore preferable to the preceding formula.

St. Thomas' formula, *"nothing can be reduced from potency to act except by a being in act"* [4] shows how the principle of causality is linked to the theory of potency and act.

The formula *"whatever is by participation is caused by another"* [5] links the principle of causality to the theory of being by essence and being by participation.

Certainty of the Principle of Causality

244. The principle of causality is not proved directly but *indirectly,* by showing that the denial of the principle involves a contradiction in terms. The truth of the principle becomes clear from a mere analysis of its terms. Hence it is said to be a *self-evident principle.*

---

[2] Motion in this formula should be taken in a broad sense and not as synonymous with a change in position. It is synonymous here with change.

[3] *Summa theol.,* Ia IIae, q.75, a.1.

[4] *Compend. theol,* c.7.

[5] Cf. *Summa theol.,* Ia, q.44, a.1, ad 1.

EFFICIENT CAUSALITY

In a principle which is self-evident to us, the predicate is necessarily connected with the subject and can be derived from it by a process of deductive reasoning. For instance, in the proposition "man is capable of speech," the predicate "capable of speech" can be derived from the subject "man" by means of an analysis of the concept "man." Once a distinct concept of man as a rational animal is obtained, the predicate "capable of speech" can be attributed to man as something which flows from man's nature, even if we had never seen a man. Let us now consider the principle of causality under the formula "every contingent being has a cause." Analysis of "contingent being"[6] shows that it is a being which is, but could also not have been because its essence is not "to be." Now, the reason why a thing is may be either purely intrinsic to the thing or not. In a contingent being this reason is not purely intrinsic to the thing precisely because its essence is not "to be." Therefore, it follows that this reason is extrinsic to it. Hence from the very analysis of contingent being it follows that such a being depends for its "to be" upon something outside itself. Now by a cause is meant a principle upon which a thing depends for its "to be." Accordingly, the very analysis of contingent being shows that every contingent being has a cause.

One cannot object that a being could be without a sufficient reason for its "to be." For such an assertion would be against the principle of sufficient reason: "Everything has a sufficient reason for its 'to be.'" A denial of the principle

[6] Note that "the relation to the cause does not enter into the definition of the thing caused; yet [this relation] follows as a consequence on that which belongs to the concept of the thing caused, because by the very fact that a thing is a being by participation it follows that it is caused by another." *Ibid.*

of sufficient reason would ultimately be against the principle of contradiction; for otherwise a thing would be "something which is" and at the same time "something which is not," because it would be without "that by which a thing is," i.e., without a sufficient reason for its "to be."

Some Axioms of Efficient Causality

245. The following axioms follow immediately from the principle of causality or are connected with it.

Cause and effect are proportionate. The effect cannot be greater than the cause; for otherwise part of the effect would be without a cause, which is against the principle of causality. By cause we mean that which really is the cause, and not that which perhaps erroneously is considered to be the cause. Likewise, the cause cannot be greater than the effect, i.e., exercise more causality than required by the effect. For otherwise part of the cause would be causing without causing something, which is a contradiction in terms.

Nothing can come from nothing. The meaning of this axiom is clear—whoever appeals to nothing as an explanation of something does not give any explanation. Non-being cannot account for being.

Every agent acts in a manner similar to itself. The meaning is that every action of an agent depends upon the nature of the agent, in the sense that no agent can exercise any action which is contrary to its nature. For no being can give what it does not have. This principle makes it possible to determine the nature of an agent from its actions.

Action follows being. This axiom, which is frequently used, may mean either that no agent can act unless it

EFFICIENT CAUSALITY

exists, or that the action of an agent is proportionate to its nature.

*Historical Notes

246. In general, those philosophers who deny the objective validity of the concept of cause either deny the principle of causality or change its meaning.

Nicholas of Autrecourt (14th cent.), a forerunner of phenomenalism, simply rejected the principle of causality. According to *Hume,* causality is a mere relation between our ideas, and "the knowledge of this relation is not, in any instance, attained by reasonings *a priori,* but arises entirely from experience when we find that certain particular objects are constantly conjoined with each other." [7] "We consider only the constantly experienced conjunctions of the events, and as we feel the customary connection between the ideas we transfer that feeling to the objects." [8]

Kant admitted the necessity and universality of the principle of causality, but only as an *a priori* law of thinking by which we classify successive phenomena. Hence for him the principle of causality has no objective value. His formula of the principle, "whatever begins has a cause," is less fortunate because it does not take into account the possibility of contingent beings existing of eternity.

Scholastic philosophers unanimously defend the objective and absolute value of the principle, although a few, such as *de Margerie* and *Descoqs,* deny that it is self-evident.

[7] *A Treatise on Human Nature,* "Works," 1890, vol. IV, p. 24.
[8] *Ibid.,* p. 62.

EFFICIENT CAUSALITY

Many modern scientists, such as *Heisenberg*, reject what they call the classical principle of causality and claim that quantum mechanics definitely shows that this principle is not valid. However, upon closer inspection, it becomes clear that they are not speaking about the metaphysical principle of causality, but about a physical principle of causality which states "when the actual condition of a closed system is accurately known in all its factors, the future condition of this system can be calculated from it." While the metaphysical principle of causality concludes from *effect to cause*, this formula seeks to conclude from *cause to effect*. Identifying this principle with the metaphysical principle of causality amounts to the arbitrary presupposition that predictibility is the same as determinism, and determinism the same as causality.

SUMMARY

247. The search for the sufficient reason why finite beings are and do change leads to the principle of causality. If the essence of a finite being is not its "to be," then the sufficient reason for this "to be" must be found outside the essence, i.e., such a being has a cause. Moreover, a being which is in potency to act cannot move itself to act. Hence it must be moved to act by something else. Now every being which changes passes from potency to act. Hence whatever is changed is changed by another.

The principle of causality is proved indirectly insofar as a denial of this principle results in a contradiction in terms. Hence it is a self-evident principle. This means that the predicate of the proposition expressing the principle is of necessity connected with the subject of the proposition and can be derived from it by analysis.

The following propositions are axioms of causality:
Cause and effect are proportionate.
Nothing can come from nothing.
Every agent acts in a manner similar to itself.
Action follows being.

II. THE CAUSALITY OF FINITE BEINGS

In this section we must investigate the two types of efficient causality which are found in finite beings, viz., secondary and instrumental causality. First, however, it will be necessary to give certain divisions of efficient causes.

Division of Efficient Causes

248. Apart from the division of efficient causes into *principal* and *instrumental* causes, and the subdivision of principal causes into *primary* and *secondary* causes, which were given above in no. 235, the following may be mentioned:

Total and partial causes. The *total* cause accounts for the whole of the effect; for instance, a horse pulling a cart is the total cause of the movement of the cart. The *partial* cause produces only part of the effect; for example, either of two horses pulling a cart.

Coordinated and subordinated causes. A *coordinated* cause is the same as a partial cause and thus accounts for only part of the effect. A *subordinated* cause is a cause which depends upon another cause. If such a cause depends upon another cause in the very exercise of its causality, it is called an *essentially subordinated* cause. Such a cause produces the whole effect, but in dependence upon the other cause. For instance, the chisel of a sculptor is a cause which exercises influence upon the whole statue, but is dependent upon the sculptor in the very exercise of its causality. If a cause depends upon another cause, but not in the exercise of its causality, it is said to be *accidentally subordinated* to this cause. For example, a man depends on his father as upon a superior cause for his existence, but in the act of begetting a son he does not depend upon him; hence he is only accidentally subordinated to his father, insofar as the act of begetting a son is concerned.

Physical and moral causes. A *physical* cause produces its effect by direct action towards this effect; e.g., the carpenter is the physical efficient cause of the table he produces. A *moral* cause produces an effect by proposing a purpose to the physical cause; e.g., a customer, by offering money, induces the carpenter to make a table.

Proximate and remote causes. The *proximate* cause is the cause from which the effect proceeds immediately. The *remote* cause acts upon another cause and thus produces the effect mediately. For instance, if I boil water, the proximate cause of the boiling is the heat of the kettle, and the fire applied to the kettle is a remote cause.

Necessary and free causes. A *necessary* cause is determined by its very nature to act in a definite way, whereas a *free* cause has control over its own action.

Direct and accidental causes. A cause is called *direct* (*per se*) if it tends to produce a certain effect either naturally or freely. For example, the act of digging naturally tends to produce a hole, and the digger freely intends to produce a hole. By an *accidental* cause is usually meant a cause which produces some effect other than that which was freely or naturally intended. For instance, the act of digging a hole may be the accidental cause of a treasure trove.

EFFICIENT CAUSALITY

Primary and Secondary Causes

249. Above, in no. 235, we have seen that principal causes act in virtue of their own power, and we divided principal causes into primary and secondary causes. Secondary causes depend upon the principal cause in a twofold manner.

In the first place, *secondary causes can act only upon pre-existing subjects;* hence they cannot exercise their causality if such subjects have not been produced by the primary cause. That secondary causes require a pre-existing subject will be clear from the following argument: A cause may either produce something where before its action there was nothing, or act upon a pre-existing reality. If a cause can produce something where before there was nothing, it is evident that it is independent in its causality from all other causes. Such a cause tends primarily and directly to produce the "to be" of a thing. But a cause which can only act upon pre-existing reality merely changes this reality into something else. For instance, when an architect builds a house, he does not produce the whole reality which is the house, but merely arranges things in such a way that they "become" a house. Likewise, when a plant produces seed, it does not produce the whole reality which is the seed, but merely causes pre-existing matter to receive the form of its seed. In other words, such causes do not effect that a thing *is*, but only that it *becomes* something. As St. Thomas expresses it, such causes "are causes of things with respect to their becoming, but not with respect to their 'to be.'" [9] Now it is clear that a cause which can account only for the "becoming" of a thing but not for its "to be," depends upon

[9] *De potentia*, q. 5, a. 1, ad 4.

the cause which accounts for the "to be" of the thing. For this reason the causes of "becoming" are called secondary causes, and the cause of "to be" is the primary cause.

Finite beings are mere secondary causes. For otherwise their causality would have to bridge the infinite gap which separates absolute non-being from being. Obviously, only an infinite being will be able to bridge an infinite gap, and the power of a finite being is finite. Hence finite beings can exercise their causality only upon pre-existing subjects and therefore are mere secondary causes.[10]

250. In the second place, *secondary causes or finite beings depend upon the primary cause in the very exercise of their causality.* The proof is as follows:

A thing is an efficient cause by the exercise of its action. Now, in a finite being substance and the exercise of its action are really distinct, because its action is an accidental determination of the substance. Hence a finite being is in potency to the exercise of its action. Now, nothing can be reduced from potency to act except by a being in act. Therefore, a finite being can exercise its action or causality only in dependence upon the primary cause. "No matter," says St. Thomas, "how perfect a corporeal or a spiritual nature is, it cannot go into act unless moved by God," [11] and "no cause gives "to be" save insofar as it participates in the operation of God." [12]

The relationship between the primary and secondary causes is a very complex problem which has given rise to endless disputes. We shall not consider it here because its

[10] Cf. St. Thomas, *op. cit.*, q.3, a.4.
[11] *Summa theol*, Ia IIae, q 109, a.1.
[12] *Quodlibet.* 12, a.5. Cf. *In II sentent.*, d.1, q.1, a.4.

proper place is in the philosophy of the Infinite Being.[13]

251. *Finite beings are truly efficient and principal causes.* Notwithstanding their utter dependence upon the primary cause, finite beings are truly efficient and principal causes. Some philosophers have thought that finite beings do not exercise any causality at all, and considered them as mere occasions for the action of the Infinite Being. For instance, in their opinion, fire does not heat anything, but when a fire is lit God directly causes heat in its surroundings. This doctrine is known as *occasionalism*.

The falsity of this doctrine becomes clear from its consequences. For if occasionalism were true, knowledge of any finite being would be impossible. "If creatures do not have any actions of their own so as to produce effects, the result will be that the nature of a created thing can never be known from its effects; and so we should be deprived of all knowledge of natural science, for in this science arguments from effects are chiefly used." [14]

Moreover, "it is against wisdom that anything should be in vain in the works of a wise being. But if creatures did nothing at all towards the production of effects, and God Himself did everything, other things would be used in vain by Him in the production of effects." [15]

That finite beings are truly efficient causes is clear also from our own internal and external experience, which does not allow any other rational interpretation. To deny the

[13] St. Thomas enumerates the ways in which secondary causes depend upon the primary cause in *De potentia*, q.3, a.7: "God is the cause of every action insofar as He gives the power to act, and insofar as He conserves it, and insofar as He applies it to the action, and insofar as through His power all other powers act."

[14] III *Contra gentes*, c.69.
[15] *Ibid.*

trustworthiness of this experience would imply the denial of the trustworthiness of our intellect, and thus lead to skepticism. Moreover, it would lead to the denial of human liberty, because no creature would be able to act according to its power and choice.

In the same way, experience leads us to admit that we are truly *principal* causes, i.e., causes acting in virtue of our own power. We move from place to place when we want; we study, walk, eat, drink, etc., when we want. Even so-called automatic movements, such as breathing and heartbeat, are controlled from within. This internal control over our physical and mental activities admits but one rational interpretation—we perform these actions in virtue of inherent powers which are truly our own.

Instrumental Causes

252. In a *wider* sense, any cause which is subordinated to another cause may be called an instrument. In this sense any secondary cause is sometimes called an instrument of the primary cause. Likewise, an agent acting under the moral influence of somebody else is an instrument in a wider sense; e.g., an ambassador, acting as such, is an instrument of his government. In a *strict* sense, however, the term "instrument" is used for any subordinate efficient cause which aids the efficient cause by which it is moved physically; for example, the saw is such an instrument in the hands of the carpenter. Instruments in the strict sense may be produced not only by man's ingenuity but also by nature itself; for instance, seed is a natural instrument by means of which a plant produces another plant. In this section we shall use the term "instrument" in the strict sense.

The Thomistic conception of the *nature of instrumental causality* is as follows:

"*The instrumental cause does not act in virtue of its own form*, but only through the motion which is imparted to it by the principal agent." [16]

"*An instrument has a twofold action*. The first is instrumental, according to which it operates, not by its own power, but by the power of the principal agent. The second is its own action, which belongs to it according to its own form; e.g., to cut belongs to an axe because of its sharpness, but to make a bed belongs to it insofar as it is an instrument of skill. However, it can perform its instrumental action only through the exercise of the action which is proper to it; for instance, an axe makes a bed by cutting." [17]

"*The effect is not proportionate to the instrument but to the principal agent;* e.g., the bed is not proportionate to the axe but to the art in the mind of the craftsman." [18] The reason is that the instrument does not act in virtue of its own form, but in virtue of the principal agent; hence it may produce an effect which is higher than itself.[19]

The instrumental power is "*a transitory and incomplete entity* in the order of nature." [20] For "the instrument acts insofar as it is moved by another, and therefore requires a power which is proportioned to its motion. But motion is not a complete being but a transitory being (*via in ens*), as it were, an entity intermediary between pure potency

---

[16] *Summa theol.*, IIIa, q. 62, a. 1.
[17] *Ibid.*, ad 2. Cf. *De potentia*, q. 3, a. 7 and *De veritate*, q. 27, a. 4.
[18] *Ibid.*
[19] *In IV sentent.*, d. 1, q. 1, a. 4, ad 3.
[20] *Summa theol.*, IIIa, q. 62, a. 3.

and pure act. . . . And therefore the power of the instrument, taken as such, i.e., insofar as the instrument acts to produce an effect which is beyond its natural powers, is not a complete being with a permanent reality in nature, but an incomplete being.[21] An instrument receives from the principal cause a physical premotion which makes it immediately fit to produce an effect above its nature because by means of this premotion the instrument participates in the power and the action of the principal cause.

*Historical Notes

253. The *monists*, who deny the real distinction between God and creatures, deny that God is the primary cause of all finite beings.

The *occasionalists* deny that finite beings can exercise any true causality. *Malebranche* (1638–1715) was the chief exponent of this theory, but in the Middle Ages *Avicenna* and *Avicebron* had already proposed similar doctrines.

The nature of instrumental causality has caused much dispute among philosophers. It has many important applications; for instance, it is used in psychology to explain the action of sense images upon the intellect and the movement of other faculties by the will. *Thomistic* philosophers unanimously explain instrumental causality as an intrinsic but transitory entity. *Suarez* conceived it as an intrinsic and permanent entity, which he called an active obediential power. The *Scotists* explain it as an

[21] *In IV sentent.*, d.1, q.1, a.4, ad 2am quest. Note that "an instrument is said to be moved by the principal agent so long as it retains the power imparted to it by the principal agent. Therefore, an arrow continues its flight so long as it retains the impulsive force given to it by the archer." *De pot.*, q 3, a.11, ad 5.

extrinsic assistance which makes the instrument act in sympathy with the principal cause. However, extrinsic assistance could never explain why an instrument would produce an effect that is above its natural power.

SUMMARY

254. A cause which can produce something where before there was nothing is independent in its causality from any other cause. Such a cause tends to produce primarily and directly the "to be" of a thing. It is called the primary cause. Causes which are able only to change pre-existing reality do not cause a thing "to be" but "to become" something. They are called secondary causes. Finite beings are secondary causes because they do not have the infinite power needed to pass the gap from absolute non-being to being. They also depend upon the primary cause in the very exercise of their causality because their essence is not their action; hence they are in potency to act and need to be moved by a being in act, i.e., ultimately by the Pure Act, who is the primary cause.

Finite beings are truly efficient and principal causes, as is clear from our experience. The theory of occasionalism, which denies this assertion, would make knowledge of any finite being impossible. For we know the nature of a thing from its action; hence, if finite beings have no actions of their own, it follows that their nature cannot be known.

An instrument is a subordinate efficient cause which aids the principal cause by which it is moved physically. An instrument, *qua* instrument, does not act in virtue of its own form but only insofar as it is moved by the principal agent. An instrument has a twofold action—namely, the instrumental action, according to which it operates through the power of the principal agent, and its own action, which flows from its own form. The instrumental action is exercised through the action which is proper to the instrument. The effect is proportionate to the principal agent; hence it can be higher than the instrument. The instrumental power is in the instrument as a transitory and incomplete entity because it consists in the motion of the instrument by the principal agent, and motion is a transitory and incomplete entity. The instrument is physically premoved by the principal agent.

SUGGESTED READINGS

255. F. X. Meehan, *Efficient Causality in Aristotle and St. Thomas,* Catholic University of America Press, 1940.

J. Maritain, *A Preface to Metaphysics,* pp. 132–140 (principle of causality).

A. G. Van Melsen, *The Philosophy of Nature,* pp. 216–253 (modern science and causality).

P. H. Van Laer, *Philosophico-Scientific Problems* (*Duquesne Studies, Philosophical Series,* vol. 3), Duquesne University Press, 1953, Chapters 5 and 6 (causality and modern science).

M. D. Mullen, *Essence and Operation in Thomistic and Modern Philosophy,* Catholic University of America Press, 1941 (causality of finite beings).

R. O. Johann, "Comment on Secondary Causality," in *The Modern Schoolman,* 1947–1948, pp. 19–25.

R. Garrigou-Lagrange, *God: His Existence and Nature,* vol. I, pp. 191–198 and vol. II, pp. 232–239 (ontological validity of the concept of cause); vol. I, pp. 181–191 (principle of sufficient reason).

Louis de Raeymaeker, *The Philosophy of Being,* Ch. X, pp. 262–268.

CHAPTER 14

Final Causality

✳✳✳ 256. As we have seen in chapter 12, the final cause is "that for the sake of which something is done."[1] In the present chapter we shall investigate whether or not the final cause is a true cause, the so-called principle of finality, the nature of final causality, and chance.

The Final Cause Is a True Cause

A final cause is a cause in the true sense of the term and not merely metaphorically. This assertion may be proved as follows:

A true cause exercises positive influence upon the "to be" of a thing. Now a final cause exercises such an influence because it moves the agent to act and thus has a positive, though mediate, influence upon the "to be" of the effect. Hence the final cause is a true cause.

Regarding the manner in which the final cause acts, it should be noted that it does not exercise its influence in the same manner as an efficient cause. The efficient cause operates through *physical influence* in the order of *execution*, whereas the final cause operates through *moral influence* in the order of *intention*.

Not only is the final cause a true cause, but "*the first cause of all causes* is the final cause. The reason is that

[1] Aristotle, *Metaphysics*, bk. V, ch. 2; 1013a, 32.

matter does not get its form unless it is moved by the agent, for nothing reduces itself from potency to act. But the agent does not move except for the sake of the end."[2]

The Principle of Finality

257. The last sentence of the preceding paragraph contains the so-called principle of finality: *Every agent acts for an end.*

Like the principle of causality, the principle of finality is a *self-evident* principle, which we understand immediately when the terms in the principle is expressed are analyzed. St. Thomas gives this analysis in the following words: "If an agent did not act for some definite effect, all effects would be indifferent to it. But that which is indifferent to many [effects] does not produce this [effect] rather than that. Hence from that which is indifferent to either of two effects no effect will result unless it be determined by something to one of them. Consequently, it would be impossible for it to act. Therefore, every agent tends to some definite effect, which is called its end."[3]

258. *How Can Irrational Agents Act for an End?* It is easy to see that *rational* agents act for an end "because when they act they first conceive in the intellect that which they attain with their action, and act according to what they have preconceived."[4] But there is some difficulty in understanding how irrational agents[5] can act for

[2] *Summa theol.*, Ia IIae, q. 1, a. 2.
[3] III *Contra gentes*, c. 2.
[4] *Summa theol.*, Ia IIae, q. 1, a. 2.
[5] Concerning the difficulty as to how God can act for an end, see St. Thomas, *In II sentent.*, d. 1, q. 2, a. 1.

FINAL CAUSALITY

an end. St. Thomas solves this difficulty in the following way:

"Something can by its action or motion tend to an end in a twofold way. In the first place, as something which *moves itself* to an end, e.g., man. Secondly, as something which *is moved* to an end by another; e.g., an arrow tends to a definite end because it is moved by the archer who directs its action towards that end. Those beings, then, who have the power of reason move themselves to an end because they have control over their actions. . . . But beings which lack reason tend to an end by a natural inclination, as if they were moved by another and not by themselves. Since they do not know what an end is, they cannot direct anything to an end, but can only be directed to an end by another." [6]

Thus it becomes clear that the principle of finality is to be understood *analogically* with respect to the various types of agents which act for an end. According as the nature of the agent varies with respect to its activity, so also its tendency towards an end; yet the proportion between the nature of the agent and the end of its action remains the same in the various types of agents tending towards an end.

We may distinguish a *threefold tendency towards an end:* [7]

a) A tendency towards an end which is known as such and freely chosen. This tendency is proper to rational beings. It is called a *rational appetite* or will.

b) A tendency towards an end which is known concretely by the agent but determined for it by another (by

[6] *Summa Theol.*, Ia IIae, q. 1, a. 2.
[7] *Ibid.*, q. 26, a. 1.

nature). This tendency, which is proper to irrational animals, is called *sense appetite*.

c) A tendency towards an end which is not known at all by the agent and determined for it by another. This tendency, which is proper to all beings that lack cognitive powers, is called in general *natural appetite*. Such an appetite may be based upon an *intrinsic* principle implanted in the very nature of the agent, as is the case with plants and minerals with respect to their natural actions, or upon an *extrinsic* principle, such as an impulse, which is exemplified by a bullet which moves towards a target.[8]

Note. The principle of finality is not, as it sometimes said: "Every effect is for an end." For an effect may be produced without being intended; for instance, when something comes about "by chance." As St. Thomas says: "Whatever happens, happens either by chance or for the sake of an end. For what comes about without being intended as an end is said to happen by chance."[9]

The Nature of Final Causality

259. Three elements may be distinguished in final causality. In the first place, we may ask what makes a thing a *potential final cause?* The answer is that a thing can be a potential final cause if it can be desired. Now nothing can be desired except what is able to move an agent to strive for it. But an agent strives only for that which is suitable for it. Hence *goodness* is what makes a thing a potential final cause.[10]

Secondly, we may ask what makes a potential final cause become an *actual final cause?* A thing is an actual

[8] *Ibid.*, Ia, q. 103, a 1, ad 3.
[9] *In II physic.*, lect. 13.
[10] III *Contra gentes*, c. 3.

final cause when it actually moves an agent to strive for it. Now an agent strives for a good by desiring it. Hence *being desired* makes a potential final cause an actual final cause.[11]

Thirdly, is there any *necessary condition* for the actualization of a potential final cause? The answer is that the good must be proposed to the appetite of the agent and become existent in the agent's intention. For the final cause does not move physically as an efficient cause, but intentionally; hence the good must become existent in the agent in the order of intention. This existence, however, presupposes knowledge of the good. Hence *knowledge of the good* or end is a necessary condition for the actualization of the potential final cause. However, as we have seen in no. 258, this knowledge may exist either in the agent which acts for the end or in another agent which makes an agent act for the end.

Chance

260. If it is true that every agent acts for an end, what can be the meaning of chance? For frequently things are said to happen "by chance" or "luck," i.e., unintentionally. For example, a man digs a well and comes across the long-forgotten treasure chest of a pirate; two friends unknowingly travel to the same city at the same time and meet there by chance. What is attributed to chance is an effect produced by the concurrence of two or more causes which operate independently and thus produce an effect which is *unforeseen* by anyone who does not know that several causes are at work or how these causes operate. If the activity of all the causes involved is foreseen, the effect is no longer attributed to chance. For instance, if I con-

[11] *De veritate*, q. 22, a. 2.

sider that a pirate buried his chest in this particular spot, and that someone else later starts digging in exactly the same place, the treasure trove is not the effect of chance with respect to me. But if I do not consider the effect produced by one of these causes, the pirate, the finding of the treasure happens "by chance" as far as I am concerned. Hence, chance exists only in the mind of one who does not know all the causes which exercise influence upon the effect.

From the foregoing, it follows that an explanation which appeals to *chance is no explanation at all*, but a confession of ignorance. Moreover, one who claims that everything happens by chance contradicts himself. For if everything happens by chance, nothing is foreseen; hence there is no knowledge of the working of any cause, and therefore there cannot be any claim that a given effect was not intended, i.e., came about by chance.

Historical Notes

261. In ancient Greece the principle of finality was denied by *Democritus* and other materialists, who explained the actions of natural agents by necessity of nature acting without a purpose. In a famous passage, which could have been inserted in the works of a nineteenth century evolutionist, Aristotle cites one of them: Why, for instance, should not "our teeth come up of necessity—the front teeth sharp, fitted for tearing, the molars broad and useful for grinding down the food? Since they did not arise for this end, but it merely was a coincident result; and so with all other parts [of the body] in which we suppose that there is a purpose? Wherever, then, all the parts came about just as they would have been if they had come to be for an end, such things survived, being organized spon-

FINAL CAUSALITY

taneously in a fitting way; whereas those which grew otherwise perished and continue to perish." [12] As we have seen above, it is precisely this necessity of nature, this determinism, which forces us to admit the principle of finality.

Final causality easily provides an argument for the existence of God; hence it is not surprising that *Epicurus* (342–270 B.C.), whose purpose in life was to rid mankind from the fear of the gods, although he was not an atheist, accepted Democritus' determinism with some modification. *William of Occam*, the father of nominalism, denied the certainty of the principle of finality.

Hume, followed by many materialists, rejected final causality. *Kant* admitted the principle, but doubted its absolute and objective value.

But from the times of *Anaxagoras* (500?–430? B.C.), who spoke like "a sober man in contrast with the random talk of his predecessors," [13] the principle of finality was admitted by the noblest of all philosophers, by *Plato, Aristotle, St. Augustine, St. Thomas, Duns Scotus,* and mostly all of the scholastics. Among modern philosophers we may mention, although not without some qualifications, *Descartes, Leibnitz, and Bergson*.

SUMMARY

262. The final cause is a true cause because it moves the agent to act and thus exercises a positive, though mediate, influence upon the effect. The final cause is called the cause of all causes because it moves the efficient cause without whose action matter does not get its form.

The principle of finality is that every agent acts for an

[12] *Physics*, bk. II, ch. 8; 198b, 18 ff.
[13] Aristotle, *Metaphysics*, bk. I, ch. 3; 948b, 17.

end. This principle is self-evident. For if the agent did not act for a definite effect, all effects would be indifferent to it; hence there would be no reason why this effect would follow rather than that. An agent which is indifferent to either of two effects has to be determined to one of them before it acts. Consequently, every agent acts for an end.

An agent may act for an end either by moving itself towards this end or by being moved to it by another. Hence, even beings which do not know an end as an end can still act towards an end, namely, insofar as they are made to act towards an end. Because not all agents act for an end in the same manner, the principle of finality is an analogous principle.

A thing is a potential final cause by being capable of moving an agent. Since an agent is moved only by what is suitable for it, it follows that goodness is what makes a thing a potential final cause. A potential final cause is actualized by being desired. Desire, however, presupposes knowledge; hence a necessary condition for the exercise of final causality is knowledge of the end. This knowledge may be either in the agent which acts for an end or in the cause which makes the agent act for an end.

An effect is attributed to chance if it is unforeseen. Hence if one knows all the causes that contribute towards a certain effect, nothing in this effect will occur by chance.

*APPENDIX

The Exemplary Cause

263. A few words may be added here concerning the so-called exemplary cause. As we have seen above in no. 234, by an exemplary cause is meant "that to the likeness of which a thing is said to be made." [14] Elsewhere St. Thomas expresses himself more precisely—the exemplary cause is "a form in imitation of which something comes to be according to the intention of an agent which determines an end for itself." [15] In this definition [16] the words, *"a form in imitation of which,"* indicate the idea which serves as a model, for the idea is the same as the form which a thing imitates. By saying, *"according to the intention of an agent,"* we exclude the possibility that the likeness comes about by accident. The words, *"which determines an end for itself,"* indicate that there can be question of exemplary causality only if the agent determines the end for itself and not if the end is determined by another; in other words, only in the case of rational agents, who are directed in their action by their ideas, is there question of exemplary causality.

The exemplary cause is a *true cause,* for it exercises a

[14] *In V metaphysic.*, lect. 2, no. 764.
[15] *De veritate*, q. 3, a. 1.
[16] *Ibid.*

positive influence upon the "to be" of the effect inasmuch as it influences the intellectual agent to act in a definite way.

The exemplary cause is *not an efficient cause* because of itself it is not the first principle of movement in the order of execution, but merely the form in imitation of which something comes to be. It belongs to the order of intention rather than to the order of execution.

The exemplary cause is *not formally the same as the final cause.* For, formally speaking, the final cause moves the agent to act insofar as it is a purpose to be reached, whereas the exemplary cause specifies the effect to be produced, since it is the form to be imitated in the effect. *Materially,* however, the final and the exemplary cause are the same because it is the specific form which, insofar as apprehended as a good, moves the agent as the final cause, and insofar as it specifies the action of the agent, directs the agent as its exemplary cause. Hence it is clear why the exemplary cause is called a *formal extrinsic* cause. It is formal because it specifies the effect, and it is extrinsic because it specifies the effect not from within but from without.

SUGGESTED READINGS

264. C. Hollencamp, *Causa Causarum. On the Nature of the Good and Final Cause,* Quebec, 1949.

E. A. Pace, "The Teleology of St. Thomas," in *The New Scholasticism,* 1927, pp. 213–231.

A. G. Van Melsen, *The Philosophy of Nature,* pp. 168–171 (concept of finality); pp. 235–241 (chance and random).

P. H. Van Laer, *Philosophico-Scientific Problems,* Ch. 6 (modern science and the principle of finality).

J. Maritain, *A Preface to Metaphysics,* pp. 141–151 (chance).

H. Renard, *The Philosophy of Being*, pp. 161–164 (exemplary cause).

Louis de Raeymaeker, *The Philosophy of Being*, Ch. X, pp. 270–275 (final causality), pp. 275–281 (exemplary causality).

CHAPTER 15

The Mutual Relations of Causes

Reciprocal Causality

✤✤✤ 265. The first point to consider in this chapter is the question whether or not causes are causes of one another. Thomistic philosophers answer in the affirmative and thus admit so-called reciprocal causality. The Thomistic position [1] may be briefly summed up as follows:

There is no reciprocal causality in the same genus of causes. The reason is that a cause is a principle and therefore prior to that which proceeds from it. Hence, if two causes which belong to the same genus, say, two efficient causes, would be causes of one another, one would have to be prior to the other as its cause, and posterior to it as its effect, both under the same respect, which is impossible. Therefore, no causes are causes of one another under the same respect, or in the same genus of causality.

There is reciprocal causality in different genera of causes. In the first place, *matter and form* are causes of one another. Matter is that which sustains the form, and the form is that which gives to matter its species. This

[1] Cf. Aristotle, *Metaphysics*, bk. V, ch. 2, 1013b, 9; St. Thomas, *In V metaphysic.*, lect. 2, nos. 774 ff.

reciprocal causality of matter and form explains why, for instance, we may say without fear of contradiction that the dispositions of matter which cause a new form to become actual are prior (but not in time) to this form in the genus of material causality, while the same form is prior to these dispositions in the genus of formal causality.

Secondly, *the efficient and the final cause* are causes of one another. For it is the agent, which by its action produces the end in the order of reality,[2] and it is the end or final cause, which in the order of intention, causes the agent to act.

*Two or More Causes of the Same Effect

266. The second point is whether or not two causes can be the causes of one and the same effect. This question can be answered only if we make a few distinctions.

In the first place, from the foregoing it is clear that one effect may have several causes if these causes belong to *different genera.* These genera are efficient, final, formal, material, and exemplary causality.

Secondly, if we limit ourselves to causes of the *same genus*, we must again distinguish. One and the same effect can have more than one cause if these causes are *subordinated.* As we have seen in no. 252, the principal and the instrumental cause are causes of one and the same effect, and the same is true of the primary and secondary cause.[3]

What about causes of the same genus which are *not subordinated?* Again, we must distinguish. Two non-subordinated *partial* causes can produce together one and the same effect; for instance, two horses pulling a cart. Strictly speaking, however, there is no question here of

[2] Or at least makes a pre-existing reality really its own.
[3] Cf. *Summa theol.*, Ia, q. 105, a. 5, ad 2, III *Contra gentes*, c. 70.

two causes producing the same effect, because the partial causes are combined into one total cause. Whether it is possible for two non-subordinated *total* causes to produce one and the same effect is a matter of dispute among scholastic philosophers—Scotus and Suarez admit its possibility, while Thomistic philosophers deny it. The latter base their argument upon the fact that any finite cause is limited both specifically and individually. Since every effect is virtually precontained in its cause, an effect of this finite cause will be *this* effect of this finite cause and therefore cannot be at the same time *that* effect of that finite cause. An application of this doctrine is found in the Thomistic denial of two substantial forms in the same matter because both these forms would be the formal cause of being with respect to one and the same thing.

This brings us to the end of our study of causes. Occasionally there has been question of the Infinite Being, God, although no formal proofs were given as yet for His existence. However, it will not be too difficult to see how the principle of causality leads to the admission of a Being which exists of itself, and how the principle of finality points to the existence of a Supreme Intelligence. Thus we can understand why Aristotle called metaphysics "theology"—it culminates in the consideration of

"THE FIRST AND SUPREME PRINCIPLE"
GOD.

Review Questions

Introduction
1. Distinguish the three levels of abstractions.
2. What is meant by the material and the formal object of a science?
3. Name the material and the formal object of metaphysics?
4. Define metaphysics.
5. Why are cosmology, rational psychology, etc. metaphysical sciences?
6. What is the importance of metaphysics?
7. Name the epistemological presuppositions of general metaphysics.

Chapter 1: The Nature of Being

I. The Concept of Being
1. State the senses of the terms "to be" and "being."
2. Show that being is the most common and most simple of all concepts.
3. Is the concept of being absolutely simple?
4. Why is a strict definition of being impossible?
5. In what sense is the concept of being the first of all concepts?

II. The Unity of Being
1. How does the human mind arrive at universal concepts such as man, cat, tree, etc.?

REVIEW QUESTIONS

2. Why is it impossible to obtain the concept of being in the same way?
3. What is meant by imperfect abstraction or abstraction of indetermination?
4. What kind of unity is possessed by the concept of being?
5. How is being contracted?
6. Why is being not a genus?

III. *The Analogy of Being*

1. Explain the meaning of equivocal, univocal, and analogous terms.
2. Describe analogy of attribution.
3. What is metaphorical analogy?
4. Define and explain analogy of proportionality.
5. Show that being is not univocal nor equivocal but analogous.
6. Prove that being is analogous by analogy of proportionality.
7. In what sense is the concept of being analogous by analogy of attribution?

IV. *Logical Being*

1. What is meant by logical being?
2. Is logical being the same as nothing?
3. Give examples of privative and relative logical beings.

Chapter 2: The Transcendental Properties of Being

I. *Transcendental Properties in General*

1. State the meaning of "transcendental."
2. What is meant by a transcendental property of being?
3. Distinguish between transcendental and predicamental predicates.
4. Name the transcendental concepts.
5. Which transcendental concepts express transcendental properties?
6. Are transcendental properties really distinct from being?

II. *Otherness*

1. Which judgment rises from the transcendental "otherness?"
2. What is meant by a principle?
3. What kind of a principle is the principle of contradiction?
4. In what sense is the principle of contradiction the first principle?
*5. Distinguish between first complex and first incomplex principle.
6. Show that the principle of contradiction is the first principle.
7. In what sense is the principle of contradiction an analytic principle?
8. Is the principle of identity prior to the principle of contradiction?
9. State the principle of excluded middle.

III. *Unity*

1. Distinguish between transcendental and predicamental unity.
2. What is the difference between multitude and number?
*3. Why does oneness not add anything positive to being?
*4. Is oneness a purely negative concept?
5. Prove that every being is one."
6. Are "being" and "one" synonymous terms?
7. What is the importance of the principle that every being is "one"?

Appendix, Identity and Distinction

1. Describe identity and distinction.
2. Distinguish between real and logical identity and give examples of both.
3. Give examples of metaphysical, physical, and moral identity.
4. What is meant by essential and accidental identity? Are

REVIEW QUESTIONS

they real or logical? Give examples of each, and also of generic and specific identity.
5. What is the difference between real and logical distinction?
6. Is real distinction the same as separability?
7. Explain the following terms: metaphysical and physical distinction, virtual and purely logical distinction, major and minor distinction.
8. Can things which are really identical be logically distinct. Can things which are logically distinct be really identical? If so, give examples.

IV. *Truth*

1. Define logical and ontological truth.
2. What is the ultimate basis of ontological truth?
3. What is the importance of the principle that every being is true?
*4. How is truth found in the Infinite Being and in finite beings?
*5. What does "true" add to being as such?
*6. What does "true" add to determined beings?
7. What is meant by truth of speech? Is it logical or ontological truth?
*8. In what sense are we justified in speaking of phenomenal truth?
*9. In what sense is truth eternal?
*10. Is created truth unchangeable?
11. What is falsity?
12. Is it possible for a thing to be absolutely false?

V. *Goodness*

1. Describe and explain what is meant by goodness.
*2. What does "good" add to being?
3. In what sense is every being good?
*4. How is goodness found in the Infinite Being and in finite beings?
5. Distinguish between the useful, the pleasant, and the virtuous or disinterested good.

REVIEW QUESTIONS

6. Distinguish between moral and physical good, absolute and relative good.
7. Explain the notion of evil. Can evil exist all by itself?
8. What is meant by absolute and relative evil, physical and moral evil?
9. In what sense does evil have a cause?
*10. Can God be the cause of evil?

*Appendix, Beauty

1. State and explain St. Thomas' description of the "beautiful."
2. Compare the "beautiful" to the "true" and the "good."
3. Is every being beautiful?
4. What causes us to judge certain things to be ugly?
5. State the conditions required for our perception of beauty.

Chapter 3: Act and Potency

I. *The Problem of Becoming*

1. State the problem of becoming.
2. How did Parmenides solve the problem?
3. What was the answer of Heraclitus?
4. How did Aristotle solve the dilemma of Parmenides?
5. May the occurrence of change be considered as a primary datum of experience?

II. *The Problem of Limitation*

1. State the problem of limitation.
2. What kind of a composition does limitation imply?

III. *St. Thomas' Synthesis*

1. How did St. Thomas connect the theory of act and potency with the theory of limitation by participation?
2. Explain the principle: act is limited by potency only.
3. Can an external agent limit the perfection of a thing?
4. What limits potency?
5. Why must a pure act be infinite?
6. Why must a pure act be unique?
7. Are potency and act really distinct?

REVIEW QUESTIONS

8. Can a thing be in potency and act at the same time?
9. Do potency and act enter into a real composition?
10. What keeps potency and act together?
11. Explain the following terms: absolutely and relatively pure act; first and second act; active and passive potency; pure and mixed potency.

Chapter 4: Multiplication of "To Be"

1. What problem is raised by the fact that many things "are"?
2. Explain the terms "essence" and "existence."
3. Is essence an act?
4. How can we explain the multiplication of "to be"?
5. Prove the real distinction of essence and its "to be."
6. Can an essence exist without "to be"?
7. Are essence and "to be" separable?
8. Does a finite essence enter into a real composition with its "to be"?
9. Show the importance of the real distinction of finite essence and its "to be" by enumerating some applications.

Chapter 5: Multiplication of Essence

I. *How Can an Essence Be Multiplied?*

1. Is it a primary datum of experience that essences are multiplied?
2. How do we solve the problem of multiplication of essence?
3. Explain the terms "matter" and "form."
4. Are matter and form really distinct?
5. Can a form be limited without matter?

II. *The Principle of Individuation*

1. What is meant by "individual"?
2. What do we mean by the principle of individuation?
3. Why can form not be the principle of individuation? What about a combination of forms?
4. Prove that matter is the principle of individuation.
5. How is matter the principle of individuation?

REVIEW QUESTIONS

6. What is meant by "matter made distinct by quantity"?
*7. How can matter be purely potential while requiring this quantity and no other?
*8. What is the reason that matter has a requirement for this quantity and no other?
*9. How are unreceived forms and pure "to be" individuated?
*10. Does individuation add anything real to an unreceived form or pure "to be"?

*Chapter 6: Possible Being

1. Distinguish between possible and actual being, and between pure possibles and possibles in a wider sense.
2. Is a possible the same as nothing? as a logical being?
3. What is meant by extrinsic and intrinsic possibility?
4. Where do we find the ultimate foundation of extrinsic possibility?
5. What is the ultimate foundation of intrinsic possibility?
6. What kind of a "to be" do possibles have?

Chapter 7: The Categories in General

1. What is meant by a "category" and how are categories distinguished from transcendentals?
2. Name the ten categories of Aristotle.
3. Is any category a purely extrinsic denomination?
4. Do categories have a common genus?
5. What is classified in the categories?
*6. In what sense are categories univocal?

Chapter 8: Substance

I. *The Necessity of Distinguishing Between Substance and Accidents*

1. What problem is raised by the primary datum of experience that the individual finite being shows itself to be manifold in the order of activity?
2. Show that non-essential mutability requires a composition of potency and act in the order of activity.

REVIEW QUESTIONS

3. Are substance and accidents really distinct?
4. How does the union of substance and accidents compare to that of essence and "to be" and of matter and form?
5. Is a composition of substance and accidents possible if there is no composition of essence and "to be"?

II. *The Concept of Substance*

1. How do we acquire the concept of substance?
2. How are we certain of the existence of substance?
3. Define "substance" and explain the definition.
*4. In what sense is God a substance?
5. What is expressed by the term "to be in itself"?
6. Show that substance is not inert but dynamic.
*7. Explain the terms complete and incomplete substance; primary and secondary substance; complete in substantiality and complete in specific perfection.
*8. How did the controversy about substance come about and develop? What is the real issue between phenomenalism and traditional philosophy?

*Chapter 9: Supposit and Person

1. Define supposit and person, and explain the definitions.
2. Is subsistence the same as individuality?
3. Are individual substance and supposit really distinct?
4. Why is subsistence not to be identified with existence?
5. In what does subsistence consist according to the view of most Thomistic philosophers?
6. Why is self-conciousness not a good definition of personality?

Chapter 10: Accidents in General

1. Distinguish predicable from predicamental accidents.
2. Define predicamental accidents.
3. Explain the terms absolute and relative accidents; intrinsic and extrinsic accidents; modal accidents.
4. Prove the reality of accidents.

5. Do accidents have their own "to be"?
6. How are accidents individuated?

Chapter 11: Relations

1. Explain the nature of relations.
2. What is meant by transcendental relations? Are they real?
3. Define accidental or predicamental relation.
4. State the conditions required for a predicamental relation.
5. Prove the existence of predicamental relations.
6. Are they distinct from their subject, term, and foundation?
*7. How are they multiplied specifically?
*8. How are they multiplied numerically?
9. Why do many philosophers object to the real distinction of predicamental relations from their foundations?

Chapter 12: Causes in General

I. *The Concept of Cause*

1. Compare the concept of cause with that of principle, condition, occasion, and sufficient reason of being.
2. Define the concept of cause.

II. *The Existence of Causes*

1. Prove metaphysically that the concept of cause corresponds with objective reality.

III. *Genera of Causes*

1. Enumerate the genera of causes and describe their meaning.
2. Why do we speak of genera of causes and not of species?
3. Explain the following terms: primary and secondary cause; principal and instrumental cause; the end which and the end for which; the end of the act and the end of the agent.

Chapter 13: Efficient Causality

I. *The Principle of Causality*

1. How do we answer the question as to why finite beings are?

REVIEW QUESTIONS

2. How do we answer the question as to why finite beings do change?
3. Derive the principle of causality from the principle of sufficient reason.
4. Explain the axioms: cause and effect are proportionate; every agent acts in a manner similiar to itself; action follows being.

II. *The Causality of Finite Beings*

1. Explain the following terms: total and partial cause; coordinated and subordinated causes; physical and moral causes; direct and accidental causes.
2. Show that secondary causes depend upon the primary cause in two ways.
3. What is occasionalism? Show its falsity.
4. What is the nature of instrumental causality?

Chapter 14: Final Causality

1. Prove that the final cause is a true cause.
2. Why is the final cause called the "cause of all causes"?
3. State the principle of finality. Show its truth.
4. How can irrational agents act for an end?
5. Why is the principle of finality an analogous principle?
6. What makes a thing a potential final cause? What makes it actual? Is there any necessary condition for the actualization of a potential final cause?
7. What is meant by chance?
8. What is the value of an explanation which appeals to chance?

*Appendix—*The Exemplary Cause*

1. Define the exemplary cause.
2. Why is it a true cause?
3. Is the exemplary cause formally the same as the final cause? Do they coincide materially?

REVIEW QUESTIONS

Chapter 15: The Mutual Relations of Causes
1. What is meant by reciprocal causality?
2. Why can there be no reciprocal causality in the same genus of causes?
3. Is there reciprocal causality in different genera of causes?
*4. Is it possible for one and the same effect to have two or more nonsubordinated total causes?

Some Translations of St. Thomas Aquinas' Writings

de Ente et Essentia—*On Being and Essence,* tr. by C. C. Riedl (St. Michael's College, Toronto), 1937.

―――― *On Being and Essence,* tr. by A Maurer (The Pontifical Institute of Mediaeval Studies, Toronto: 1949).

de Veritate—*Truth,* tr. by R. W. Mulligan (Chicago: Regnery, 1952, 3 vols.).

in Boethium de Trinitate—*The Trinity,* tr. by Rose E. Brennan (St. Louis: Herder, 1943).

―――― *On the Division and Method of the Sciences,* tr. by A. Maurer (Pontifical Institute of Mediaeval Studies, Toronto: 1953). A translation of questions 5 and 6 of the Latin work.

Summa Contra Gentes (Gentiles)—*The Summa Contra Gentiles of St. Thomas Aquinas,* literally translated by the English Dominican Fathers (New York: Benziger, 1929 ff. 5 vols.).

―――― *Of God and His Creatures,* abridged translation of the Latin work by J. Rickaby (St. Louis: Herder, 1905).

de Potentia—*On the Power of God,* literally translated by the English Dominican Fathers (London: Burnes, Oates & Washbourne, 1932 ff., 3 vols.). Also available in a one vol. ed. of the Newman Press, 1952.

Summa Theologica,—*The Summa Theologica,* literally translated by the Fathers of the English Dominican Province (London: Washbourne, 1927 ff. 22 vols.). Also available in American edition, 3 vols., Benziger, 1947 f.

de Spiritualibus Creaturis—On Spiritual Creatures, tr. by Mary C. Fitzpatrick in collaboration with John J. Wellmuth (Milwaukee: Marquette University Press, 1949).

de Anima—The Soul, tr. by John P. Rowan (St. Louis: Herder, 1949).

in Aristotelis Librum de Anima—Aristotle's de Anima in the Version of William of Moerbeke; and the Commentary of St. Thomas Aquinas, tr. by Kenelm Foster and Silvester Humpries (New Haven: Yale University Press, 1951).

Compendium Theologiae—Compendium of Theology, tr. by Cyril Vollert (St. Louis: Herder, 1949).

Mention must also be made of Anton C. Pegis, *The Basic Writings of St. Thomas Aquinas* (New York: Random House, 2 vols, 1945), which has the first part of the *Summa Theologica* and certain sections of the *Summa Contra Gentes,* and of *Thomas Aquinas, Selected Writings,* ed. by Martin C. D'Arcy (London: 1939).

Index of Names

Numbers refer to the margin

Aegidius the Roman, 146
Albert the Great, 146, 163
Albertson, J. S., 215
Alexander of Hales, 73
Alfarabi, 146
Anaxagoras, 261
Anderson, J. F., 50
Andronicus of Rhodes, 1
Aristotle, 1, 6, 9, 14, 61, 66, 92, 94, 103, 115, 117, 122, 129, 133, 146, 152, 163, 176, 179, 192, 217, 224, 227, 233, 238, 256, 261, 265, 266
Augustine, 101, 103, 110, 111, 120, 146, 163, 261
Averroes, 14, 192
Avicebron, 253
Avicenna, 14, 73, 146, 253

Benedictis, J. de, 146
Bergson, H., 261
Berkeley, G., 192, 195
Billot, L., 146, 202, 205
Boethius, 146
Bonaventure, 73, 146
Bourke, V. J., 17
Buckley, G., 17
Bushinski, E. A., 50

Cajetan (Thomas de Vio), 27, 29, 37, 45, 50, 163, 175, 192, 199, 208, 205
Capreolus, 205

Carpenter, H., 148
Casey, J. T., 17
Cicero, 103
Claire, V. H., 113
Clarke, W. N., 120, 123, 134
Coffey, P., 148, 174, 215, 240
Comte, A., 14
Coursey, M. E., 113

Dario, J., 179
Descartes, R., 79, 146, 172, 192, 193, 196, 204, 213, 238, 261
Descoqs, P., 246
Democritus, 92, 117, 261
Duggan, G., 207

Empedocles, 92
Epicurus, 261

Garrigou-Lagrange, R., 113, 255
Gilson, E., 17
Ginsburg, N. D., 226
Gredt, J., 55, 78, 163, 176

Hartmann, N., 179
Hegel, G., 66, 146, 179
Heisenberg, W., 246
Henle, R. J., 17
Henry of Ghent, 172
Heraclitus, 116, 117, 133
Herrera, 172
Hilary, 146

INDEX OF NAMES

Hoenen, P., 179
Hollencamp, C., 264
Hume, D., 15, 192, 193, 195, 246, 261
Huxley, T, 193

Isaac Israeli, 90

Johann, R. O, 255
John of St. Thomas, 163, 177

Kant, I., 14, 51, 63, 111, 179 192, 195, 224, 238, 246, 261
Keeler, L. D., 113
Koren, H. J, 17, 50
Kossel, C. G., 226

Leibnitz, G., 66, 103, 196, 238, 261
Locke, J., 192, 204

McCall, R J., 113
McMahon, F. E., 215
Malebranche, N, 253
Manes, 103
Marc, A, 198
Margerie, A. de, 246
Maritain, J., 50, 113, 255, 264
Markus, R, 198
Mattiussi, G., 146
Meehan, F. X, 255
Mercier, D., 64, 92, 169, 172, 192, 205, 213
Mill, J. Stuart, 179, 192, 193
Moseley, F. S., 198
Moses, Maimonides, 146
Mullen, M. D, 255

Nicholas of Autrecourt, 246

O'Neill, C. J., 113

Pace, E. A, 264
Parmenides, 14, 32, 115, 116, 117, 133
Paulsen, F., 192

Pauson, J J, 31
Phelan, G. B., 50, 113
Phillips, R. P, 63, 163, 205, 207
Plato, 73, 120, 146, 163, 261
Plotinus, 122, 146
Plutarch, 1
Porphyry, 1
Prado, N del, 145, 205
Proclus, 122
Protagoras, 172
Pseudo-Areopagite, 146
Pythagoras, 73

Raeymaker, L. de, 17, 50, 64, 77, 148, 165, 174, 198, 207, 240, 255, 264
Remer, V., 146, 163
Renard, H, 113, 134, 146, 148, 163, 165, 174, 198, 205, 264
Renoirt, F., 165
Roland-Gosselin, M. D., 146
Rosmini, A., 163
Ross, W. D., 9

Scheu, M., 181
Schiffini, S, 146, 224
Schopenhauer, A., 116
Scotus, J. Duns, 32, 45, 79, 132, 146, 163, 192, 205, 224, 261
Slavin, R. J., 165
Smith, E., 113
Smith, V. E, 50
Spencer, L., 192
Spinoza, B., 116, 146, 196
Strabo, 1
Suarez, F., 32, 45, 79, 132, 146, 163, 192, 205, 213, 224, 253
Sully-Prudhomme, 108
Sylvester of Ferrara, 163

Taille, A. de la, 146
Taine, H, 146
Thomas Aquinas, *passim*.
Thomas, I, 240
Toohey, J. J, 49

Van Laer, P. H., 17, 255, 264

INDEX OF NAMES

Van Melsen, A G., 12, 17, 149, 153, 165, 255, 264
Van Roo, W., 134
Van Steenberghen, F., 55, 113, 134
Vasquez, 92

Wall, J. B., 165

Walton, W. M., 148
William of Auvergne, 146
William of Occam (Ockam), 172, 224, 261
Wolff, C., 1

Zoroaster, 103

Index of Subject Matter

No references are made to the Summaries
The numbers refer to the margin

Abstraction, science and, 2 ff, levels of, 2 ff, of universals, 27, of being, 28 f.

Accidents, to be distinguished from substance, 182 ff; are not supposits, 199, definition, 208, predicable and predicamental, 208, division of, 209, reality of, 200, have their own "to be," 211, individuation of, 212

Act and Potency, 114 ff, change and, 117 ff, divide real being, 128, definition, 129, division, 130 f, synthesis of theory of participation with theory of, 123 ff, act limited by potency, 123 f.; finite and infinite act, 125, real distinction of, 126, union of, 127; analogy of, 127, in the order of "to be," 135 ff, in the order of essence, 150 ff; in the order of activity, 182 ff; causality and, 241 ff

Activity, the order of, 182 f

Analogy, notion of, 34 ff., modes of, 37 ff, of attribution, 38, metaphorical, 39, of proportionality, 40, of being, 43 f, of transcendental properties, 52, of mathematical truth, 81; of limitation by participation, 121, 150; within a category, 175, of substance as applied to God, 188, of relation, 223, of cause, 237, of final causality, 258

Analytic proposition, sense of term in Thomistic and Kantian philosophy, 63

Appetite, goodness and, 94, beauty and, 105 f

Beauty, 105 ff., description, 105, relationship to truth and goodness, 106, present in every being, 107, conditions for perception, 109, definition, 110

Becoming, the problem of, 114 ff. See also *Change*

Being, object of metaphysics, 6; senses of, 18 f., definition of, 21, most common and most simple, 20; not absolutely simple, 20, first of all concepts, 22, unity of concept of, 25 ff, abstraction of, 27 f, not a genus, 31, analogy of, 43 f; logical, 47 f., properties of, 51 ff, and otherness, 57 ff, and unity, 68 ff, and truth, 81 ff; and goodness, 94 ff, and beauty, 107 ff, and change, 114 ff, divided by act and potency, 128; nature of finite, 135 ff; possible,

288

INDEX OF SUBJECT MATTER

166 ff; finite, 175 ff; contingent, 232, 242, divided by substance and accidents, 175 ff; and supposit, 199 ff.

Cartesians, 79
Categories, 175 f.; Kantian, 179, 195
Cause, of evil, 101 f.; can limit perfection of effect, 123, concept of, 228 ff., and principle, 228; and condition, 229, and occasion, 230, and sufficient reason, 231; existence of, 232; genera of, 233 f., 237
  Efficient Cause, 235; division, 235, 248. See *Efficient Causality*
  Exemplary Cause, 234. See *Exemplary Cause*
  Final Cause, 236. See *Final Cause*
  Formal Cause, 234. See *Form*
  Material Cause, 234. See *Matter*
Chance, 260
Change, intelligibility of, 114 ff.; objectivity of, 118, non-essential, 182 ff; problem of, 114 ff.
Christian Scientists, 103
Composition, of act and potency, 123, of essence and "to be," 144, of matter and form, 152; of substance and accidents, 183 ff.
Conceptualism, 28
Consciousness, personality and, 204
Contingent Being, 232, 242
Contraction of Being, 30
Contradiction, principle of, 57 ff.; of being and change, 114 ff.

Degrees of Abstraction, 2 ff.
Distinction, nature and kinds of, 77 f., of act and potency, 126; of essence and "to be," 140 ff., of matter and form, 152; of substance and accidents, 182 ff.; of cause and effect, 231; of supposit and substance, 203
Dualism, 103
Dynamism of Substance, 190 ff.

Effect, distinct from cause, 231; has cause, 242 ff.; two causes of one, 266
Efficient Causality, 241 ff.; act and potency and, 241 ff., principle of, 242 ff; participation and, 243, certainty of principle of, 244; axioms of, 245, science and the principle of, 246, of finite beings, 248 ff, of secondary causes, 249 ff.; of instrumental causes, 252
Empiricists, 79
End, see *Final Cause*
Equivocal Terms, 34
Essence, 21, 135; definition of, 136 f.; as a perfection, 137; distinction from "to be," 140 ff; multiplication of specific, 149 ff.; constituent principles of, 150 ff.; substance and, 187
Ethics, metaphysics and, 12
Excluded Middle, Principle of, 65
Exemplary Cause, 234, definition, 263, its causality, 263
Existence, implied by "to be," 18 f. See *"To Be"*
Experience, as starting point of all science, 2 ff; of problem of limitation, 119, of distinction of essence and "to be," 135 f.; of distinction of matter and form, 149; of distinction of substance and accidents, 182 ff.; causality and, 232, 238

Falsity, 91
Fatalists, 172
Final Causality, 256 ff.; is true causality, 256; principle of, 257; in irrational agents, 258; nature of, 259

289

INDEX OF SUBJECT MATTER

Form, 130, act of specific essence, 150 ff., individuation and, 157

Genus, being is not a, 31; categories have no common, 178
God, possible being and, 168 ff.; categories and, 178, a substance in an analogous sense, 188
Goodness, transcendental, 53 ff.; 94 ff., beauty and, 106, as final cause, 259; kinds of, 98

Hylomorphism, 150 ff.
Hypostasis, 199 ff.

Idealists, 14, 66
Identity, principle of, 64; kinds of, 75 f.
Imagination, science and, 2 ff; role in mathematics, 4; metaphysics and, 5, 223, relations and, 223
Individual, 155
Individuation, principle of, 154 ff; of unreceived forms and pure "to be," 162
Instrumental Cause, see *Efficient Cause*
Intellect, science and, 2 ff; truth and, 53 ff, 81 ff, beauty and, 105 ff, substance and, 185
Intelligibility, principle of, 84 f., of change, 115 ff.

Limitation, problem of, 119 f.; of act, 123 f, extrinsic and intrinsic principle of, 123, of potency, 124, of "to be," 135 ff; of specific essence, 149 ff.; of form by matter, 152

Materialists, 261
Mathematics, abstraction and, 4; physical science and, 8
Matter, abstraction from, 2 ff., limits form, 151 ff; nature of, 150 ff; primary and secondary, 151; as principle of individuation, 157 ff.
Metaphysics, names, 1; abstraction of, 5, object of, 6, division of, 7; importance of, 9; origin and history, 13; epistemological presuppositions of, 15; imagination and, 5, 223
Modes, of analogy, 37 ff.; of being, 52 ff, 175 ff., 183 ff; substantial, 203, 205
Monists, 23, 115 f., 132, 253
Motion, see *Change*
Multiplication, problem of, 119 ff.; of "to be," 135 ff.; of specific essence, 149 ff.; of unreceived forms, 153, in order of activity, 182 ff; of relation, 222

Nature, essence and, 136
Neo-Platonists, 120, 123, 238
Nominalists, 23, 32, 45, 146, 163, 172, 224, 261

Object of Metaphysics, 6
Occasionalists, 251, 253
One, as a transcendental, 53 ff. See *Unity*
Ontology, 1
Otherness, transcendental, 53 ff., 57 ff.

Participation, unity and, 71, truth and, 86, goodness and, 97; beauty and, 107; limitation through, 121 f; meaning of, 121 f, synthesis of theory of participation with theory of act and potency, 122 ff; multiplication of "to be" and, 135 ff, multiplication of specific essence and, 150 ff, analogy of limitation by, 150, possible being and, 169; causality and, 243
Perfection, see *Act and Potency*
Person, 199 ff.
Personality, consciousness and, 204
Phenomenalists, 89, 132, 192 ff., 238, 246
Philosophy, modern, and substance, 192 ff.

INDEX OF SUBJECT MATTER

Platonists, 179
Possibility, ultimate foundation of, 166 ff
Positivists, 14, 224
Potency, definition of, 129, limits act, 128; division, 131. See also *Act and Potency*
Predicaments, 52
Presuppositions, epistemological, of metaphysics, 15
Principle(s), metaphysics and absolute, 12, of contradiction, 57 ff.; notion and kinds of, 58, 228; sense of first, 59, complex and incomplex, 59, of identity, 64, of excluded middle, 65, of intelligibility, 84 f., of limitation, 119 ff.; of individuation, 154 ff.; cause and, 228
Priority, kinds of, 228
Properties, transcendental, of being, 54 ff.
Pythagoreans, 179

Quantity, object of mathematics, 4; individuation and, 158 ff; individuation of, 212
Quiddity, essence and, 136

Relation, as logical being, 48; of being and truth, 87 f., of being and goodness 95 f ; transcendental, of act and potency, 127, of matter and quantity, 159 ff ; nature of, 217; predicamental and transcendental, 218; conditions of predicamental, 219, existence of predicamental, 220; distinction of predicamental, from subject, term, and foundation, 221, multiplication of, 222; reality of, 223, mutual, of causes, 265 ff.

Science, abstraction and, 2 ff.; physical, 2 ff ; mathematics, 4, metaphysics and, 5; substance and physical, 187; principle of causality and modern, 246

Scotists, 172, 253
Sense Experience, see *Experience*
Skeptics, 116, 238
Species, multiplication of individuals in, 154 ff.
Speech, truth of, 88
Subsistence, 202 ff.
Substance, to be distinguished from accidents, 182 ff , concept of, 185 ff.; definition of, 187, dynamism of, 190, division of, 191; modern philosophy and, 192 ff.; in physical sense, 187; supposit and, 199 ff
Supposit, 199 ff ; definition, 199; nature, 200 ff.

Theology, as name of metaphysics, 1, 266; notion of supposit and, 199
"To Be," senses of, 18 f ; multiplication of, 135 ff ; description of, 138, really distinct from essence, 140 ff ; and individuation, 157; of possible being, 171; of accidents, 184, 211, in itself, 189, subsistence and, 202 ff.; cause and, of finite beings, 232, cause of, and cause of coming to be, 249
Transcendental, meaning of, 51; concepts, 52 f ; properties, 54; relation of being and truth, 87; beauty as a, 107; relations, 218
Truth, as a transcendental, 53 ff , 81 ff , kinds of, 81 ff , of speech, 88; phenomenal, 89; eternal, 90, unchangeable, 90, beauty and, 106

Union, of act and potency, 127; of essence and "to be," 144; of matter and form, 152; of substance and accidents, 184
Unity, of a science, 7, of concept of being, 28, as a transcendental, 53 ff , 68 ff ; of individual substance, 211
Univocal Terms, 34

291

www.ingramcontent.com/pod-product-compliance
Lightning Source LLC
Chambersburg PA
CBHW050839230426
43667CB00012B/2062